'Ainscow, Chapman, and Hadfield combine their experiences to offer evidence for change built on relational collaboratives that value local knowledge and deep learning through rapid communication networks among and between the worlds of policy, research, and practice. They are academics in action. Approaching systems change through generative collaboration, they advance educational equity through engaged and reflexive work with practitioners and policy makers. This is valuable reading for educators who want to contribute to ensuring that our educational systems are the drivers for equity and opportunity for every learner.'

Professor Elizabeth Kozleski,
Stanford Graduate School of Education, USA

'*Changing Education Systems: A Research-based Approach* is a timely and substantial new contribution to the school improvement field. The authors are an experienced and formidable team who have built on their research and work with schools and policy-makers over more than three decades. Their book focusses on the 'big issues' in research and improvement. The authors are striking examples of engaged researchers with a common commitment to enhancing equity, promoting inclusion and improving the quality of education and outcomes for all. They provide a timely account and critique of three major improvement initiatives in England, Scotland and Wales, identifying successes, challenges and lessons learned. They show the importance of research knowledge and the use of data as catalysts for change. Their book reveals that such knowledge needs to be combined with sustained engagement with practitioners to have a positive and sustained impact. Their analyses reveal the difficulties in promoting excellence and equity in highly unequal societies and the need for long-term commitment from policy-makers (local and national) as well as respect for and involvement with practitioners to support improvement. Achieving sustained change is, as these authors acknowledge, difficult, but this volume provides important new insights on the policy-making process and enhances our understanding of the potential of research to support work with schools and their staff. Written in clear and accessible language without over simplification, it provides an important resource to guide policy-makers and practitioners seeking to foster positive change to enhance educational equity and excellence to the benefit of all students.'

Professor Pamela Sammons,
'ersity of Oxford, UK

'The most pressing challenge facing educators, regardless of where we live, is how to influence school education to positively address educational disadvantage at scale, and how to make this last. As this continues to confound, some recent research is making real inroads into how to move ahead – this book presents such scholarship. Bringing a collective wisdom built on years of research assembled through engaged partnerships with teachers, head teachers and policy shapers on three major change initiatives, the authors offer genuinely exciting insights into the promises and pitfalls of system change. This book is for anyone interested in understanding the realities of change in education systems.'

Professor Allan Walker,
The Education University of Hong Kong

CHANGING EDUCATION SYSTEMS

As countries seek to develop their education systems, achieving sustainable improvements amongst students from disadvantaged backgrounds remains a major challenge. This has considerable implications for those in the research community as they seek to influence developments in the field.

Drawing on the authors' extensive experiences as researchers, policy advisers and influencers, *Changing Education Systems* offers key insights on how to promote equity within education systems. Exploring three large-scale national reform programmes, the book:

- Presents a series of propositions that are the basis of a research-based approach to system change
- Explains the creation of relationships in which academic researchers collaborate in the process of development
- Considers smaller place-based projects that are set within policy contexts dominated by the idea of market forces as a strategy for improvement
- Explores the steps needed to overcome locally specific barriers

Changing Education Systems is a must-read for policy-makers and practitioners involved in educational reforms, as well as researchers wishing to contribute to and learn from such developments.

Mel Ainscow is Emeritus Professor of Education at the University of Manchester and Professor of Education at the University of Glasgow, UK.

Christopher Chapman is Professor of Educational Policy and Practice at the University of Glasgow, UK.

Mark Hadfield is Professor of Education at Cardiff University, UK.

CHANGING EDUCATION SYSTEMS

A Research-based Approach

Mel Ainscow, Christopher Chapman
and Mark Hadfield

LONDON AND NEW YORK

First published 2020
by Routledge
2 Park Square, Milton Park, Abingdon, Oxon, OX14 4RN

and by Routledge
52 Vanderbilt Avenue, New York, NY 10017

Routledge is an imprint of the Taylor & Francis Group, an informa business

© 2020 Mel Ainscow, Christopher Chapman and Mark Hadfield

The right of Mel Ainscow, Christopher Chapman and Mark Hadfield to be identified as authors of this work has been asserted by them in accordance with sections 77 and 78 of the Copyright, Designs and Patents Act 1988.

All rights reserved. No part of this book may be reprinted or reproduced or utilised in any form or by any electronic, mechanical, or other means, now known or hereafter invented, including photocopying and recording, or in any information storage or retrieval system, without permission in writing from the publishers.

Trademark notice: Product or corporate names may be trademarks or registered trademarks, and are used only for identification and explanation without intent to infringe.

British Library Cataloguing-in-Publication Data
A catalogue record for this book is available from the British Library

Library of Congress Cataloging-in-Publication Data
A catalogue record has been requested for this book

ISBN: 978-0-367-22177-5 (hbk)
ISBN: 978-0-367-22186-7 (pbk)
ISBN: 978-0-429-27367-4 (ebk)

Typeset in Bembo
by Cenveo® Publisher Services

CONTENTS

Foreword	*viii*
Preface	*xiv*

1	Changing education systems	1
2	City Challenge in England: Drawing the lessons	15
3	Schools Challenge Cymru: A catalyst for change	42
4	Developing a regional self-improving school system: Collaboration, competition and transition	70
5	The Scottish Attainment Challenge: Addressing poverty-related outcomes	91
6	New challenges: Managing change in an educational marketplace	112
7	Addressing barriers to change	136
8	A research-based approach	162

References	*170*
Index	*180*

FOREWORD

When the authors asked me if I would be interested in writing a forward to their book, I said: 'Probably not – I am discouraged about the future of systemic reform.' Their response was, 'Just take a look – we think that you will be surprised.' I was, and am pleased to start with my conclusion: *This book offers an experientially wise perspective on how to foster change in both energetic and more ossified educational systems.*

What distinguishes this from other books on systemic change is the underlying assumption, which the authors have tested in multiple contexts, that relationships are fundamental to system change. Structures and policies are important, but without closer links among policy-makers, external advisers and educational professionals, the inevitable small failures that accompany big ideas for change result in distrust, pessimism, and withdrawal (Rinehart, 2017). They show that reliable positive relationships, on the other hand, increase the assets and energy available to schools, advisers, and local agencies to continue.

But, back to the beginning . . .

Two decades ago, I wrote an essay titled 'A light feeling of chaos' (Louis, 1998), in which I examined three U.S. educational policy trends that carried unacknowledged internal contradictions. I am sure that the authors of this book never saw this essay but, based on their intimate engagement with both the research and practice of school reform, their book elaborates on my underdeveloped ideas. The three trends I identified – systemic reform, decentralization/site autonomy, and choice – are the key pillars of educational policies that are usually lumped together under the category of neo-liberal New Public Management (Osborne, 2006). This braid of reform elements persists in spite of the fact that achieving a balance among them has proven elusive because they carry internal contradictions that are unarticulated or incompatible. However, in spite of the critiques by both conservative and critical pundits, they continue to hold promise. This book shies away from illusion and focuses on what can be seen from inside-out.

One of the issues in education is that all policies are a compromise between the hope that changing structures will quickly make schools work better (largely unrealistic, particularly given the divergent assumptions about what constitutes a better school), and the reality that school cultures and practices must change, which requires a great deal of time. Quick fixes, whether structural (permitting charter or academy schools), curricular (focusing on 'bright spots' and 'evidence-based practices' purported to rapidly increase student achievement), or staffing (regimented instructional protocols, differentiated pay or promotion), work in some places but not others and have limited lasting effects. Slow fixes (attacking underlying causes of poor learning or gradually raising standards, or expectations for professionals and for students) appear promising, but are watered down or disappear when new governments with differing priorities takeover. Recommendations for systemic reform in education (Schleicher, 2018) often appear vapid when they are reduced to bullet points rather than contextualized to a specific country.

The brilliance of this book is that, through the complex stories of 'how it really worked' in various settings in the United Kingdom, it highlights the promise, the shortcomings, and the new insights about the levers for long-term success in system change. The realistic picture is not always pretty, but it consistently balances a critical perspective with a conviction that as we learn more about the internal contradictions in school reform 'policy bundles' we equip ourselves for the next step on the journey. By consistently acknowledging that systemic reform is a 'wicked problem' (Rittel & Webber, 1973) that has no final solution, the authors also provide insights into the components of disappointing social experiments that lead to next steps.

The issue of power is fundamental to systemic reform, and the authors treat that topic boldly in this volume, but without ideological baggage. Who gets to decide what in a state or national education system is more highly fraught than many other public services: children spend most of their time in families (who are responsible for most of their development), in communities (where many of them are expected to contribute to and reflect its values) and are future contributors to increasingly globalized nations. But, as the cases analyzed in this book demonstrate, decisions about who gets to decide often seem motivated by (1) a sense that tired governments, whether central or 'middle tier,' have run out of ideas; (2) a belief that authorities are incompetent; or (3) general mistrust. This is a subtext of all of the cases in this book, although it is interwoven with the hope that change will build on the deep enthusiasm that most educators and families have to improve the lives and learning of children. The book begins with the optimistic story that emerged from the visible early successes (and wide publicity) associated with the London Challenge, but guides the reader slowly through the nuanced experiences of Manchester, Wales, and finally Scotland.

The arguments for more autonomy and quasi-privatization are driven by competing theories ranging from the 'invisible hand' (or boot) of neo-liberal economics (Apple, 2004), to the argument that the wisdom of teachers and families generates more educational innovation than bureaucracies (Junge, 2014). However, great hopes for the consequence of relatively small shifts in responsibility and authority, where choice and quasi-autonomy are constrained by heavy-handed accountability (Salokangas & Ainscow, 2017), seem misplaced, particularly when such shifts occur at a time of financial cutbacks. This old story emerges, again, as a thread in the complicated, multi-year experiences of authors who were in the middle of the change enterprise.

The evidence of research on school-based management suggests that it is difficult to carry out and often fails to touch the classroom. Under some circumstances, it is associated with better teaching, but the accumulating evidence over more than 20 years is hardly sufficient to argue that it is a basis for broad reform (Hingston, 2018; Louis, 1998). Furthermore, the logic of place-based educational reform that is sensitive to particular circumstances and local wisdom (Gruenewald & Smith, 2014) is powerful when applied to particular learning opportunities, but erodes when it confronts existing place-based inequities. Still, underlying the story of failures to meet the highest expectations is always the equally profound insight that, in spite of the challenges, some things worked and persisted in making a difference in London, Manchester, Wales and Scotland. Thus, rather than reading failure into each of the chapters, I came away further convinced that school reform requires 'steady work' rather than glitzy novelty (Elmore & McLaughlin, 1988).

Another example of their insights is networking. Early enthusiasm for networking, supported by a wide variety of scholars, focused on topics ranging from technology integration across schools (Schrum & Levin, 2009) to professional development for teachers (Stoll & Louis, 2007), to the development of systems of support between highly effective schools and those striving to become more effective (Earl & Katz, 2007; Wohlstetter, Malloy, Chau, & Polhemus, 2003). The authors of this book have all previously published extensively on the topic of school-to-school networks, and they retain a belief that the evidence supports the potential for networks in the four system change projects that form the heart of this book. They see it in political terms, as the power to create professionally centred relationships that are an alternative to top-down management of change. Although they believe in networks, the book explores in detail the ways in which they also have the potential to increase inequity, often because of policies that provide 'an unusual cocktail of competition and cooperation' and cannot guarantee rapid improvements. Although I have read some of the authors' previous work on this topic, the rich details of how policies support or constrain networks from achieving their promise are critical for anyone who is interested in designing or implementing efforts to break down the siloes between schools.

The book also provides a potential counterpoint to the apparently infinite capacity of local policies to divert broader national or state reform policies.

Cohen (1995) noted that expanding systemic reform policies in the United States 'pawned more agencies and increased political and administrative traffic without greatly increasing the capacity for instruction' (p. 13) – an observation that continues to resonate more than 20 years later. In contrast, this book points directly to the critical role of a relationship-centred 'middle tier' in countering administrative bloat, fragmentation and competition. Each of the four cases highlights how school networks and relationships with other local agencies have the potential to promote 'steady work.' The authors have introduced a focus on the middle tier in previous publications (Ainscow, 2015; Chapman & Hadfield, 2010), but here they deepen our understanding through their detailed descriptions of the variability among the middle tier arrangements. There is no 'one-size-fits-all' model for the middle tier: networks that create energy for reform emerge from the capacities and histories of the locations where they emerge. They also deteriorate when capacity erodes or old patterns re-emerge. This is not bottom-up or top-down reform, but 'centre-out' – adaptive structures and agencies influencing both school initiatives and (in the best circumstances) central government.

A final notable contribution of this book is its use of data and rich case material to explore theories of the relationship between policy and complex social change. A *technical policy perspective* is found in most policy analysis texts and among those advocating rational policy models (Ostrom, 1999). Policy-makers need information, including frameworks for understanding the sector that they are trying to affect, in order to make sensible legislative and regulatory decisions and to monitor policy impacts. This book provides much grist for the mill of school reform work because it illuminates the common causes of weakened policy impact. This requires a close read of each case because the ways in which policy can go off track are numerous. Other scholars emphasize a *political perspective*, focusing on a naturalistic explanation of how policies are made, and how they spread. Both the indeterminate nature of the policy-making process and the inevitable slippage that occurs as additional policy refinements accrue during implementation are fodder for explaining how policies succeed or fail (Forrester & Adams, 1997; Kingdon, 1995). Again each of the cases points to the way in which 'steady work' in the different contexts made a difference in overcoming distrust, creating more enduring partnerships, and building capacities where they did not previously exist. A *practitioner perspective* emerges from studies of public sector administrators and civil servants, and examines how the strain toward autonomy in interpreting policies affects the broader process of complex change. Professionals who will be affected by proposed changes often see new policies and regulations as distractions from their 'real work,' and therefore interpret them to fit their needs (Weatherly & Lipsky, 1977). Rather than being passive recipients of policy, educators are creative actors in the policy-making process (Honig & Hatch, 2004) as they orchestrate the *local* policy process (Pocklington & Wallace, 2014; Wallace, 2003).

Each of these perspectives has validity, but they are seldom integrated in applied policy analyses, creating frustration for everyone who wants to

xii Foreword

understand how we ended up in our most current public service messes. How are clusters of policies – systemic efforts at reform – embedded and transmitted to create impact? How does local autonomy shift the process of system change? This book suggests that there are no easy answers. However, if we hope for real change that affects most schools in most local contexts, we cannot rely on the top (system policy is not enough) nor the bottom (the energy and enthusiasm of individual schools will not change a system), but must also create effective middle tier systems that are relational rather than procedural. I applaud the message of complexity, critique and hope as well as the depth and detail with which it is conveyed.

Karen Seashore Louis
Regents Professor of Organizational Leadership, Policy and Development
Robert H. Beck Chair of Ideas in Education
University of Minnesota
May 2019

References

Ainscow, M. (2015). *Towards self-improving school systems: Lessons from a city challenge.* Abingdon-on-Thames: Routledge.

Apple, M. W. (2004). Creating difference: Neo-liberalism, neo-conservatism and the politics of educational reform. *Educational Policy, 18*(1), 12–44.

Chapman, C., & Hadfield, M. (2010). Supporting the middle tier to engage with school-based networks: Change strategies for influencing and cohering. *Journal of Educational Change, 11*(3), 221–240.

Cohen, D. K. (1995). What is the system in systemic reform? *Educational Researcher, 24*(9), 11–31.

Earl, L., & Katz, S. (2007). Leadership in networked learning communities: Defining the terrain. *School Leadership and Management, 27*(3), 239–258.

Elmore, R. F., & McLaughlin, M. W. (1988). *Steady Work. Policy, Practice, and the Reform of American Education.* Santa Monica, CA: Rand Corporation.

Forrester, J. P., & Adams, G. B. (1997). Budgetary reform through organizational learning - Toward an organizational theory of budgeting. *Administration & Society, 28*(4), 466–488.

Gruenewald, D. A., & Smith, G. A. (2014). *Place-based education in the global age: Local diversity*: Routledge.

Hingston, J. (2018). *The Impact of School Autonomy Reform on Secondary Principals.* Ph.D. dissertation. School of Education. University of Newcastle. Newcastle, New South Wales, AU.

Honig, M., & Hatch, T. (2004). Crafting coherence: How schools strategically manage multiple, conflicting demands. *Educational Researcher, 33*(8), 16–30.

Junge, E. R. (2014). Charter school path paved with choice, compromise, common sense.

Kingdon, J. W. (1995). *Agendas, alternatives, and public policies* (2nd ed.). New York: Harper Collins.

Louis, K. S. (1998). A light feeling of chaos: Educational reform and policy in the United States. *Daedalus, 127*(4), 13–40.

Osborne, S. P. (2006). The New Public Governance? *Public Management Review, 8*(3), 377–387. doi:10.1080/14719030600853022

Ostrom, E. (1999). Institutional rational choice: An assessment of the institutional analysis and development framework. In P. A. Sabatier (Ed.), *Theories of the Policy Process* (pp. 21–64). Boulder, CO: Westview Press.

Pocklington, K., & Wallace, M. (2014). *Managing complex educational change: Large scale reorganisation of schools*: Routledge.

Rinehart, R. M. (2017). *Intergroup dynamics in education reform: How identity, power, and emotions hinder systemic reform*. Paper presented at the Academy of Management Proceedings.

Rittel, H., & Webber, M. (1973). Dilemmas in a general theory of planning. *Policy sciences, 4*(2), 155–169.

Salokangas, M., & Ainscow, M. (2017). *Inside the autonomous school: making sense of a global educational trend*: Routledge.

Schleicher, A. (2018). *World Class: How to Build a 21st-Century School System*. Paris: OECD Publishing.

Schrum, L., & Levin, B. B. (2009). *Leading 21st-century schools: Harnessing technology for engagement and achievement*: Corwin Press.

Stoll, L., & Louis, K. S. (2007). *Professional learning communities: Divergence, depth and dilemmas.* New York: McGraw Hill.

Wallace, M. (2003). Managing the unmanageale?: Coping with complex educational change. *Educational Management and Administration, 31*(1), 9–29.

Weatherly, R., & Lipsky, M. (1977). Street level bureaucrats and institutional innovation: Implementing special education reform. *Harvard Educational Review, 47*(2), 171–197.

Wohlstetter, P., Malloy, C. L., Chau, D., & Polhemus, J. L. (2003). Improving schools through networks: A new approach to urban school reform. *Educational Policy, 17*(4), 399–430.

PREFACE

The material we present in this book derives from a programme of development and research going back almost 30 years. It began with a small-scale project in England, known as Improving the Quality of Education for All (IQEA), and led on to a series of other initiatives, some small and some large. Many of these took place in the United Kingdom. In addition, we have been privileged to participate in related developments in other parts of the world.

Common to all these initiatives is a focus on equity. Taking a lead from the OECD, we see this as involving the principles of inclusion and fairness. A further common feature was that all these developments involved teams of academic researchers working alongside practitioners and, sometimes, policy-makers, using ideas from research to inform and guide developments in the field.

In carrying out this work we have frequently found ourselves struggling to determine how best to position ourselves. Our ideal stance is that of researchers who are 'at the table' when important decisions are being discussed. At the same time, we want to be able to offer views that may sometimes challenge what is being said. This is a fine line to walk. Choosing not to challenge becomes a form of collusion in the worst sense of the term. On the other hand, too much challenge is likely to lead to the invitation to be at the table being withdrawn, which, as we explain, occasionally became a feature of some of the experiences we describe in this book.

An implication of all of this is that the accounts we present draw on the work and ideas of lots of people, far too many to name. These include practitioners, community representatives, civil servants and politicians, including, in some instances, government ministers. Inevitably, some of these colleagues will disagree with our interpretations and the conclusions we draw. We hope, however, that they will recognise their contributions, all of which have helped stimulate our thinking. In thanking them, we dedicate the book to everybody who has been part of the stories we tell.

Nearer to home, we must acknowledge the support and professional stimulation we have had from colleagues over the years at the Universities of Cambridge, Nottingham, Warwick and Wolverhampton, and more recently at Cardiff, Glasgow and Manchester, and, much further away, at the Queensland University of Technology. Particular thanks to Paul Armstrong for his contributions to Chapter 6.

We must also thank those who have supported each of us at a more personal level. Mel thanks Kiki Messiou for her continuing inspiration, support and challenge. He also acknowledges the influence of two brilliant school teachers: his son, Dan, and his daughter, Lucy, both of whom provide frequent reminders of the pressures facing those who work in our schools. Chris thanks Ann, Aonghas, Mairead and Calum for their unconditional support and encouragement. Mark would like to thank all the lobsters who got out of the pot in South Wales and tried to make a difference.

Finally, we must thank Professor Karen Seashore Louis for providing a splendid foreword that relates our experiences to international developments.

Mel Ainscow, Christopher Chapman and Mark Hadfield
May 2019

1
CHANGING EDUCATION SYSTEMS

Change is high on the agenda of education systems around the world. In particular, there is widespread concern to bring about sustainable improvements in the way schools serve learners from disadvantaged and minority backgrounds. This focus on equity is evident in both the developed and the developing world (OECD, 2012; UNESCO, 2015).

With this theme as our overall focus, in this book we ask, *how can equitable change in education systems be best achieved?* Recognising that this has considerable implications for those of us in the research community, we also ask, *how can our work be used to inform efforts to address the equity policy challenge?*

In this introductory chapter, we provide an overview of the evidence we use to address these two questions. We discuss our involvement in a series of system-level improvement initiatives in various parts of the United Kingdom. Unusually, wherever possible, we do this by combining evidence collected from an insider perspective with data generated from independent research and evaluations. First, however, we contextualise these developments in relation to international efforts to promote equity within education systems.

The international change agenda

Since 1990, the United Nation's Education for All movement has worked to make quality basic education available to all learners (Opertti, Walker & Zhang, 2014). Reflecting on progress over the 15 years that followed, a Global Monitoring Report pointed out that, despite improvements, there were still 58 million children out of school globally and around 100 million children who do not complete primary education (UNESCO, 2015). The report goes on to conclude that inequality in education has increased, with the poorest and

2 Changing education systems

most disadvantaged shouldering the heaviest burden. Indeed, it suggests that the world's poorest children are 'four times more likely not to go to school than the world's richest children, and five times more likely not to complete primary school' (p. ii).

Whilst this situation is most acute in the developing world, there are similar concerns in many wealthier countries, as noted by the OECD (2018), which reports that across its member countries, almost one in five students does not reach a basic minimum level of skills to function in today's societies. It also states that students from low socio-economic background are twice as likely to be low performers, implying that an individual's social circumstances present obstacles to them achieving their educational potential.

An earlier OECD report, *'No more failures: ten steps to equity in education'* (2007), argued that educational equity has two dimensions. First, it is a matter of *fairness*, which implies ensuring that individuals' social circumstances – for example gender, socio-economic status or ethnic origin – should not be an obstacle to achieving educational potential. Second, it is to do with *inclusion*, which is about ensuring a basic minimum standard of education for all. The report noted that the two dimensions are closely intertwined: 'tackling school failure helps to overcome the effects of social deprivation which often causes school failure' (p. 11).

The report goes on to argue that a fair and inclusive education is desirable because of the human rights imperative for people to be able to develop their capacities and participate fully in society. It also reminds us of the long-term social and financial costs of educational failure: those without the skills to participate socially and economically generate higher costs for health, income support, child welfare and security. In addition, increased migration poses new challenges for social cohesion in more and more countries.

Despite the efforts made in response to these arguments, in many parts of the world a gap remains between the achievements of students from rich and poor families (UNESCO, 2010). The extent of this gap varies significantly between countries. So, for example:

> In a world-class system like Finland's, socioeconomic standing is far less predictive of student achievement. All things being equal, a low-income student in the United States is far less likely to do well in school than a low-income student in Finland. Given the enormous economic impact of educational achievement, this is one of the best indicators of equal opportunity in a society.
>
> (Mourshed, Chijioke & Barber, 2010, pp. 8–9)

However, more recent international comparisons indicate that the best performing school systems manage to provide high-quality education for all of their students. School systems cannot easily buck wider social trends, however, and

Changing education systems **3**

growing social inequality leads to increases in educational inequality, and not just for the poorest families:

> Inequalities in educational attainment and outcomes have a social gradient. It is not just poor children who do less well than everybody else: across the social spectrum children do less well than those with household social position just above their own families.
>
> (Pickett & Vanderbloemen, 2015, p. 24)

The implication is that whilst it is possible for countries to develop education systems that are both excellent and equitable, the more socially unequal a society the more profoundly problematic this is.

Encouragement for a more optimistic view is provided by the recent 'Report Card' prepared for Unicef (2018) by the Innocenti Centre. Focusing on high- and middle-income countries, it concludes:

> Tackling educational inequality does not mean sacrificing high standards. Countries with higher average achievement tend to have lower levels of inequality. . . . Bringing the worst performing students up does not mean pulling the best-performing students down. (p. 3)

Warning against the temptation to copy what more successful countries do well, the authors of the report argue that lessons undoubtedly can be learned from these countries, but they must be replicated with care. There are, it argues, many sources of inequality in education related to political, economic, social, cultural and institutional contexts, and these vary across countries. What works in one country may not work elsewhere. To take a specific example, Fullan (2009) notes that Finland has no system of national testing, but that does not mean that the absence of testing is always a good thing. An emphasis on system change strategies being contextually sensitive is one of the pervading themes in the following chapters.

Bringing our brief review of the international policy context up to date, the year 2016 was particularly significant. Building on the Incheon Declaration agreed at the World Forum on Education in May 2015, UNESCO published the Education 2030 Framework for Action in 2016. This emphasizes inclusion and equity as laying the foundations for quality education. It also stresses the need to address all forms of exclusion and marginalization, disparities and inequalities in access, participation, and learning processes and outcomes. In this way, it is made clear that the international Education for All policy agenda really has to be about 'all' and that social and educational inequality cannot simply be disentangled.

Taking account of this international policy agenda, in the chapters that follow we argue that effective system change requires the coming together of processes of social learning and actions within settings that stretch from multiple classrooms to the committee rooms of senior policy-makers. In order to contribute,

4 Changing education systems

researchers have to develop new skills in creating collaborative partnerships that cross borders between actors who have different professional experiences. As we will show, this is a messy rather than a linear process – technically simple but socially complex. Subsequent chapters illustrate how the different roles and socio-cultural contexts of policy-makers/practitioners and academics create a complex set of power relations that have to be factored into processes as simple as introducing ideas from research to the complexities of co-producing knowledge and joint action.

Research and policy-making

The belief that research can simply be 'applied to practice' and have direct effects in the field has now largely been abandoned, even though it may still be held by some researchers, who, it has been suggested, 'seem surprised or even dismayed that their work is not immediately adopted into policy or practice' (Levin, 2011, p. 17). Reimers and McGinn (1997) argue that education systems are 'arenas of conflict' rather than machines, and what they do is a reflection of how different actors within the system construct their roles. In this book, we draw on our privileged positions as researchers who have worked across arenas of conflict through our involvement in a series of large-scale improvement programmes in the United Kingdom. This leads us to offer advice on how research and, indeed, researchers can best contribute to improvements in the field. We argue that education systems will only be able to use research effectively if steps are taken to overcome locally specific social, political and cultural barriers. As we explain, this analysis has implications for policy-makers, practitioners and, indeed, for those of us working in the world of academic research.

Much has been written about the relationship between research and policy, some of which has focused on the quality of educational research itself. For example, over a decade ago, Whitty (2006) summarised what he saw as the abuse of educational research. Although much has changed in the United Kingdom since this was written, these perceptions remain as strong as ever. However, for the purposes of this book, we put issues about the quality of the research to one side in order to focus on two key sets of relationships: between research and policy-making and, just as significantly, between researchers and practitioners.

Some of the literature sets up divisions between those involved in the production of research and those involved in the construction of policies in public services (e.g., Innvaer et al., 2002). In contrast to this polarised position, Katherine Smith (2013, pp. 38–39) offers five contrasting ways of conceptualising the relationship between research and policy. These relate specifically to public health, but they seem to hold true for broader public policy as well. Smith's conceptualisations point to a set of useful pointers for action, as follows:

1. **Technocratic and instrumental:** Whilst research should be one of the key factors influencing policy-makers, politics often gets in the way. This

means that, in order to improve impact, researchers need to develop better relationships with policy-makers and must produce policy-relevant findings.

2. **Complex and messy:** Although many factors influence policy-making, relatively small factors can sometimes lead to significant changes. Chance can also play a significant role. Therefore, researchers who want to have an impact need to work as policy entrepreneurs, promoting solutions to appropriate audiences and adapting solutions to exploit emergent policy windows.

3. **Normative, political and interest-based:** Policy decisions are often the result of political ideologies and interests. Whilst research findings may play a role in influencing ideology, they are rarely adopted unless they fit with established positions. By developing closer relationships with policy-makers, researchers can increase the impact of their research but only when it supports the dominant ideological discourse.

4. **Democratic and conceptual:** Public perceptions and values influence policy decisions and research cumulatively over long time frames. Therefore, whilst research may occasionally influence research directly, the more common influence is through contributing knowledge that shifts conceptualisations of particular issues. This highlights the importance of sensitivity regarding concepts, language and discourses.

5. **Constructivist and sociological:** The relationship between research and policy is a 'multi-directional interplay.' Here, language and discourse are again important, particularly as the knowledge exchanged is translated and transformed as it moves between actors. It is therefore helpful to think about ideas, rather than evidence, as the unit of analysis.

Smith's five conceptualisations are underpinned by social, political and cultural factors that act as facilitators to and/or barriers of efforts to influence policy-making. Any system may hold elements of each of them at any one time, although the blend may vary both over time and between different teams and units within a given context. This suggests that, in order for research to influence policy, researchers are likely to require a sophisticated understanding of the policy landscape and a range of tools and approaches to ensure that evidence influences decisions.

Smith still seems to see researchers as adopting a traditional stance, that of the interested spectator, who gathers evidence and finds ways of feeding the findings into the field of play. We adopt a radically different stance, that of *engaged researchers*, who work alongside policy-makers and practitioners in the field, using our research-based knowledge to inform decision-making as it occurs. Being an engaged researcher, embedded within central government policy-making but also working alongside practitioners as they reconstruct policy at different levels of an education system, not least the level of the school, is a difficult stance to adopt. The accounts we provide in subsequent chapters throw light on the nature of these difficulties.

6 Changing education systems

Influencing policy-making

With regard to education policy-making, the uptake of research findings often remains limited. For example, Harris et al. (2013) argue that, despite a valid knowledge base about what works and why at classroom, school and increasingly system levels, policy-making communities have been reluctant to engage with research findings, and when they have, this has tended to be selective. This can lead to situations where political ideology, anecdote and, on occasion, whim dominate policy-making.

One system where research evidence does appear to have had an impact on decision making is in Ontario, Canada. Reasons for this that have been suggested include the strong influence of international assessments and global exchanges in generating the desire to have leading-edge knowledge to inform improvements, and the key role of individual researchers in working in and with the education system (Harris et al., 2013). This reiterates the argument that there is a need for strong relationships between researchers, policy-makers and practitioners, plus fluidity of movement of researchers into and out of government positions of the sort described later in this book. In this way, the flow of communication and influence can build shared understandings and strengthen social and professional capital between research and policy communities. However, the situation in Ontario changed following the election of a new provincial government in 2018, reminding us that political processes and timelines create their own set of barriers to educational change. Further examples of this are illustrated in the accounts we provide, which may be relevant to those colleagues involved in the developments in Ontario.

The lack of evidence-based policy-making in other national systems has been explained by communication, institutional, and cultural gaps between researchers and policy-makers (Mitton et al., 2007). Such gaps can have an adverse effect, leading to professional divides, suspicion and mistrust that become mutually reinforcing in ways that create a downward spiral that further minimises research influence on policy-making.

Policy change in education usually involves a process of complex negotiation between competing interests. This is another explanation for the paucity of research utilisation within the policy-making process (Reimers & McGinn, 1997). Levin (2011) provides a helpful practical model to consider how knowledge mobilisation occurs, using three interconnected contexts: production, use and mediation. These contexts are not necessarily structures. Rather, they are better thought of as functions, with some people, organisations or groups operating in one or more of the contexts. Those that attempt to move between research and policy communities operate across all three contexts. Sullivan and Skelcher (2002) refer to such individuals as 'reticulists' who build capacity and collaborative practices to enhance their influence. They tend to be:

- *Skilled communicators* – adapting their language to specific settings and empathising with others through negotiation and seeing a situation from a range of perspectives.

- *Excellent networkers* – gaining access to a range of settings, seeking out and connecting with others with common interests and goals.
- *Strategic in orientation* – seeing the 'big picture' and understanding how different partners can contribute to achieve common goals.
- *Contextually astute* – understanding how opportunities and constraints within the organisation can influence individual's behaviour.
- *Problem-solvers* – thinking laterally and creatively to seek solutions to the challenges they face.
- *Self-managing* – taking risks within a framework that understands organisational capacity. In this sense they have sound organisational skills.

Even with such qualities, however, the challenge of knowledge mobilization and research uptake remains a complex process involving varied influences, from the motivation and skills of decision-makers to the ability of researchers to effect decision-making structures and processes. A sense of what this can mean is well illustrated by David Laws, a former Schools' Minister in the UK government, who commented:

> A lot of decision-making is not based on evidence but on hunch. I had little coming to me from civil servants that presented the latest academic evidence. Too often, they just serve up practical advice about how the minister can do what he or she wants. But politicians are prone to make decisions based on ideology and personal experience.[1]

This graphically highlights some of the challenges faced by researchers working in the spaces between research and policy-making/practitioner communities. With this in mind, in what follows we explain our experiences of attempting to navigate these spaces within various education systems.

Generating data

The arguments we develop draw on our 'insider' involvement as researchers employed as advisers and facilitators within a series of system change initiatives in different parts of the United Kingdom over the last ten years or so.[2] The largest of these projects are City Challenge in England (2003-11), Schools Challenge Cymru in Wales (2014-17), and the Scottish Attainment Challenge (2015-18). Each of these has had a strong central government mandate and represented massive financial and resource investments in national systems. In addition, we draw on our experiences within a series of smaller scale developments that embedded us even more deeply in the action in the field.

Whilst the three of us were not all directly involved in all of these developments, throughout their existence we acted as critical friends to one another as we worked individually in one or more of the contexts. In this way, we have been able to share experiences, provide mutual support and develop a shared

8 Changing education systems

intelligence about how to mobilise the use of research evidence and influence key decision-making processes at different levels of systems.

As we show in later chapters, this shared intelligence was based upon some successes in using research knowledge to inform decision making, as well as some disappointments. These experiences confirm for us the advice of Jane Tinkler (2012), who argued that when *'those in power seek academics out, they usually want the result of experience and expertise built up over an academic's career, rather than just the findings from a particular piece of research'* (p. 1). This means that as engaged researchers we had to find the right balance in slowly opening up certain cultures to the idea of using research, and developing the critical capacity of individuals and groups in its use with on-the-hoof decisions as to when to make contributions and challenge existing assumptions.

To varying degrees, the projects we describe each adopt an overall 'development and research' approach (Ainscow et al., 2012a). This is one of a family of methodologies referred to by Fishman et al. (2013) as 'design-based implementation research.' They aim to transcend traditional research/practice barriers in order to facilitate the design of educational interventions that are 'effective, sustainable, and scalable.' This is seen as occurring when researcher and practitioner knowledge meet in particular sites, aimed at producing new knowledge about ways in which broad values might better be realized in future practice. Our interest in this form of engagement goes back to the early 1990s when we were all three involved in the Improving the Quality of Education for All (IQEA) initiative, with its emphasis on researchers collaborating with networks of schools, using collaborative inquiry to promote equitable developments (Hopkins, Ainscow & West, 1994).

Our involvement in the projects we describe was as advisers and facilitators working on a part-time basis, wherever possible using our knowledge of evidence from relevant research to guide decision making and to affect decision-making structures and processes. At the same time, we viewed our involvements as opportunities to generate evidence to answer our own research questions in relation to themes that would be of interest to a wider audience of practitioners, policy-makers and researchers. This points to a rather obvious methodological challenge regarding the analysis we provide in later chapters. As researchers, we were given remarkable opportunities to put into practice ideas that had emerged from many years of investigating ways of developing more equitable schools and education systems. At the same time, we were provided with privileged access to information about how decisions are made within a national education system. On the other hand, as engaged players, often charged with the task of championing the projects, how far can our interpretations be trusted, not least because efforts to collect data about the processes involved were mainly carried out in an incidental way?

Wherever possible, this methodological challenge is addressed in the book by triangulating data generated in different ways. First, it is based on an analysis of our archive of documents that record the development of the projects, including observation notes and records of meetings with stakeholders. Second, when available, sets of data are drawn from independent evaluations commissioned by governments or local authorities. Usually these studies provided an analysis of statistics that track the progress of students on national tests. In some instances, they also generated qualitative data collected through surveys of staff in schools, plus interviews with samples of stakeholders, including students, politicians, national and local administrators, advisers and school leaders.

The accounts presented also draw on records of our many discussions with those involved in the initiatives, as we moved in and out of the action in the field. In addition, we use evidence collected more directly through policy documents, statistical data, informal observations and interviews with participants. As we have indicated, our involvement placed us in a position of having privileged access to information regarding the way decisions are made within an education system, from the levels of government ministers and senior civil servants through to that of teachers in the classroom. All of this provided frequent reminders of the cultural, social and political complexities involved when trying to bring about changes in the way that an education system does its business.

Our decision to adopt the stance of engaged researchers, rather than what we have referred to as spectator researchers, presents complex ethical challenges. These occur during periods of engagement in the field and then later when writing accounts of the sort we present in this book. As far as possible, in our working relations in the field, we made it clear that we saw ourselves as commentators on what happens, with an intension to publish our findings. However, given the numbers of people involved and the many encounters that occurred, we know that some colleagues were not aware that this was part of our purpose, particularly those we met in passing. In relation to those with whom we had more intensive working relationships, one of our strategies was to produce written summaries and discussion documents that were shared and discussed with stakeholders. Indeed, these texts are part of the evidence we have drawn on in writing the accounts that follow.

In terms of writing these accounts, we have been careful to ensure that particular stakeholders cannot be identified. However, given the public profile of the various initiatives and, especially, the key political figures involved, it is sometimes impossible to avoid naming individuals.

Common features

Although each of the projects that we describe had its own design, they do share common features. In particular, they each sought to explore new, more fruitful working relationships: between national and local government; between administrators and practitioners; within and between schools; and between schools and their local communities. They also led to the evolution of a way of thinking about educational change as we drew lessons from the various initiatives. Broadly stated, this involves processes of collaborative inquiry that require analysis to

10 Changing education systems

formulate change strategies that relate to particular contexts. At the heart of this approach is a social learning process within which different types of knowledge and theories, both professional and academic, stimulate reflection, debate and, most important, practice experimentations at all levels of a system. The role of the engaged researcher involves stimulating professional dialogues within a relationship based on the collaborative 'joint production' of knowledge, rather than one of trying to broker in 'external research.' Such collaborative co-production requires those involved to be aware of internal power dynamics and to recognise and value the differences and limitations of the forms of theorizing and knowledge each brings to the field of practice.

A useful theoretical interpretation of this approach is that it seeks to strengthen social capital, a factor known to be a feature of education systems that are more able to foster greater equity (Payne, 2008; Putman, 2000). In other words, it requires relationships across different levels of the system in order to establish new pathways through which energy, expertise and lessons from innovations can spread. At the same time, the greater awareness of what was happening elsewhere often challenged expectations as to what is possible, particularly with regard to the progress of students from economically disadvantaged backgrounds.

The use of this approach was influenced by our earlier research that placed an emphasis on mutual critique, within and between schools, based on an engagement with shared data (Ainscow et al., 2006, 2012b). This, in turn, involves strong collective commitment from senior school staff and a willingness to share responsibility for system reform (Chapman, 2008).

We argue that this requires the coming together of different perspectives in a process of social learning and knowledge creation within particular settings. To have a worthwhile role, researchers have to develop new skills in establishing collaborative partnerships that cross borders between actors who have different professional experiences. They also need to mobilise support in dealing with the pressures this involves. In subsequent chapters, we illustrate how the different roles and socio-cultural contexts of policy-makers/practitioners and academics create a complex set of power relations that have to be factored into the process of introducing ideas from research.

Conclusion

In the seven chapters that follow we describe, analyse and reflect on our experiences working as engaged researchers to a series of system change initiatives in the United Kingdom. We begin in the next chapter with the largest of these developments, City Challenge in England. Launched in London in 2003, the success of City Challenge has been widely reported, leading to extensive debates about the key factors that led to its impact. Since its completion it has had an ongoing influence on other developments, not least the ones we describe in subsequent chapters. Relevant to the later developments in Wales and Scotland, each with a strong inclusive ethos, there is evidence that London's success can be explained, at least in part, by the ways in which schools have responded to increased diversity within the student population.

In this chapter, we examine the evidence regarding what has been called the 'London effect' before focusing more specifically on the work of the Greater Manchester Challenge between 2008 and 2011. This was a follow-on project that involved a partnership between national government, local authorities, schools and other stakeholders, and it had a government investment of around £50 million. The decision to invest such a large amount reflected a concern regarding educational standards in the region, particularly amongst children and young people from disadvantaged backgrounds. The approach adopted, which was influenced by the earlier initiative in London, was based on an analysis of local context and used processes of networking and collaboration to make better use of available expertise.

In Chapter 3, we provide an account of Schools Challenge Cymru, the Welsh government's three-year flagship initiative to promote equity across its education system. Starting in 2014, its aims were to bring about rapid improvements in the performance of 40 secondary schools serving the more disadvantaged communities, and then to use lessons from these developments to strengthen the capacity of the education system to improve itself. The design of the initiative was informed by lessons from the City Challenge programme in England. In particular, it was based on an assumption that education systems have potential to improve themselves, provided policy-makers allow the space for practitioners to make use of the expertise and creativity that lies trapped within individual schools and classrooms. Therefore, the aim was to 'move knowledge around,' and it was assumed that the best way to do this would be through strengthening collaboration within schools, between schools and beyond schools.

We explain that the barriers experienced in Wales mainly related to existing ways of working, which, although well intended, were seen to consume time and resources and to delay action in the field. We also discuss how, despite a highly positive independent evaluation, the project was discontinued as a result of changes in political leadership. Nevertheless, there is evidence that the programme has continued to influence thinking and practice across the Welsh education system, suggesting that, as intended, it has acted as a catalyst for change. In the chapter, we provide an analysis of the particular dynamics of change within the Welsh context.

Staying in Wales and moving closer to the action in the field, in Chapter 4 we look at what is involved when education systems seek to strengthening links between schools to provide mutual support and challenge. Drawing on our involvement over a four-year period, we analyse more closely what happened as one of four regional education consortia, Central South Wales, explored such a move. In particular, we look at the challenges involved in strengthening collaboration between schools within policy contexts that emphasise competition as a means of achieving improvements. We also examine the nature of the transitional arrangements that are required to move a system from a bureaucratic and hierarchical approach to governance to a more collaborative and polycentric one.

12 Changing education systems

Whilst there was significant progress in developing a self-improving system across schools in the five local authorities that make up the Central South Wales region, this remained fragile for a variety of reasons, including the tendency for governments to revert to top-down decision making when faced with major policy changes. There was also the continuing impact of national accountability systems. Publication of school test scores and inspection reports, and grading schools in terms of the degree of support that they require, tended to discourage cooperation between schools.

Moving on to Scotland, in Chapter 5 we describe and analyse the Scottish Attainment Challenge, a national change initiative that was launched in 2015 with high levels of political commitment. The programme is still developing, and there is scant independent evidence assessing the impact of the programme to date. It is, however, clear that the experiences in England and Wales, referred to in earlier chapters, influenced the way the policy was designed and implemented.

The Scottish initiative has a strong national mandate and high levels of funding, and it has already stimulated interesting developments in some parts of the country. At the same time, it has faced barriers rather similar to those in England and Wales. The most striking of these relates to the ways in which decisions are made. Put simply, this involves constant tensions between national and local politicians and administrators, a matter that has been further illuminated through attempts to create a series of regional collaboratives similar to those in Wales. In this context, school leaders have far less influence on decision making than their counterparts in England, a factor that is currently under review. We go on to consider what needs to happen to move the programme forward.

Chapter 6 continues the focus on how contextual factors, not least competing national policies, can act as barriers to change within education systems. Looking at more recent developments in a number of English school districts, we examine the role of the middle tier in a national education system, where schools are increasingly autonomous, within a policy context that emphasises competition and choice. A major strand of development has been the rapid expansion of the academies programme. This involves schools being funded directly by the national government rather than through a local authority.

These developments are set within a policy context in which the dominant model has become schools linking together in multi-academy trusts. All of this is leading to a worrying level of system fragmentation that is further disadvantaging learners from poorer backgrounds and increasing the marginalization and exclusion of certain groups of students. We argue that, despite this trend, greater autonomy for schools still makes sense, particularly if it provides space for practitioners to innovate. The problem, in the English context, is that other policies based on competition between schools have tended to prevent this from happening. Rather, they have led to a search for one-size-fits-all strategies for improving examination and test scores that can be imposed on teachers. Reflecting on developments in various parts of the country, we go on to recommend actions needed to make school autonomy more effective in promoting equity within education systems in which policy is based on market forces.

It is important to stress that this book does not offer a toolkit of techniques that can be moved from place to place. Rather, it describes and explains the development of a form of intelligence, a way of thinking that should be used flexibly in response to local circumstances. In Chapter 7, we argue that this approach has the potential to create the conditions within which researchers can contribute directly to system change. Putting ideas from research into play in such developments, however, remains difficult because of certain forms of contextual barriers. These barriers include *social factors*, including the extent to which relationships exist that encourage the sharing of expertise in an atmosphere of mutual respect and challenge; *political factors*, due to the impact of the attitudes and preferences of key partners, and their varied views as to project goals, and the relative openness or closed nature of local leadership and decision-making structures; and *cultural factors*, related to local traditions and the expectations of those involved as to what is possible and the role research and researchers should play in system reform.

In this chapter, we draw on a series of further studies that have involved the use of collaborative inquiry within networks of schools in order to consider how these barriers can be addressed. This leads us to suggest a strategic model that sets out to clarify the positions and relationships between practitioners and policymakers, on the one hand, and researchers on the other.

Finally, in Chapter 8, we draw together the argument developed throughout the book and provide a series of propositions that can be used to think about how school systems can be supported in making better use of research knowledge and researcher engagement. We argue that this has the potential to create new spaces within which academic researchers can become partners in the process of improvement, adding their expertise to that which exists within a school system. What connects these propositions and gives them coherence is the way they focus attention on the importance of managing and interconnecting individual, organisational and system level learning within complex transitional dynamics. In such contexts, researchers – acting as critical friends, drawing attention to relevant research evidence from elsewhere and advising how processes of inquiry can be built into strategies that are trialled – can make significant contributions.

We end by contrasting this thinking with a very different approach to the use of research knowledge in education that is becoming dominant in an increasing number of countries, not least in the United Kingdom. Sometimes referred to as the 'what works' approach, it operates with a set of assumptions regarding the use of research knowledge based on a logic model that frames the problem in terms of how to convince practitioners to change their practices in the light of external research evidence (Tripney et al., 2018). The implication is that practitioners are there to 'deliver' practices that have been designed and evaluated by researchers. In this way, practitioners are framed as knowledge users rather than

14 Changing education systems

knowledge creators, an overly passive image that has undermined the attempts of many external researchers to engage them in professional dialogues around their decision making and practices.

Notes

1 *The Guardian*, August 1, 2017.
2 It should be noted that the four countries that make up the United Kingdom – England, Northern Ireland, Scotland and Wales – each has its own education policies.

2

CITY CHALLENGE IN ENGLAND

Drawing the lessons

Staying with our focus on achieving equitable changes within education systems and how research and researchers can support such processes, in this chapter we look at the City Challenge programme in England. This large-scale initiative, which has had a major impact on thinking in the field, generated a series of ideas that have subsequently informed the projects we describe in the later chapters.

In writing about City Challenge, we are conscious that a wide range of publications have already attempted to make sense of the successes of the initiative, first in London, and then later in the Black Country (in the West Midlands) and Greater Manchester (e.g., Blanden et al., 2015; Barrs et al., 2014; Claeys, Kempton & Paterson, 2014; Greaves, Macmillan & Sibieta, 2014; Hutchings et al., 2012; Hutchings & Mansaray, 2013; Kidson & Norris, 2014; Ofsted, 2010). What is distinctive about our contribution, however, is that as participant observers we are able to examine what happened from the inside.[1] This enables us to draw lessons that we believe will be useful to those in other parts of the world who are interested in system-level change in relation to equity.

Building on the findings of our earlier research, these lessons point to an approach to system change based on an analysis of local contexts, and processes of networking and collaboration in order to make better use of available expertise. Our analysis of what happened also throws light on some of the difficulties involved in trying to use research knowledge to assist in the design of such projects.

The context of England

The English education system is a particularly interesting context to consider when thinking about the challenge of equity, as noted in a 2007 OECD study, which reported that the impact of socio-economic circumstances on young people's

16 City Challenge in England

attainment was more marked in the UK than in any other of the 52 countries considered. Illustrating the complex nature of the patterns of inequality that exist, Kerr and West (2011) suggest that we see poverty, as indicated by eligibility for free school meals,[2] is strongly associated with low attainment, more so for white British students than for other ethnic groups; children from homes with single and/or unemployed parents, and parents who have few educational qualifications themselves, often do less well at school; and, of the minority ethnic groups, British students of Chinese and Indian heritage are generally the most successful and African-Caribbean students the least successful. Summing this up, Benn and Millar (2006) argue that one of the biggest problems the country faces is 'the gap between rich and poor, and the enormous disparity in children's home backgrounds and the social and cultural capital they bring to the educational table' (p. 145).

London Challenge was introduced during a period of successive Labour Governments (1997 to 2010), which saw extensive efforts to address growing social and educational inequality. These developments were part of an intensification of political interest in education, especially regarding standards and management of the state system (Whitty, 2010). This led to a series of highly centralised national strategies to strengthen practices of teaching and leadership. At the same time, competition between schools was seen to be one of the keys to 'driving up standards,' whilst at the same time further reducing the control of local authorities over provision.[3] All of this was intended to 'liberate' schools from the bureaucracy of local government and establish a form of marketplace. In this way, families would have greater choice as to which school their youngsters would attend, informed by school reports from the national inspection agency, the Office for Standards in Education (Ofsted), and the annual publication of school test and examination results.

During that period, a number of policy efforts also addressed factors that lie beyond schools. These recognised that children's academic performance cannot be divorced from other aspects of their development and what happens to them outside school in their families, neighbourhoods, and more widely. These initiatives sought to improve and equalise educational outcomes by aligning schools' core activities of teaching and learning with interventions targeting other aspects of children's lives. All of this was part of a Children's Plan that set out a framework for organising child and family services based on the principle that Every Child Matters, i.e., that all children should be healthy, stay safe, enjoy and achieve, make a positive contribution and achieve economic well-being.

Government statements at the time pointed to improvements in test and examination scores, arguing that these were as a result of their various policies. Within the research community, however, there was a variety of views, including some that argued that there has been very little impact, particularly amongst learners from disadvantaged backgrounds, and that the apparent improvements in measured performance were not supported by detailed analysis of national data (Meadows et al., 2007; Sammons, 2008; Tymms, 2004). Concern was also expressed that improvements in test and examination scores may have been achieved by the use of particular tactics – some of which are, to say the least, dubious – such as orchestrated changes in school populations, the exclusion of some students and the careful selection of the courses students follow. In addition, there was an argument that improvements in measured performance did not necessarily result in increased access to higher education, particularly in more competitive universities, nor into higher-status employment (Gorrard, 2008). All of this casted doubt on both the authenticity of improvement claims and the sustainability of whatever progress was made (Gray, 2010). Meanwhile, there was a worry that the various national strategies, whatever their benefits, had tended to reduce the flexibility with which schools can respond to the diverse characteristics of their students (Ainscow & West, 2006).

It was also argued that the development of the educational marketplace, coupled with the emphasis on policies fostering greater diversity of schools, had created a quasi-selective system in which the poorest children, by and large, attend the lowest-performing schools (Ainscow et al., 2012a). Consequently, the low-achieving and, many would argue, the least advantaged schools, had fallen progressively further and further behind their high-performing counterparts. In terms of these effects, through selective advantaging and disadvantaging of schools, the very policies that had generally led to increased standards also increased, rather than decreased, disparities in education quality and opportunity between advantaged and less privileged groups. The policy priority, therefore, was to find ways of continuing to improve the education system that would foster equity, a concern often referred to as 'closing the gap.' This, then, was the agenda at the centre of what happened in London during the early years of this century.

The London Challenge

Instigated in 2003 by the then Labour government led by Tony Blair, London Challenge set out to address what was seen as the problem of London schools, particularly in the secondary sector where there was increasing concern that parents were choosing private education. This occurred during the period of unprecedented centralisation of national education policy described previously. In this context, London was, in effect, given permission to experiment in order to find new ways of improving the performance of its schools.

Five years later there was considerable evidence that these experiments had led to significant change, which, it should be noted, had only focused on secondary schools up to 2007. So, for example, it was reported that London schools had improved 'dramatically' and that the capital had recorded its best ever GCSE results,[4] showing London state school pupils leading the rest of the country for the third year running (Ofsted, 2010).

Our discussions at the time with academic colleagues working in London confirmed the view we had picked up from policy-makers and practitioners

18 City Challenge in England

that considerable changes had occurred in relation to the way secondary schools across London went about their business. However, doubts were expressed about the extent to which these improvements had made a significant difference to students from the most disadvantaged backgrounds.

A key person in relation to all of this was Sir Tim Brighouse, who led the London Challenge. In an article describing his experiences, he tells the story of the first five years of the initiative and presents his reflections on what had occurred (Brighouse, 2007). In so doing, he quotes from his foreword to the prospectus for the programme, 'The London Challenge; Transforming London Secondary Schools,' which included a passage setting out the origins and intentions of the scheme:

> This great city needs and deserves a truly world-class education system, which serves every community and enables every person in the city to fulfil their own individual creative potential. That is what the proposals published in this document are intended to achieve.
>
> London already does have some world class universities, some world class colleges and some world class schools. It has some world class teachers and some world class educational facilities. And the educational performance of London's schools has improved significantly in recent years. Fewer than 11% of children in inner London achieved 5 good O levels in 1987 – more than 40% achieve the equivalent now.
>
> But there are still far too many schools which are failing to inspire and lead their communities and far too many areas where educational aspirations are low. Too many parents are anguished and fearful, rather than proud or confident, when choosing their child's secondary school. And there are far too many who feel that either expensive private education or lengthy journeys across the city from home to school are the only satisfactory answer.
>
> This situation is unacceptable and it is the reason why we are determined to establish an education system which is truly world class everywhere in London. That system has to be founded more on creativity and diversity, which is the city's strength, rather than uniformity. It has to provoke and challenge rather than accepting mediocrity. And it has everywhere to stimulate excellence and establish world standards. In short, the exhilarating achievement which characterises some London schools must become the trademark of all London schools.
>
> Though the Government is allocating more resources to London, and we are prepared to allocate still more, I do not fundamentally believe that London's educational problems are problems of resources. It is much more about significant and radical reform that will mobilise the vision and leadership of the London educational community to achieve educational excellence. We need to make a visible and radical break with the past to transform aspiration and create a culture of achievement (p. 70).

To that end, Brighouse went on to set out what he saw as three essential components:

> First, we have to focus on the two areas of London where we consider the problems to be greatest. These are the north London group of three local authorities (Haringey, Hackney and Islington) and the south London group of two (Lambeth and Southwark). In these areas we need to establish an educational organisation and systematic drive for excellence which rewards success and does not tolerate failure. We have to develop a diverse system of academies and specialist schools which ensures that parents have a choice between excellent alternatives.
>
> Second, we have to work exceptionally closely with schools which are failing to reach acceptable standards and to take whatever decisions are necessary to raise the quality of these schools, so that their local communities can have full confidence in what they can achieve.
>
> And third, we must strengthen, across the whole of London, the standing of London's education. We must celebrate and enhance the quality of London's teachers and create better educational opportunities for students. We will create a new and better deal for students, teachers and headteachers – so that London becomes seen as a highly attractive part of the country in which to study and teach. (p.7)

In his chapter, Brighouse comments on his frequent use of the phrase 'world class,' which he argues draws attention to the 'pre-occupation in the developed world with producing ever higher standards of educational outcomes in a quest to be economically competitive, and in the knowledge that unskilled jobs are disappearing and that those that remain are increasingly filled by immigrants' (p. 71).

It is important to note at this stage that, from the outset, London Challenge had the active involvement of a Government Minister. In the early period this had been Stephen Twigg MP, who was later followed by Andrew Adonis, who, having been made a life peer in 2005, was appointed soon after as Minister of State for Education. As the story of London Challenge and the projects that followed evolve through this and subsequent chapters, the importance of a high-status political mandate is a pervading theme, even though it can sometimes bring its own problems.

Another important feature of London Challenge was the importance placed on contextual analysis as a means of creating a strategy that was relevant to the particularly circumstances within the capital city. Commenting on this, Kidson and Norris (2014) argue that this went well beyond a consideration of statistical trends in order to explore how local factors were influencing the progress of students in particular schools.

Bearing all of this background information in mind, in late 2007 one of us spent a period working alongside London Challenge colleagues. This included attendance at the fortnightly meetings of the Challenge advisers, a team of highly

20 City Challenge in England

experienced former school leaders, who worked part-time within the initiative. It was also possible to shadow some of them as they visited their 'Keys to Success' schools; that is, schools designated as requiring more intensive support.

The team meetings were in two parts. One of these involved civil servants in updating the advisers on current policy developments. The other part of the meeting was described as the 'professional hour.' This was a time when strategies were debated and opportunities provided to share experiences from the field. During one of these discussions, an adviser whispered: 'We like to try quirky things you know.' This seemed to confirm the importance of the advisers having freedom to use their extensive experience to assess situations and to try out novel ways of moving schools forward.

Typically, each of the Challenge advisers worked with four or five Keys to Success schools, remembering, of course, that at this stage the focus was only on the secondary sector. Most of these schools had also established a project board, which usually included the headteacher, the chair of governors and a local authority officer. This approach, which was later replicated with some success in projects described in later chapters, provided opportunities for the Challenge advisers to keep up to date with implementation processes. In this respect, it was evident that the writing of field notes following school visits was seen as an important strategy, not least in helping the civil servants keep an eye on developments in the field.

There was evidence of an overall pattern of activity to these interventions. This involved the development of a bespoke improvement package for each of the schools, often with an element of support from other schools. Important here was the skill of the Challenge adviser in working with a school's senior staff to assess the context. What was also important was the freedom the advisers were given to act quickly and decisively, albeit within a context in which they were held accountable for their schools' progress. In this way, the adviser was in a position to determine the nature of any external support that might be needed. Then, through the combined knowledge base that existed within the London Challenge team regarding where relevant expertise was likely to be available, the adviser was able to commission appropriate support, whether that be from another school or an external agency.

One source of information regarding sources of support was provided through the Families of Schools data system, within which schools across London were grouped on the basis of the profiles of the communities they served. In this way, schools could compare their current levels of student achievement with those found in similar schools. And, in so doing, they could locate schools with relevant strengths that they might choose to approach for support. Commenting on this in 2013, Tim Brighouse argued:

> If schools really are going to crack the issue of chronic educational underachievement among traditionally disadvantaged groups of pupils, they need two sorts of evidence. The first is reliable data on the scale and varied

nature of their attainment gap, and how they compare to other schools in a similar context. The second is reliable research and evidence from other schools about how to improve their performance. (p. 17)

Through the adviser's involvement in the process of assessing the context and formulating a plan of action, he or she was in a position to evaluate whether other, more drastic actions were needed to secure the school's improvement. In some instances, this might mean a decision that the headteacher, or other senior staff, did not have the capabilities to lead the process. In such situations, individual advisers could draw on the experience of their colleagues in determining appropriate ways forward. The fact that they carried the authority of a minister also gave them a mandate to insist that local authority staff make use of their statutory powers to intervene.

Commenting on all of this, Kidson and Norris (2014), who studied the process of implementation within the London Challenge, argued that sustainability of the model required high levels of trust and accountability for the outcomes of the work. Furthermore, their research led them to conclude that, for the advisers, this accountability came increasingly from their peers, rather than from the department. The space to exercise professional judgement was, the researchers suggest, a crucial element in all of this. It was also important to be able to work with a team of civil servants that did not 'leap to intervention' but was 'on hand and aware of what was going on.' Kidson and Norris quote the most senior civil servant involved as saying the aim was 'not micro-managing them, but being close to them.'

In addition to the direct work with schools, London Challenge developed its own leadership strategy. Led by headteachers, with support from the National College for School Leadership, this introduced the concept of successful headteachers working as consultant leaders, providing support for schools experiencing difficulties. In Chapter 6 we explain how this idea was later to become a feature of national policy. Another idea that was then emerging was that of 'teaching schools,' a concept that also was later to become part of English policy.

Our sense was that the London Challenge strategy largely by-passed the 33 local authorities, apart from the support provided to five that were seen as a cause for concern. Indeed, several of the advisers gave the impression that they saw the authorities as an irrelevance. For example, one said, "We do not ask the permission of LAs (local authorities) before we act.' Another added, 'It's the challenge to the schools that matters.'

Commenting on the London Challenge strategy, Kidson and Norris (2014) argue that this presented ministers and officials with a number of 'knotty implementation challenges.' These included the importance of managing the public profile of the project in the context of media criticism of London schools and a sense of 'crisis' in school standards among parents and politicians; the need to bring in and utilise credible professionals to provide underperforming schools with the bespoke support they needed to improve, while ensuring they were

22 City Challenge in England

accountable to the department; ensuring that advisers, teachers and school leaders had access to high-quality resources and models for school improvement, whilst also drawing on strengths already within the system; overcoming possible suspicion and defensiveness from local authorities that might prevent support reaching the schools most in need, particularly in councils with political control that was different to the government; and maintaining the coherence of the policy as it was implemented across a large city and alongside the Department for Education and Skills' other national priorities for schools. We return to these difficulties in Chapter 7.

The 'London effect'

In the light of the success of the first phase of London Challenge, in 2007 the government took the decision to extend the programme for a further three years and to include primary schools. At the same time, the creation of a generic City Challenge programme was announced that would include new initiatives in two other regions, the Black Country, in the West Midlands, and Greater Manchester. Meanwhile, there began what is, to this day, a continuing debate within academic circles to determine the key features of what came to be known as the 'London effect.'

As a result of their research into implementation of the London Challenge, Kidson and Norris (2014) conclude that it was a distinctive example of public service improvement that was practitioner-focused, highly collaborative and applied across a system. They note, too, that all the people they interviewed felt the initiative had made a major contribution to the exceptional improvement in the capital's schools despite other factors at play. This was attributed to the way credible professionals played a challenge and support role to their peers; the powerful sense of moral purpose and positive framing; and the close working relationships of officials, advisers and ministers, which was focused on a shared, data-led view of where there was strength and weakness in the schools.

There are, however, a range of other views as to what made the difference in London. In a helpful summary of these positions, Josh Lowe (2015) points out that other government interventions that took place around the same time may also have had an impact. He mentions, for example, Teach First, a graduate recruitment scheme launched in 2002 to coax top young graduates into the classroom, which was widely used in London. He also notes the possible impact of Ofsted and the new transparency in relation to school results. In addition, Lowe argues that the role of primary schools cannot be ignored, noting that the national strategies in literacy and numeracy were perhaps taken up far more enthusiastically in London than elsewhere. It is worth noting, too, that there is a view in the field that London schools have benefited from preferential financing.

Simon Burgess, a researcher at the University of Bristol, introduces another perspective, suggesting that the basis for London's progress was the ethnic composition of its school population. In particular, he concludes that a key factor had been the attraction to London of migrants and others aspiring to a better life. This led Burgess to argue:

> First, integrated multi-ethnic school systems can be very productive, allowing the ethnic minority pupils to achieve the grades they seek, and (potentially) raising the scores of white British pupils as well. Here is a role for school leadership, in managing multi-ethnic school system – it could have gone less well. Second, in parts of England where there simply isn't a large community of recent immigrants, a focus on how to encourage pupils' engagement with school, hard work and aspiration may pay strong dividends.
>
> (Burgess, 2014, p. 16)

A further worrying factor that cannot be overlooked are more recent reports suggesting that London schools have seen increases in both temporary and permanent exclusion rates.[5] Which reminds us of a comment made by a key figure involved in London Challenge who referred to how they had learnt to 'pull some tricks' in order to improve results.

All of this underlines the complexities involved in system change and the problems that exist when trying to establish the nature of the 'local causality' (Hadfield & Jopling, 2018) at play within in it.

The Greater Manchester Challenge

Drawing on lessons from London, between 2007 and 2011 one of us was seconded from his university to be Chief Adviser of a follow-on initiative that set out to address the equity agenda across 10 local authorities[6] in the north-west of England. Known as the Greater Manchester Challenge, the project involved a partnership between national government, local authorities, schools, leaders, teachers and other stakeholders, and had a government investment of around £50 million. The decision to invest such a large budget reflected a concern regarding educational standards in the region, particularly amongst children and young people from disadvantaged backgrounds. As in London, the programme had its own government minister.

At the time, the Greater Manchester city region was home to a population of 2.5 million people and had over 600,000 children and young people. Across the region, there were approximately 1,150 schools and colleges. The area is diverse in a number of ways, with very high levels of poverty. Children and young people come from a range of ethnic and cultural backgrounds, with a high proportion whose families have Asian heritage. Nearly 16% have a first language other than English, and in the city of Manchester over 60% of school students are bilingual.

A detailed study of patterns of school attendance in Greater Manchester confirmed the concerns noted earlier about the perverse impact of national policies on the educational experiences of young people from disadvantaged backgrounds (Robson et al., 2009). In particular, it showed that deprived students who attended low-performing schools did worse in terms of examination results than deprived students who attended higher-performing schools. And, because such students go disproportionately to poor-performing schools, this exacerbates the gulf between the results of deprived and nondeprived students, thereby acting as a significant driver of social polarisation.

This being the case, it seemed curious that in a densely populated conurbation like Greater Manchester there had been little attempt previously to develop cross-local authority policy in the interests of the city region as a whole. In designing the Challenge it seemed logical to adopt such a strategy as a way of narrowing the gap between low- and high-performing groups of learners. At the same time, there was a need to be sensitive to the possibilities that exist within urban environments. Here the comments of Hargreaves (2003) regarding cities are a useful reference point. Drawing on the classic book, *The Death and Life of Great American Cities*, written in the early 1960s by Jane Jacobs, he reminds us that large cities are usually characterised by social and cultural diversity that has enormous potential for promoting innovation. Furthermore, cities tend to attract creative people whose energy and resources can be mobilised to support educational improvement efforts.

The overall aims of the Challenge were to raise the educational achievement of all children and young people, and to narrow the gap in educational achievement between learners from disadvantaged backgrounds and their peers. A vision document, developed through consultation between national and local partners, led to a worrying proliferation of what were described as 'pledges' as the various stakeholders – nationally and locally – attempted to promote their own areas of interest. These intended outcomes involved an uncomfortable mix of narrow indicators related to rapid improvements in test and examination results, much favoured by civil servants, and wider concerns to enrich the educational experiences and life chances of young people of the sort that we favour.

In an attempt to create a sense of common purpose within this overambitious and somewhat contradictory agenda for change, it was eventually agreed that the focus of Challenge activities would be on 'three As.' These were that all children and young people should have high *Aspirations* for their own learning and life chances; are ensured *Access* to high-quality educational experiences; and *Achieve* the highest possible standards in learning. It was immediately obvious that these goals would necessitate reforms at all levels of the education service. This being the case, the aim was to encourage experimentation and innovation rather than simply doing more of the same.

Bearing in mind the arguments presented earlier, the Greater Manchester Challenge also set out to take advantage of new opportunities provided as a result of adopting an approach that drew on the strengths that existed in different parts of the city region. These included possibilities for tackling educational issues that cut across local authority boundaries (such as declining school performance at the secondary school stage, the development of personalised learning pathways for older students); linking educational issues to broader social and economic agendas (such as population mobility, employment, transport, housing, community safety, health), none of which respect local authority boundaries; and the freer exchange of expertise, resources and lessons from innovations, not least through the linking of schools and colleges in different local authorities.

Three years on, the impact of all of this was significant in respect to overall improvements in test and examination results and, indeed, in the way the education system carried out its business. However, as in London, within such a large scale and socially complex project it is difficult to make causal claims in respect to the factors that led to these improvements, particularly within an initiative that incorporated such a wide range of strategies.

In what follows we reflect on statistical data compiled as part of the formal monitoring of the impact of the project and qualitative evidence collected through numerous informal observations and conversations, plus more occasional formal interviews with stakeholders, in order to draw out some lessons. This leads us to conclude that two overall strategies, together, contributed to the improvements that have occurred:

- Increased collaboration within the education system, such that the best practices were made available to a wider range of children and young people; and
- The active involvement of community partners, including local businesses, universities and colleges, faith groups, voluntary organisations, academy sponsors and the media.

In explaining these conclusions, we also throw further light on some of the difficulties involved in putting these strategies into operation, many of which relate to matters of power regarding decisions about priorities, ways of working and the use of resources.

Moving knowledge around

As in London, the overall approach of the City Challenge programme in Greater Manchester emerged from a detailed analysis of the local context, using both statistical data and local intelligence provided by stakeholders through a series of formal and informal consultations. This drew attention to areas of concern and also helped to pinpoint a range of human resources that could be mobilized to support improvement efforts. Recognising the potential of these resources, it was decided that networking and collaboration – within and across schools – should be the key strategies for strengthening the overall improvement capacity of the system.

This approach was informed by our earlier research evidence which suggested that, under appropriate conditions, greater collaboration within schools is a means of fostering improvements (Ainscow, Booth & Dyson, 2006; West, Ainscow &

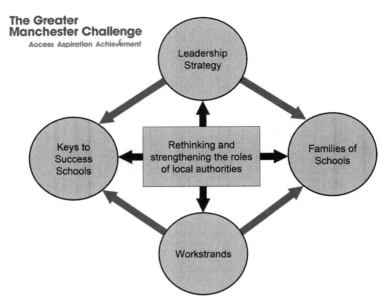

FIGURE 2.1 The elements of the Greater Manchester Challenge.

Stanford, 2005); and that collaboration between differently performing schools can reduce polarization within education systems, to the particular benefit of learners who are performing relatively poorly (Ainscow, 2010; Ainscow & Howes, 2007; Ainscow, Muijs & West, 2006; Ainscow & West, 2006). It does this by both transferring existing knowledge and, more important, generating context-specific new knowledge.

With this in mind, during the first year of the Challenge various methods were introduced to 'move knowledge around,' a phrase that was much used in promoting the strategy. The ways in which these methods were linked are summarized in Figure 2.1 to illustrate the complexity of the approaches that were introduced.

Initially, arrangements were coordinated by the small team of Challenge advisers[7] and civil servants, but subsequently they were mainly led by headteachers. In what follows we summarise the elements of the approach, noting that most of these were adapted from what had happened previously in London.

Families of schools

In an attempt to engage all schools in the city region in processes of networking and collaboration, as in London, Families of Schools were set up, using a data system that groups schools on the basis of the prior attainment of their students and their socio-economic home backgrounds. There were 58 primary and 11 secondary Families, each of which had between 12 and 20 schools from different local authorities. The strength of this approach is that it grouped together schools

City Challenge in England   27

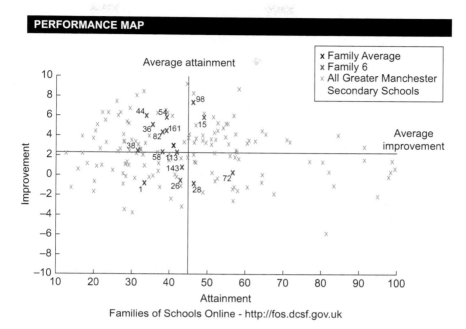

FIGURE 2.2 Data display for Family 6, secondary schools (from Ainscow, 2012).

that served similar populations whilst, at the same time, encouraging partnerships amongst schools that were not in direct competition with one another because they did not serve the same neighbourhoods.

Figure 2.2 is a graph taken from the Families of Schools data system. It illustrates how schools within a Family can be compared in terms of the overall attainment levels of their students (i.e., the horizontal axis) and the improvements that have occurred over the previous three years (i.e., the vertical axis). So, for example, in this case: which is for secondary Family 6, and why does school number 1 seem to be doing so poorly compared with schools 15 and 98?

Such varied performance amongst Family members offers possibilities for using differences as a resource to stimulate the sharing of expertise and joint efforts to innovate to improve the performance of every school; increase the numbers of outstanding schools; reduce the gap between high- and low-performing groups of learners; and improve outcomes for particular vulnerable groups of students.

We found, however, that for this to happen schools had to dig more deeply into the comparative data to expose areas of strength that can be used to influence performance across their Family, whilst also identifying areas for improvement in every school. In so doing, they must be wary of the dangers associated with what Simon (1978) refers to as 'satisficing.' Put simply, this involves attempts to meet criteria for adequacy, leading to acceptance of a merely satisfactory outcome, rather than aiming for the best possible levels of improvement.

28 City Challenge in England

With this in mind, the average performance for each Family – both in terms of overall attainment and recent improvement trends – provided a benchmark against which overall goals for each of the partner schools could be set. At the same time, the analysis of data with regard to subgroups of students (e.g., boys and girls; those eligible to free school meals; minority groups) and different subject areas also enabled a Family to work on the issue of within-school variations. The collective goal was then to move all of the Family members in a 'north-easterly' direction on the performance graph.

In thinking about how to make this happen, we found that it was important to be sensitive to the limitations of statistical information. What brings such data to life is when 'insiders' start to scrutinise and ask questions as to their significance, bringing their detailed experiences and knowledge to bear on the process of interpretation. The occasional involvement of colleagues from partner schools can deepen such processes, not least because of the ways in which they may see things, or ask questions, that those within a school may be overlooking.

Even then, limitations remain that need to be kept in mind. Statistics present patterns of what exists: they tell us what things are like but give little understanding as to why things are as they are, or how they came to be like that. This is why qualitative evidence is needed to supplement statistical data. For example, our earlier research had demonstrated how mutual observation amongst colleagues and listening to the views of learners can be a powerful means of challenging thinking and provoking experimentation (Ainscow, Booth & Dyson, 2006). Again, here, there is potential for schools to support one another in collecting and engaging with such evidence in a way that has the potential to make the familiar unfamiliar.

Led by headteachers, the Families of Schools proved to be successful in strengthening collaborative processes within the city region. So, for example, primary schools in one Family worked together to strengthen leadership in each school. This included headteachers visiting one another to carry out 'learning walks' during which colleagues had opportunities to reflect upon and debate noticeable differences in practices. Eight schools in another primary Family identified a shared desire to build stronger relationships with the children's homes – for example, parents of children with English as an additional language where there were communication issues, or groups of students with lower attendance.

In the secondary sector, schools within one of the Families used a web-based system where students could showcase their work via podcasts, videos and blogs, allowing teachers, parents and students from their own and other schools to view and comment on their efforts. Talking about his school's involvement, a highly respected secondary headteacher commented, *'This is the most powerful strategy for school improvement I have experienced.'*

However, involvement of schools in the Families remained patchy, and there were concerns that too often those that might most benefit chose not to do so. Our monitoring of what went on suggested certain conditions that lead to higher involvement and a greater impact on student achievement. These are a collective commitment to improve the learning of every student, in every school in the group; an analysis of statistical data, using professional insights to identify areas that need addressing; pinpointing expertise within the schools that can be used to address these concerns; collaborative activities involving people at different levels, including, in some instances, children and young people; and a small number of headteachers taking on the role of leading these collaborative activities.

In moving collaboration forward in a way that supports development within a Family of Schools, we found that shared leadership was a central driver. This required the development of leadership practices that involve many stakeholders in collectively sharing responsibility. Often this necessitated significant changes in beliefs and attitude, and new relationships, as well as improvements in practice. The goal was to ensure that collaboration was between school communities, and not restricted to headteachers, because arrangements that rely on one person are unlikely to survive the departure of those individuals who brokered them.

Keys to success

In terms of schools working in highly disadvantaged contexts, evidence from City Challenge (in Greater Manchester and London) suggests that school-to-school partnerships (pairs or sometimes trios) can be a powerful means of fostering improvements. Most notably, what we referred to as the Keys to Success programme led to striking improvements in the performance of some 200 Greater Manchester schools facing the most challenging circumstances. There was also evidence that the progress these schools made helped to trigger improvement across the system.

It must be stressed that the approach used in each of these schools, as in London, was unique, based on a detailed analysis of the local context and the development of an improvement strategy that fit the circumstances. The team of Challenge advisers had a central role here, working alongside senior school staff in carrying out the initial analysis and mobilizing external support. A common feature of almost all of these interventions, however, was that progress was achieved through carefully matched pairings of schools that cut across social 'boundaries' of various kinds, including those that separate schools in different local authorities. In this way, expertise that was previously trapped in particular contexts was made more widely available.

Crossing boundaries sometimes involved what seemed like unlikely partnerships. For example, a highly successful school that caters for children from Jewish Orthodox families worked with an inner-city primary school – the largest primary school in the city region – to develop more effective use of assessment data and boost the quality of teaching and learning. This school had a high percentage of Muslim children, many of whom were learning English as an additional language. Over a period of 18 months, the partnership contributed to significant improvements in test results, and throughout the school the majority of students reached national expectations for their ethnic groups. This also led to a series of activities around wider school issues, such as the creative arts and the use of student voice, where the two schools shared their expertise. The headteacher of the Jewish school commented: '*It's been a totally positive experience, built on mutual respect. This (i.e., the partner school) is a great school, and the learning is definitely a two-way process.*'

Another partnership involved a primary school that had developed considerable expertise in teaching children to read, supporting a secondary school in another local authority where low levels of literacy had acted as a barrier to student progress. Describing what happened, the head of the primary school commented: '*Together we have developed the use of a letters and sounds phonics strategy to support improvements in literacy among the three lowest English sets in Year 7, including students with special educational needs. We had seen real impact using a more multi-sensory approach to the teaching of phonics within in our own school, and I couldn't see any reason why it shouldn't be used to similar effect with older students.*' She went on to talk with enthusiasm about the professional development opportunities all of this had provided for her own staff.

In another example, a grammar school[8] partnered with a low-performing inner city comprehensive school in another local authority. The impact on attendance, behaviour and examination results was remarkable. Reflecting on this, the headteacher of the grammar school said, '*I spend about three days a week at the school, and one of my assistant heads works 50% of the time with the senior leadership team to build capacity. It was apparent from the outset that the team had the skills to move the school forward, but its members were not forged into a team and were not made accountable.*' She also commented on the benefits gained for her own school.

Through these examples we saw how boundaries to do with cultures, religion, age group of students and selection could be crossed to facilitate the exchange of expertise. Significantly, these examples also indicated that such arrangements can have a positive impact on the learning of students in both of the partner schools. This is an important finding in that it draws attention to a way of strengthening relatively low-performing schools that can, at the same time, help to foster wider improvements in the system. It also offers a convincing argument for why a relatively strong school should support other schools. Put simply, the evidence is that by helping others you help yourself.

Whilst increased collaboration of this sort is vital as a strategy for developing more effective ways of working, the experience of Greater Manchester shows that it is not enough. The essential additional ingredient is an engagement with evidence that can bring an element of mutual challenge to such collaborative processes, echoing the suggestions of Tim Brighouse mentioned earlier about the importance of engaging with reliable data to improve outcomes.

We found that evidence was particularly essential when partnering schools. Collaboration is at its most powerful when partner schools are carefully matched and know what they are trying to achieve. Evidence also matters so that schools go beyond cosy relationships that have no impact on outcomes. Consequently, schools needed to base their relationships on evidence about each other's strengths and weaknesses, so they can challenge each other to improve.

To facilitate this kind of contextual analysis, various strategies and frameworks were devised to help schools support one another in carrying out reviews. In the primary sector, this involved colleagues from another school acting as critical friends to internally driven review processes; whilst in secondary schools, subject departments were involved in 'deep dives,' where skilled specialists from another school visited to observe and analyse practice to promote improvement activities.

The power of these approaches is in the way they provide teachers with opportunities to have strategic conversations with colleagues from another school. For example, in one primary school this helped senior staff raise attainment and build leadership capacity. The school was judged 'satisfactory with good features' as a result of an inspection in 2007, but the following year its test scores in mathematics dipped dramatically. Eighteen months after enlisting support from another school, attainment was significantly higher. The headteacher explained: *'The rise in standards is largely down to quality conversations between senior leaders at our school and another primary school in the neighbouring borough. This has reinvigorated leadership, helped set direction and boosted confidence going forward.'* In describing her involvement, the headteacher of the partner school explained: *'I feel my school has benefited a great deal too. The main impact has been for me and the senior leadership team, as I have been able to have challenging and confidential discussions about the strategic direction of the school and make changes in the way members of the leadership team work together. This has, in turn, given me the confidence to distribute leadership more effectively and delegate with confidence.'*

The leadership strategy

Within the Greater Manchester Challenge, headteachers were seen as having a central role as what Hopkins (2007) refers to as 'system leaders.' The good news is that our experience suggested that many successful headteachers were motivated by the idea of taking on such roles. Reflecting on his experience of working as a system leader, one headteacher commented: *'I have a strong conviction that impact is maximized through a willingness to learn oneself when giving support and to ensure that, at all times, the client school is at the centre. In other words, no matter how experienced or skilled you might believe yourself to be, it is important to be flexible and meet the school where it is at – rather than to go in with a template of answers. To do this, strong professional and objective relationships have to be established with all key players you are working with and supporting.'*

Another headteacher explained that, for her, the key to successful partnership working across schools is mutual trust and an understanding that there are opportunities for the development for both schools. She explained, *'It's just about working together to try to support each other and making sure we are doing something really useful, not just reinventing the same thing.'* Using the image of an orchestra, she added, '*The school's own staff are the principle instruments, the external partners are just helping with the conducting.*'

By the end of the Greater Manchester Challenge, there were some 170 or so headteachers designated as system leaders.[9] Increasingly, over the three years, they drove forward improvement efforts across the city region. In addition to their involvement in the Families of Schools and the partnerships set up to support Keys to Success schools, they explored other mechanisms for making better use of the expertise that exists within the schools.

One important strategy to facilitate the movement of expertise was provided through the creation of various types of hub schools. So, for example, there were hub schools that provided specialist support for students with English as an additional language. These schools engaged enthusiastically in the process of sharing practice through workshops attended by practitioners from across the region. Similarly, there developed what were called teaching schools,[10] which provided professional development programmes focused on bringing about improvements in classroom practice. Over 1,000 teachers from across the city region took part in these programmes that involved powerful adult learning strategies, such as the modelling of effective classroom techniques, practice and feedback and peer coaching. Once again, here, there was strong evidence of mutual benefit in this approach; it had a positive impact on the quality of classroom practice and student learning in both the schools receiving support and within the teaching schools themselves.

Other hub schools offered support in relation to particular subject areas, and in responding to groups of potentially vulnerable groups, such as those seen as having special educational needs. In this latter context, a further significant development involved new roles for special schools in supporting developments in the mainstream.

The work strands

In talking about the various strategies for moving knowledge around, many headteachers reported that it was important that the partnerships involved schools from different local authorities. Indeed, one head commented that, for him, all of this had been the 'game-changer.' This suggests that cross-border collaboration can provide a mechanism for encouraging innovation, although, sometimes, it can simply lead to time-consuming meetings that have little direct impact on learners in classrooms.

As part of the Challenge, we introduced a series of what we referred to as work strands in an attempt to use cross-border collaboration to inject further innovation and pace into the system. Each of these initiatives was led by one of the local authority partners and focused on educational issues facing all local authorities, linking improvement efforts to broader social and economic agendas. Part of the reason for adopting this approach was to ensure that colleagues within the local authorities were seen to have a role, not least to avoid them becoming barriers to a change process that, in effect, reduced their involvement in school improvement.

The work strands proved to be reasonably effective in facilitating the exchange of expertise, resources and lessons from innovations across the city region in relation to issues such as raising aspirations, strengthening the contributions of governors and closing the gap between high- and low-achieving groups of students. Importantly, this led to the involvement of local businesses, professional sports clubs, universities and media organizations. For example, the four universities in Greater Manchester worked together on a project known as 'Higher Futures for You.' The overall aim was to raise self-belief and aspirations amongst primary school children from disadvantaged backgrounds. Through carefully orchestrated visits to local places of employment, students were helped to understand the career opportunities that are available to them. During a final workshop, the children shared their knowledge with their parents. This initiative, which worked with some 200 primary schools, was originally developed by the headteacher of one school.

Another of the work strands set out to explore the use of learner voice as a strategy for rethinking what schools offer to their students. In carrying out this work, a partnership was developed with an independent national charity that promotes democratic citizenship and citizenship life skills. This led to an additional focus on the experience of young people outside of school. As a result, schools across Greater Manchester collaborated in addressing this question: *In developing children as participative citizens in designing the way things are in school, can we achieve greater civic participation beyond school?* The schools involved were enthused by the opportunity provided and, in some instances, became committed to widen and deepen the involvement of students (and parents).

In another experimental initiative known as Better Futures, 16 students from disadvantaged backgrounds shared jobs in three major companies. Each student attended their internship one day per week throughout the year and caught up with missed schoolwork during the rest of the week. The evidence suggested that parents were very positive once they saw the impact on children's social skills in their home environment. Meanwhile, within schools, aspirations changed, so did attitudes to catch up on missed schoolwork, as the students made links between a good career and attaining targets at school. There was evidence, too, of shifts in aspirations; for example, from mechanic to engineer, childcare to business, and 'don't knows' to IT and Law. The approach has subsequently been developed in many more schools, involving other business organisations.

Rethinking the roles of local authorities

The creation of a system for improvement that is driven by schools themselves, and that involves cooperation between schools and other community organisations, begs questions regarding the roles of local authorities. Indeed, it raises the possibility that involvement of a middle-level administrative structure may not even be necessary.

34 City Challenge in England

The authors of the influential McKinsey report (Mourshed, Chijioke & Barber, 2010), having analysed 'how the world's most improved school systems keep getting better,' express surprise at the critical role of what they call the 'mediating layer' plays between school delivery and central government. This led them to conclude that sustaining system improvement in the longer term requires 'integration and intermediation' across each level of the system, 'from the classroom to the superintendent or minister's office.' They explain:

> The operating system of the mediating layer acts as the integrator and mediator between the classrooms and the centre. This is not to suggest that school reforms should begin here. In every system we looked at, the first focus of school reforms was on the schools and the centre. Efforts to strengthen the mediating layer usually came later, as the need for an active intermediary in delivering the system improvements became clearer.
>
> (Mourshed, Chijioke & Barber, 2010, p. 82)

The authors of the report go on to suggest that the specific functions the mediating layer plays are providing targeted support to schools; acting as a buffer between the centre and the schools, while interpreting and communicating the improvement objectives in order to manage any resistance to change; and enhancing the collaborative exchange between schools, by facilitating the sharing of best practices, helping them to support each other, share learning and standardise practices.

Certainly, the experience of Greater Manchester suggests that local authority staff can have an important role to play, not least in acting as the conscience of the system – making sure that all children and young people are getting a fair deal within an increasingly diverse system of education. To do this, they need to know the big picture about what is happening in their communities, identifying priorities for action and brokering collaboration. This required significant structural and cultural changes, with local authorities moving away from a command and control perspective, solely focused within their own boundaries, toward one of enabling and facilitating collaborative action across the city region. At times, local authority colleagues found these changes challenging, particularly during a time of reducing budgets. The strengthening of cross-border cooperation at many levels provided contexts within which mutual support could be provided in addressing these concerns. In this way, officers and support staff at various levels were able to assist one another in addressing new policy demands.

In some instances, local authorities were supported by experienced consultants in carrying out thorough reviews of their school improvement arrangements. Encouragement for these radical changes was provided by the chief executives of the 10 local authorities, who saw further improvements in their school systems as a key element of their overall strategy for the economic and social development of the city region.

Assessing the impact

After three years the impact of the Greater Manchester Challenge was significant in respect to overall improvements in test and examination results and, indeed, the way the education system operates so; for example, by 2011, primary schools outperformed national averages on the tests taken by all children in England. And, in the public examinations taken in 2011 by almost all young people at 16, secondary schools in Greater Manchester improved faster than schools nationally, with the schools serving the most disadvantaged communities making three times more improvement than schools across the country. Importantly, the two local authorities with the lowest levels of attainment were the ones that showed the greatest progress between 2007 and 2011. Both authorities had a mix of community and faith schools, alongside a range of sponsored academies. During the same period, the number of schools below the government's floor standard[11] decreased more than it did in other areas of the country. In addition, the proportion of 'good' and 'outstanding' schools, as determined by the national inspection system, increased despite the introduction of a more challenging framework.

An independent evaluation of the City Challenge programme in the Black Country, Greater Manchester and London concluded that, overall, it had been successful in achieving its objectives (Hutchings et al., 2012). Commenting on this, the authors of the report argue:

> Clearly a great many factors contributed to these improvements, including national policies and strategies and the considerable efforts of headteachers and staff. However, these factors apply everywhere in the country. The most plausible explanation for the greater improvement in Challenge areas is that the City Challenge programme was responsible. The vast majority of stakeholders at all levels who contributed to this evaluation attributed the additional improvements that have been made in these areas to the work of City Challenge. (p. vi)

The evaluators concluded that the strategic factors contributing to its success were the time scale; the focus on specific urban areas; the flexibility of approach; use of expert advisers and bespoke solutions; school staff learning from practice in other schools; and the programme ethos of trust, support and encouragement. At the same time, it should be noted that others have offered alternative possible explanations for the positive impact, including Greaves, Macmillan and Sibieta (2014) who, echoing the research of Burgess referred to earlier, point to the positive impact of the increase in the proportion of pupils from ethnic minorities in London and Manchester.

The evaluations that took place also noted that City Challenge had left a wide range of legacies nationally, as signalled by the content of a White Paper issued shortly after the election of a new, coalition Government (Department

36 City Challenge in England

for Education, 2010). This set out the Government's vision for a self-improving education system, stating that:

> Our aim should be to create a school system which is more effectively self-improving. . . . It is also important that we design the system in a way which allows the most effective practice to spread more quickly and the best schools and leaders to take greater responsibility and extend their reach. (p. 73)

On June 11, 2011, the Secretary of State for Education, Michael Gove, gave a speech in which he argued that, in order to address the issue of educational underperformance, particularly amongst disadvantaged groups of learners, there was a need to develop a 'culture of collaboration.' With this in mind, he noted that it was good to see the development of more networks of schools and the expansion of teaching schools, and to see how efforts were being made to 'embed the success of the Greater Manchester Challenge.' Echoing similar ideas, in a speech on November 13, 2012, the then Shadow Secretary of State, Stephen Twigg, also made reference to building on the progress in Greater Manchester, emphasising in particular the idea of 'evidence-based collaboration.'

A further impact of City Challenge was the emergence of locally led arrangements to continue the practices that had been developed (Hutchings & Mansaray, 2013). In each of the three areas, organisations with a strong focus on schools learning from each other was created to take forward the Challenge approaches. In London and Greater Manchester, these were led by groups of headteachers and continue to today. Meanwhile, other organisations adopted aspects of the Challenge approach to school improvement, including some local authorities that encouraged school-led partnerships; groups of faith schools; and a growing number of academy chains (Claeys et al., 2014). Commenting on such developments, a report from the House of Commons Education Committee (2013) concluded:

> Partnership working and cooperation between schools has long been part of the education landscape, whether encouraged by government or not. Nevertheless, in recent years and alongside the changing role of local authorities, school partnerships and cooperation have become an increasingly important part of what has been referred to as a 'self-improving' or 'school-led' system. This has been seen particularly in the successful London Challenge and City Challenge programmes which led to significant improvements in the schools in the areas involved. It has also been a key driver behind the rapid expansion of the academies programme. (p. 7)

In a review of the longer-term impact of City Challenge, Hutchings and Mansaray (2013) conclude that the improvements were sustained in London and Manchester, but less so in the Black Country, where our own informal

City Challenge in England **37**

observations suggest that differences of view regarding goals and strategies between local politicians and government representatives were never resolved. Nevertheless, the evaluators argue that all of the areas had benefited from important legacy activities. They also identified a number of reasons behind the continuing impact of each of the Challenges, such as the timescale of the programmes, the continuity of the personnel involved and the extent to which those in the area felt 'ownership' of the Challenge. Importantly, the authors noted that 'the challenges were comprehensive area-based initiatives that tackled all elements of schooling. It cannot be assumed that taking certain elements in isolation will be as effective as the combination of elements' (p. 7).

Hutchings and Mansaray went on to suggest that, in the Challenge areas, the legacy had included a more outward-looking approach; more effective processes and strategies; higher expectations of pupils; stronger coaching skills among middle and senior leaders; and a greater awareness of what to do to improve further. Although this is a substantial record, the authors noted that the current arrangements and structures for school improvement still had considerable limitations. Most important among these was fragmentation and lack of structure, which, it was argued, may result in vulnerable schools not getting the support they need. All of which pointed to the need for coordination of further efforts to support the maturing of self-improving systems, a theme we address in subsequent chapters.

Drawing out the lessons

So, what can we learn from this ambitious and socially complex project in London and Greater Manchester? In particular, what does it suggest about how to develop education systems that are more effective for all young people, particularly those from less advantaged backgrounds?

At the heart of the strategies we have summarized are attempts to develop new, more fruitful working relationships: between national and local government; between administrators and practitioners; within and between schools; and between schools and their local communities. A helpful theoretical interpretation that can be made of these strategies is that, together, they have helped to strengthen social capital within these two city regions. In other words, they have established pathways through which energy, expertise and lessons from innovations can spread.

In recent years, the work of Robert Putnam (2000) has been most influential in making the idea of social capital a focus for research and policy discussion. In so doing, he has demonstrated how it can help to mitigate the insidious effects of socio-economic disadvantage. Writing about the United States, for example, Putnam states that 'what many high-achieving school districts have in abundance is social capital, which is educationally more important than financial capital' (p. 306).

In relation to schools, Mulford (2007) defines social capital in terms of the groups, networks, norms and trust that people have available to them for

38 City Challenge in England

productive purposes. He goes on to suggest that by treating social relationships as a form of capital, they can be seen as a resource, which people can then draw on to achieve their goals. There are, he explains, three types of social capital, each of which throws further light on the processes that developed within City Challenge. The first of these is 'bonding social capital,' which relates to what can happen amongst work colleagues within a school; 'bridging social capital' is what can be developed between schools through various forms of networking and collaboration; and finally, 'linking social capital' relates to the formation of stronger relationships between a school and wider community resources.

The evidence we have summarized in this chapter suggests a series of interconnected strategies that have fostered the development of stronger social capital of all three types. As we have seen, these strategies can help to break down social barriers between schools – and between schools and other stakeholders – in order to facilitate the sorts of mutual benefit we have described when schools learn how to learn from one another. In this sense, the strategies provide the basis for what Hargreaves (2010) describes as a 'self-improving school system.'

That said, an account of these experiences would be misleading if it did not also mention the struggles that occurred in trying to ensure the support and involvement of so many different stakeholders. This had the potential to create tensions that would delay progress within an initiative where pace had to be an essential feature, not least because of the pressures to deliver on the requirement of government that there should be rapid improvements in student outcomes.

In reflecting on all of this, we are reminded of Robert Bales' theory of group systems used in earlier research (see Ainscow, Hargreaves & Hopkins, 1995). As Bales predicts, attempts to get different stakeholders to pull together leads to tensions between the need to establish cohesion amongst groups, whilst, at the same time, taking actions to achieve project goals. Put simply, it is relatively easy to maintain cooperation until the moments when hard decisions had to be made, most particularly regarding the setting of priorities and the allocation of resources. We return to this issue in Chapter 7.

Meanwhile, as far as Greater Manchester is concerned, the urgent task at the end of the three years was to use these strategies to ensure continuing improvement beyond the period of the Challenge. With this in mind, a School Improvement Partnership Board was formed, with headteacher and local authority representation. Its purpose was to continue the process of analysing the city region to encourage further collaboration in responding to new areas of concern. At the same time, an agency was established that took on the role of coordinating the various forms of school-to-school partnerships. Known as By Schools for Schools, it was led by a group of 25 outstanding headteachers who were representative of the different types of school and local authorities. In Chapter 6, we go on to explain how the legacy of these arrangements has continued into an era of very different national policies.

In moving forward, the success of the strategies we have described provides grounds for optimism. At the same time, we must be wary of falling into the trap of thinking all of this is simple and straightforward. For example, writing about the idea of school networks as an improvement strategy, Lima (2008) argues:

> Despite their growing prevalence, networks have become popular mainly because of faith and fads, rather than solid evidence on their benefits or rigorous analyses of their characteristics, substance and form . . . there is nothing inherently positive or negative about a network: it can be flexible and organic, or rigid and bureaucratic; it can be liberating and empowering, or stifling and inhibiting; it can be democratic, but it may also be dominated by particular interests. (p. 2)

It is also important to recognise that the gains made were hard won and often remained fragile. Here, continuing tensions regarding priorities and preferred ways of working between national and local policy-makers, and, indeed, between schools and local authorities, continued to be factors creating barriers to further progress. In particular, those near to central government remained preoccupied with achieving short-term gains in test and examination scores in ways that can create barriers to efforts for promoting sustainable improvements. Coupled with this was their mistrust of local authorities – the staff of which are often seen as part of the problem, rather than part of the solution – and doubts about the need to have separate strategies that fit particular contexts. At the same time, within local authorities there has been and still is an understandable uncertainty about the motives and agendas of government officials who had chosen to impose an intervention upon their work.

It must also be remembered that, despite the overall improvements that occurred, the school systems in Greater Manchester and London continue to let down significant numbers of learners. Whilst remarkable progress has been made in terms of schools that serve the most disadvantaged districts, there remains a worrying overall pattern in terms of the attainment levels of those students who are from poorer backgrounds, particularly white working-class boys. These youngsters are present in most schools to varying degrees, and, sometimes, improvements in test and examination results have been achieved by overlooking them.

Having said that, through the work of City Challenge we now have many examples of schools that have improved their performance in ways that take account of all of their students. Consequently, ways have to be found to maintain the momentum, focusing on high-leverage activities that can reduce variations within schools and further strengthen the capacity of education systems to move knowledge around.

Conclusion

In thinking about how the strategies that emerged from City Challenge might be used in other contexts, it is essential to recognise that they do not offer a simple recipe that can be lifted and transferred to other contexts. Rather, they offer an approach to improvement that uses processes of contextual analysis to create strategies that fit particular circumstances. What is also distinctive in the

40 City Challenge in England

approach is that it is mainly led from within schools, with headteachers and other senior school staff having a central role as system leaders. Added value is provided by linking schools together through networks and partnerships of various kinds that cut across social barriers.

A central factor in all of this is the importance of developing change strategies that relate to particular circumstances. In this respect, a key message from City Challenge in England is the importance of processes of contextual analysis. As we have seen in both London and Greater Manchester, the teams of Challenge advisers played key roles in all of this, using their extensive experience to dig below the surface of statistical trends and throw greater light of the barriers experienced by some students, whilst at the same time identifying untapped resources for addressing these difficulties. It is worth adding here that this factor has had limited attention in the extensive literature that has focused on City Challenge.

All of this has implications for the various key stakeholders within education systems. In particular, teachers, especially those in senior positions, have to see themselves as having a wider responsibility for all children and young people, not just those that attend their own schools. They also have to develop patterns of working that enable them to have the flexibility to cooperate with other schools and with stakeholders beyond the school gate. It means, too, that those who administer area school systems have to adjust their priorities and ways of working in response to improvement efforts that are led from within schools.

It also has to be recognised that 'closing the gap' in outcomes between those from more and less advantaged backgrounds will only happen when what happens to children *outside* as well as *inside* the school changes. This means changing how families and communities work, and enriching what they offer to children. As we have explained, there is encouraging evidence from London and Greater Manchester of what can happen when schools align in a coherent strategy with the efforts of other local players: employers, community groups, universities and public services. This does not necessarily mean schools doing more, but it does imply partnerships beyond the school, where partners multiply the impacts of each other's efforts.

Finally, there is a key role for the central government in all of this. The evidence from the English experience over the last 20 years suggests that attempts to command and control from the centre stifle as many local developments as they stimulate (Ainscow & West, 2006). Consequently, central government needs to act as an enabler, encouraging developments, disseminating good practice, and holding local leaders to account for outcomes. All of this depends on the currency of knowledge exchange and, therefore, requires cultural change, a theme we return to in later chapters.

Notes

1 An earlier and much fuller account of City Challenge is provided in Ainscow (2015).
2 In England, children from economically poor backgrounds are entitled to a free lunch in schools. This is used as a proxy indicator of the numbers of disadvantaged children.

City Challenge in England **41**

3 There are 152 English local authorities. They are democratically accountable for providing a range of services for their local communities, including education.

4 The examination taken by almost all students in England around the age of 16.

5 www.london.gov.uk/press-releases/assembly/the-link-between-school-exclusions-violent-crime

6 The 10 local authorities in Greater Manchester are Bolton, Bury, Oldham, Manchester, Rochdale, Salford, Stockport, Tameside, Trafford and Wigan.

7 As in London, Challenge advisers were independent, experienced education practitioners, employed through the Department of Education to provide support for Challenge activities, particularly in the lowest performing schools.

8 Grammar schools select students academically at the age of 11. In general, they do not cater to young people from economically disadvantaged backgrounds.

9 This became part of a national scheme in which outstanding headteachers are designated as National Leaders of Education. As such, they are expected to provide support to other schools. They receive additional training in relation to their support roles.

10 Teaching schools are seen as having a similar role as teaching hospitals. On the basis of the excellent practice that exists, they offer professional development to staff from other schools. This approach, which was developed within City Challenge, subsequently became part of national policy.

11 This is the minimum standard set by government, below which schools are subject to some form of intervention.

3

SCHOOLS CHALLENGE CYMRU

A catalyst for change

In this chapter we continue with our series of accounts of large-scale improvement initiatives by focusing on Schools Challenge Cymru, the Welsh government's flagship programme to promote greater equity across its education system. Beginning in 2014, the aims were to bring about rapid improvements in the performance of 40 secondary schools serving the more disadvantaged communities, and to use lessons from these developments to strengthen the capacity of the education system to improve itself. In this way, the programme was expected to be a catalyst for systemic change.

The design of the initiative was informed by lessons from City Challenge in England, described in Chapter 2. As we have seen, this was based on the assumption that education systems have the potential to improve themselves, provided policy-makers allow the space for practitioners to make use of the expertise and creativity that lies trapped within individual schools and classrooms, and confined within traditional administrative boundaries. The aim was to 'move knowledge around,' and it was assumed that the best way to do this would be through strengthening collaboration within schools, between schools and beyond schools.

Our account of the Welsh project throws light on the barriers experienced when we attempted to apply aspects of our collective intelligence developed in other settings within a context culturally resistant to ideas imported from elsewhere. Significant, too, were the historically low levels of trust between those leading at different levels of the system. Other barriers beyond the political and cultural included vested interest groups wishing to hold onto existing ways of working; although well intended, these ideas were seen to consume time and resources, delay action in the field, and were based on different views regarding the goals of the initiative. We also describe how, despite a highly positive independent evaluation, the project was discontinued as a result of changes in political leadership. Nevertheless, there is evidence that the programme has continued to influence thinking and practice across the Welsh education system, suggesting that it has, to some degree, acted as a catalyst for change.

The Welsh context

Wales is a particularly interesting context for addressing educational equity. Like many school systems that are said to be successful (e.g., Alberta, Finland, Hong Kong, Singapore), it is small. Despite its size, however, the performance of its school system is a cause for concern (Evans, 2015), and outcomes for learners from low-income families are a particular worry, as noted in a country review conducted by OECD in 2014. Most significant, the review argued that whilst the pace of reform had been high, it lacked a long-term vision, an adequate school improvement infrastructure and a clear implementation strategy that all stakeholders shared. Concern was also expressed that Wales had struggled to strike a balance between accountability and improvement.

Wales shares a close political and social history with the rest of Great Britain, and almost everyone speaks English. However, the country has retained a distinct cultural identity and is officially bilingual. Welsh is spoken by about 20% of the population, mostly in the north and west of the country. Although it is part of the United Kingdom, Wales has a form of self-government, the National Assembly, created in 1998 following a referendum. There are 22 local authorities responsible for a range of public services, including education. Some of these are small, and although there has been much talk of mergers in recent years, little progress has been made in this regard.

In the main, the Welsh system, although underperforming in international comparisons, is still relatively equitable, in the sense that 'the performance of 15-year-old students is not as closely related to their socio-economic background as it is in most other OECD countries' (OECD, 2014, p. 21), and inclusive, in that most students attend a local neighbourhood school. After noting these positive features, the OECD review suggested a number of concrete policy options that could strengthen the Welsh education system over the longer term. In particular, it argued for the development of a long-term vision translated into measurable objectives. With this in mind, the Welsh government published a five-year reform plan (Department for Education and Skills [DfES], 2014). This provided a timeline for key activities and identified immediate measures to be taken.

A key element of the plan was government's interpretation of the idea of a self-improving school system, which, influenced by our advice, involved the following:

- Transforming school improvement from being something that was once 'done to' schools to something that is being 'done by' schools.
- An end to the top-down improvement 'service' being delivered to schools and instead seek to empower school leaders to work together, taking control of their futures and their development.

44 Schools Challenge Cymru

- Those within schools taking responsibility for raising standards within their own organisations.
- A strengthening of the partnerships between schools, such that they are able to support and challenge one another. (DfES, 2014, p. 21)

The model proposed by the government lacked detail into how such new collaborative arrangements should be developed or co-ordinated. It stated that this would form part of the work of the new regional school improvement structures it had initiated earlier.

Following a review of existing arrangements, it was decided that the school improvement services of the existing 22 local authorities would be grouped together in four regional consortia (DfES, 2013). They were allowed a degree of freedom as to how they operated in practice, and they received varying degrees of support and autonomy from the local authorities with which they are associated. Each had its own 'managing director.'

Early on in the development of the regional consortia, concerns were raised about their understanding of and commitment to the proposed new way of working. Indeed, a report for Welsh government (Hill, 2013) described the arrangements as being *'profoundly unsatisfactory'* (p. 14) because too much of the existing collaborative work between schools was of the *'come and see what we are doing'* variety (p. 63), rather than being based around leaders and teachers sharing data and then working jointly to improve learning. The consortia were also criticised for spending their budgets on appointing 'system leaders,' usually former local authority staff, rather than investing in effective collaborative school improvement processes.

For the new approach to work effectively, it was argued, regional partnerships had to create their own collaborative arrangements that reflected local needs. At the national level, however, an apparent lack of trust between different tiers in the system limited the sharing of issues and possible solutions (Evans, 2015). This also contributed to the consortia becoming defensive about the difficulties they faced and led to competition between them as they set out to prove their effectiveness as new school improvement services (Dixon, 2016). Meanwhile, at the local level, consortia faced the issue of how to balance their role in developing collaborative work between schools with challenging those that underperformed according to national accountability measures. This was a balance that the national inspection service felt they had failed to get right in their assessments of the consortia, when it was concluded that they were *'better at challenging schools about their current performance than supporting them to improve'* (Estyn, 2015, p. 7).

Questions of trust also arose locally between schools, local authorities and the consortia. This seemed to be influenced by experiences in previous reform eras, when policies had swung sharply between encouraging local collaboration and imposing centrally prescribed accountability measures (Dixon, 2016). As a result, uncertainty as to whether the new arrangements would undergo similar reverses created a degree of scepticism about how genuinely committed different local actors were to collaborative approaches.

Schools Challenge Cymru

As we have explained, the Welsh initiative was intended to act as a catalyst for the implementation of the suggestions made by the OECD. Specifically, it set out to accelerate progress across the Welsh education system, focusing in particular on improving outcomes for young people from low-income families. The overall aims were:

- To bring about rapid improvements in the performance of schools serving the more disadvantaged communities; and
- To use lessons from these developments to strengthen the capacity of the education system to improve itself.

Alongside the other national reforms then being implemented in relation to the curriculum, professional learning, teacher education and educational leadership, Schools Challenge Cymru was expected to contribute to the development of a world-class education system. However, as we will explain, the preoccupation of politicians and administrators with improving test and examination scores as rapidly as possible created tensions regarding exactly what the main goals were.

The design of Schools Challenge Cymru drew extensively on lessons from the City Challenge programme in England. However, there was a political concern to show that the initiative retained a strong Welsh flavour. So, for example, terms such as 'chief adviser' and 'keys to success' that had been used in London and Greater Manchester were changed.

The project was launched in the summer of 2014, with a budget of approximately £20 million for each of the following two years, with the possibility of a further year's extension. One of us was closely involved as 'the champion,' a role analogous to that of chief adviser in the English projects. The focus was on 40 secondary schools that, to varying degrees, served disadvantaged communities (they were designated as the Pathways to Success) and, to a lesser extent, their local primary school partners.

The schools were chosen on the basis of a range of deprivation-related factors, as well as the performance of their students on examinations. Whilst this led to a sample of schools at varied stages of development, reference was made in the media to them being the 'naughty forty,' which hardly helped to get the initiative off to a positive start.

Further advice on the choice of schools was provided by local authorities and the four regional consortia. From the outset they indicated that there was to be extensive consultation with local stakeholders. Although in many ways appropriate, this had the potential to cause tensions and delay progress. To provide a flavour, on the day the list of 40 schools was announced in the press, one of us was with the Minister when a call came through to say that one of the local authorities wished to withdraw one of the nominated schools. Having hesitated for a few seconds and then noted our response, he announced that this would definitely not be possible.

Further complications occurred because the finances and administration for the project, although provided as a separate national budget, had to be processed through the four regional consortia that provided the school improvement services for local authorities. This led to difficulties regarding the appointment of advisers and issues related to their accountability in carrying out their duties. The nature of these complications varied between the four consortia, reflecting their existing working practices.

As we have explained, the expectation was that innovations involving the Pathways to Success schools would eventually have a wider impact on the way the Welsh education system works. The aim was to create the kind of 'ripple effect' that had been a feature of the projects in England (Ainscow, 2015). In particular, the programme set out to make better use of resources, and most important, the expertise that exists within the system. With this in mind, it aimed to foster new, more fruitful working relationships: within and between schools; between schools and their local communities; and between national and local government.

A national team of Challenge advisers was involved in facilitating these relationships. Approximately half of these were from outside of Wales. A small team of champions also advised on the overall strategic direction of the initiative. These were people with a strong track record of successful school leadership. As a result of our recommendations, from the outset it was made clear that the advisers and champions were to be directly accountable to the Minister for Education and Skills, a feature that met with various degrees of irritation amongst some senior officers and elected members in local authorities, as well as some union representatives.

One of the key implementation issues was that the appointment of a new team of advisers for this national programme was perceived by some in the field as a critique of the quality of the existing local advisers, who were managed by the consortia, and the historical approaches adopted by local authorities. This sense of being criticised, along with the imposition of new external structures, processes and personnel, led many of the local middle tier organisations to distance themselves from the Challenge at the outset.

Getting started

In the introduction document launching the Challenge in June 2014 (Welsh Government, 2014), the Minister for Education and Skills, Huw Lewis, stated:

> The Challenge provides resources and expertise to schools, but does not give them the solutions on a plate. Pathways to Success schools will be given support in finding, owning and being accountable for their own solutions to the challenges they face, and in ensuring they can get it right for every learner.

Wales's long-term economic health depends on unlocking the potential of all pupils, but there is a further moral purpose. Education can transform lives, and I want all children to have the best education, regardless of personal circumstance. By working together, by sharing a commitment to all children and by wanting the best to be normal, I believe that all children can achieve. Schools Challenge Cymru seeks to remove the obstacles to that achievement.

The document went on to state that the Pathways to Success schools would have four entitlements. First, each school would be provided with a 'School on a Page' template. This would provide a simple framework summarising the situation in the school. In this way, the schools involved would have a common language to compare their situations and explore possible areas of cooperation. This framework was based on an approach that was already working well in the Central South Wales region, about which we say more in Chapter 4, and was intended to help schools in identifying where their efforts may be best concentrated.

Second, each Pathways to Success school was to be assigned a Schools Challenge Cymru adviser who was to take an active role in each school's improvement process, with an expected commitment of up to 25 days of support to each school per annum. The advisers were to be highly experienced individuals, each with a track record of achieving school improvement. They would provide support and challenge to Pathways to Success schools in preparing their plans for improvement, working with senior staff in analysing their context and providing them with support in formulating appropriate and effective improvement strategies. In so doing, they would be in a position to locate and broker additional support from other schools and external agencies that could help to strengthen these improvement efforts – acting as a gatekeeper to ensure improvement efforts were fully aligned and effective.

Third, the Pathways to Success schools would be supported by their adviser in drafting a single school development plan – a comprehensive map of the next stage of the school's improvement journey, with stretching targets for success. These were to be completed by the end of the summer term (i.e., July 2014). These plans would set out the targets for improvement schools would set themselves, demonstrating how they intended to achieve these through involvement in the Challenge. They would also provide the context for practitioners' performance management and professional development, indicating how the school intended to develop its staff in relation to its priorities and targets. Through the involvement of its adviser, the schools would define how the additional resources provided through Schools Challenge Cymru would be used to support rapid improvement. In addition, the plans were expected to identify any additional resources required in terms of infrastructure investment.

Finally, each participating school's efforts were to be supported by the establishment of an accelerated improvement board, to be convened and chaired by the headteacher. The other members of this board would be the chair of governors, a

48 Schools Challenge Cymru

representative of the local authority, a headteacher from a cluster primary school and the adviser. Based on practices that had proved effective in London and Greater Manchester, these boards would meet monthly. The main task was to ensure that the improvement strategies were being implemented effectively and that rapid progress was made.

The team of advisers had members drawn from both Wales and England, providing a helpful blend of local knowledge and new perspectives. As had been the pattern in London and Greater Manchester, they met every few weeks. During these day-long meetings, which were held in government offices in Cardiff, advisers were updated on national policy developments and reported on progress in the schools they were supporting. A further important feature of the meetings was a case study discussion of a particular school, where members of the team shared their thoughts on how improvement could be fostered. These discussions proved to be a powerful vehicle for collaborative problem solving, as well as a rich form of professional development for everybody involved.

Meanwhile, acting as the champion, one of us met with the Minister and, on some occasions, other department officials, every six weeks or so to review progress in the 40 schools. During the first year of the project, the Minister visited each of the 40 schools, usually alongside the school's adviser. There is little doubt that these formal visits gave a strong sense of the importance given to the work going on in the schools.

Moving forward

We have been able to track the progress of Schools Challenge Cymru through the term progress reports written by one of us to update the Minister. The first of these, written in December 2014, described the positive things that had occurred during the first few months, whilst also pinpointing some barriers to progress:

> The programme is now up and running. Importantly, much of the early uncertainty and, indeed, confused ideas amongst some stakeholders about what it involves have now largely disappeared. Nevertheless, we still need to maintain an on-going debate with stakeholder groups across the country in order to maintain support for our strategy as it develops. It is also vital that we do everything possible to promote interesting developments that are going on in the schools.
>
> We are confident that there will be significant progress in the 40 Pathways to Success schools over the next 18 months. There seems to be growing enthusiasm in the schools for the approach we are taking, particularly amongst the heads. Each school has a well thought through action plan and additional resources to make this work. We will, of course, continue to monitor the use of these resources to ensure they are having the desired impact. In most cases, too, the Pathways to Success schools have a carefully chosen partner school – usually from another local authority – to

support their efforts. The Advisers will make sure that these partnerships are leading to improvements in practices with the intention that the benefits will be for both schools. In this way the strategy is already extending its reach beyond the Pathways to Success schools.

(Report to Minister, December, 2014)

The report went on to explain:

There are, however, a small number of schools where, despite these arrangements, we have concerns about their capacity to improve without significant changes in leadership and/or governance arrangements. There appears to be a worrying pattern here in respect to the failure of the system to pick up these cases at an earlier stage and step in to prevent further deterioration. Currently we are in urgent discussion with representatives of the local authorities involved in order to formulate rapid interventions in these schools. This may require changes in key personnel or in the governing body, some form of federation, or closure of the school followed by a fresh start of some kind. It is essential that we keep a close eye on these situations in order to prevent further delays. Pace must be maintained, whilst, of course, keeping a keen eye on legal process.

(Report to Minister, December, 2014)

The report concluded by arguing that Schools Challenge Cymru was offering an 'invitation to innovate.' Some of this related to new forms of school-to-school partnerships, crossing borders of various kinds that had traditionally prevented the movement of expertise between different types of schools. Other innovations involved working in new ways with partners from outside the school sector, such as universities, voluntary organisations and businesses, through what was called 'The Pupil Offer.'

Further progress

A second report to the Minister in April 2015 noted that there was already 'much to celebrate,' not least in the ways in which the 40 Pathways to Success schools and their partner schools were using the programme to explore more effective ways of bringing about improvements in their work. At the same time, it was noted that this was throwing further light on the barriers to change referred to in our earlier report.

Examples of the developments that had taken place had been presented by schools at a workshop for the 40 headteachers held in March of that year. These included accounts that focused on areas such as teacher professional development; pupil leadership; transition between schools; strengthening literacy in science lessons; involving hard-to-reach parents; and restorative practice in relationship to behaviour. There were also encouraging accounts of how schools were

50 Schools Challenge Cymru

cooperating in taking these initiatives forward. What came through the discussions at the workshop was a new sense of optimism as to what was possible. There was also evidence of a growing pride in being part of such an important national initiative, as well as a feeling that being a Pathway to Success school was becoming a badge of honour.

Alongside these developments, significant progress had been made in making interventions in the small number of schools identified by the advisers as a cause for concern. In the report to the Minister, these were described as 'desperately bad situations' that have been allowed to deteriorate over many years. It was also clear that existing arrangements for monitoring schools had failed to identify and address the extent of their problems.

The analysis of the advisers had led them to conclude that, even with additional support, improvements in these schools were unlikely without substantial changes regarding management, leadership and governance. As a result, firm strategies were being put in place in all of these schools. In some cases, this meant changes in leadership and governance personnel, and the introduction of new people. Partnerships had also been created with schools that had the capacity to provide powerful support for rapid improvements in areas such as attendance (students and staff), behaviour, teaching, student tracking, and middle and senior leadership. These interventions required radically different thinking and responses – plus a much greater sense of urgency – in local authorities and, indeed, within the DfES. Some of this had led to moments of tension with colleagues in the field as a result of our mandate from the Minister being used to demand that actions be taken in respect to those schools experiencing severe difficulties of various kinds.

It was noted that lessons from these experiences would be helpful in making systemwide changes to ensure that, in the future, schools experiencing decline are identified and dealt with much earlier than in the past. This theme was part of the agenda of a one-day seminar for Local Authority Directors and Consortia Managing Directors, held in February 2015.

Moving into the second year

The report to the Minister at the end of the first year of the programme explained that an increased emphasis had been place on working with the primary schools in the 40 local area clusters. This was based on an assumption that significant progress in breaking the link between poverty and educational achievement would require coordinated effort on a district basis, starting as soon as possible in a child's life, a theme that was supported passionately by the Minister.

Further impetus for this had been achieved through a successful two-day conference attended by primary school leaders from across the 40 clusters. Discussions during that event were stimulated by accounts of existing practice from different parts of the country, plus evidence from international research. A powerful feature of this event, as with the earlier ones, was that most of the input came from within the schools themselves. This new emphasis reflected a commitment to the view that most of the expertise needed to improve the performance of Welsh education was there within the system. The presence of the Minister at these events was particularly valuable in signalling the government's commitment to the initiative.

The announcement of the provisional GCSE results in August 2015 provided an early indication of the impact of the programme. Overall, the picture for Pathways to Success schools was beyond our expectations. Across the country there were impressive improvements, staggering in some cases. Given the unfortunate situations inherited in some of these schools, this was remarkable. There was also evidence that partnerships between schools had been a powerful factor in bringing about these improvements. To put all of this into a wider context, neither the London nor Manchester Challenges had made similar progress after just one year. This provided a strong foundation for our efforts to have a wider impact during the following year.

There were, however, a few results that were disappointing. In some cases, these were schools with extremely difficult circumstances, such that significant changes in leadership and/or governance were necessary. Inevitably, this had been time-consuming. Meanwhile, we negotiated significant contracts with high-performing schools that would provide intensive support for these schools. Given these arrangements, we expected to see improvements in the performance of the schools in the following 12 months.

In looking to the second year, we wanted to build on the strategies that had proved to be successful during the previous 12 months. In summary, it was reported to the Minister that these were as follows:

- **The work of the advisers** – this had been arguably the most powerful lever for change. The emphasis we had placed on 'high trust, high accountability' meant that team members had been given considerable autonomy to analyse particular contexts and get behind those within the schools in implementing changes. It was clear that members of the team had brought different skills and experiences to this work. The regular team meetings had been an important context for sharing this expertise. This being the case, we intended to encourage greater emphasis on advisers calling on other colleagues to support their efforts, particularly in those schools facing particularly difficulties in bringing about change. We also anticipated that support for schools would be differentiated in relation to the levels of progress already made. In a few instances, advisers who had been less effective did not have their contracts renewed.

- **Accelerated Improvement Boards** – we were particularly surprised by the impact of these arrangements. Their power seemed to be that they emphasised the importance of headteachers themselves taking responsibility for improvement strategies, using a small number of key outsiders as sources of support and challenge. The fact that the boards met monthly ensured that

52 Schools Challenge Cymru

pace was maintained and that those involved held one another accountable for carrying out agreed tasks. The notes of the meetings provided an efficient means of keeping stakeholders informed in ways that avoided time-wasting reporting arrangements. It was encouraging, too, that this strategy was now being introduced more widely across Wales.

- **Professional learning** – the rapid progress that has been achieved in many of the schools had resulted from the introduction of new forms of professional learning for practitioners. These were based on the findings of international research regarding what makes professional development powerful as a strategy for school improvement (see Messiou & Ainscow, 2015). In summary, the evidence is that effective professional development needs to involve a collaborative process that is located mainly in classrooms; involves opportunities for teachers to see colleagues at work; promotes in-depth discussion, leading to the development of a language of practice; is based on an engagement with evidence, such that individuals are challenged to reconsider their taken for granted assumptions as to what is possible; and is facilitated by someone who has the expertise to help teachers understand the difference between what they are doing and what they aspire to do. It is worth adding that these strategies seemed to have been particularly successful when they involved more than one school.

It was also pleasing to report at this stage that, after a period of some tensions regarding the locus of decision making with regard to support for the 40 schools, progress had been made in working with senior staff in the four consortia to build on the lessons from the Challenge. This had led each of them to formulate plans for capacity building that would be supported by Challenge funding. This was to be allocated on the basis of recommendations of the champions group, taking account of the following criteria:

Relevance to the implementation of the self-improving approach outlined in national policy;

A central concern to achieve rapid improvements in the achievements of all pupils, in all schools, focusing in particular on learners from economically disadvantaged backgrounds;

Significant involvement of school leaders in designing and coordinating the strategies to be used;

An emphasis on cooperation between schools and, where relevant, community partners; and

Attention to ways of ensuring that strategies will be sustainable beyond the period of additional funding.

Given the different contexts, it was inevitable that these plans varied across the country, taking account of existing practices that could be built upon and bearing in mind the diversity of these contexts.

Making sense of the impact

By the early part of 2016, discussions were beginning to take place about the possible future of Schools Challenge Cymru. With this in mind, another report to the Minister made reference to the following three types of impact (Report to the Minister, February 2016).

Type 1: Evidence of direct impact

1.1. **The use of intensive school partnerships in order to promote rapid progress with other schools where progress is a cause for concern.** Across the four regional consortia, further schools were being given more intensive, customised support of the sort provided for Pathways to Success schools. This often involved carefully brokered support from other schools that were able to provide appropriate expertise. In this way, practices that were previously trapped in particular contexts were being made more widely available.

1.2. **Efforts to develop the working practices of consortia advisers.** The work of Schools Challenge Cymru's small team of expert advisers was proving to be vital to the success of the programme. Working closely with schools in new ways, they were themselves proving to be a powerful catalyst for change. Recognising the impact of all of this, the four regional consortia had begun developing the work of their own teams of advisers in order to replicate this approach. In some instances, this involved Schools Challenge Cymru advisers in providing professional development opportunities for consortia staff. Sometimes these involved joint school visits that provided possibilities for mutual coaching.

1.3. **Introduction of Accelerated Improvement Boards at other schools where progress is a cause for concern.** Meeting once a month and chaired by the headteacher, these boards involved a handful of key stakeholders who planned activities to move their schools forward with pace. The process involved a new, more powerful form of accountability. This was unlike traditional top-down approaches, with their emphasis on reporting to external agencies. Instead, it involves a form of mutual accountability, where those involved share responsibility and hold one another accountable for making things happen. The introduction of this approach in other schools across Wales was very encouraging.

Type 2: Evidence of how the programme is supporting new practices

2.1. **The creation of various types of improvement hub in relation to teaching and leadership.** These had been established in three of the consortia and usually involved partnerships of schools. Working together, they were providing programmes of professional learning for teachers in their own schools and for others in their local areas. In supporting these important initiatives, Schools Challenge Cymu was seeking to make better use of the expertise that was there within the teaching force.

2.2. **The emergence of groups of successful headteachers who are taking on the role of system leaders.** This meant that heads had to see themselves as having a wider responsibility for all children and young people, not just those that attend their own schools. It also required them to develop patterns of working that enabled them to have the flexibility to cooperate with other schools and with their wider communities. In so doing, it opened up new possibilities for their professional development regarding the management of change. It could also be an important factor in the implementation of other national reforms. However, the extent to which this approach had developed varied across the consortia.

2.3. **Experimentation with peer review approaches within groups of schools.** This approach was being developed in two of the consortia regions. It echoes the recommendations of international research that argues for a move away from a heavy reliance on external accountability toward an investment in the professional capital of teachers and school leaders (e.g., Fullan et al., 2015). However, this has to be challenging and credible. In other words, it must not involve forms of collusion within which partner schools endorse one another in an acceptance of mediocrity.

2.4. **The strengthening of collaboration within local area school clusters.** In general, local area cluster work is a relative strength within the Welsh education system. Building on this, Schools Challenge Cymru was encouraging the use of these groupings to address particular areas of concern, such as the need to improve standards of literacy and numeracy. In some instance, too, local area clusters were being used as vehicles for strengthening professional development amongst practitioners. Here, again, the importance of leadership from within schools is vital, as is the need for shared responsibility for progress across a group of schools.

Type 3: Indications that the programme is helping to change thinking

3.1. **Raised expectations regarding how rapidly improvements can be achieved.** Whilst this was difficult to measure, there were suggestions in some parts of the country that the rapid improvements being achieved in the Pathways to Success schools was beginning to challenge assumptions regarding what is possible. This had particular implications for efforts to improve outcomes for learners from low-income families.

3.2. **A greater willingness by local authorities to make use of their powers of intervention.** Whilst this remained a challenge, the focus on a small number of the Pathways to Success schools facing multiple difficulties had led to examples of such interventions. These mainly involved changes in management and/or governance arrangements. In some cases, we had also seen the benefits of more intensive partnerships with a support school, including a consideration of the future possibility of these becoming federations. It was anticipated that accounts of these developments would filter across the system, encouraging a greater confidence that such changes can be undertaken successfully.

3.3. **Further cooperation between local authorities.** There are important implications in all of this for the future roles of local authorities. They have to adjust their ways of working in response to the development of improvement strategies that are increasingly led from within schools. Specifically, they must monitor and challenge schools in relation to the agreed goals of collaborative activities, whilst senior staff within schools share responsibility for the overall management of improvement efforts. The problem is, of course, that local authorities are not equally strong. A way to reduce this variation is to promote collaboration among them so they share resources, ideasand expertise, and exercise collective responsibility for the improvement of all of their schools. With this in mind, efforts were being made to encourage local authorities to undertake peer reviews. The strengthening of the roles of the consortia was also important in signalling the benefits of local authorities sharing their resources.

Looking to the next phase of Schools Challenge Cymru, then, it was argued that the intention was to work even more closely with the four regional consortia to further widen the impact of the programme. With this in mind, a series of what proved to be positive meetings took place with local authority directors to discuss how the Challenge could be used to support their improvement efforts. In addition, a member of the champions group was now attached to each consortium to facilitate close cooperation around these developments.

Moving into a new era

As a national election loomed in the spring of 2016, the Minister announced that he would not be standing for re-election to the National Assembly of Wales. This caused concern amongst senior civil servants, who felt that it was possible that Schools Challenge Cymru would have less support from a new Minister, who might well want to introduce their own initiatives.

Writing about this to two senior civil servants just after the election, one of us noted:

> I thought it might be helpful to underline a few points in preparation for your discussions with the new Minister about the future of Schools Challenge Cymru. These have been partly stimulated by my visits this last week to three of the Pathways to Success schools.

56 Schools Challenge Cymru

My professional assessment is that, whilst a small number of the project schools have proved slower to shift because of deep routed structural difficulties, the rapid progress made by the vast majority of them is quite remarkable. I am also optimistic that this progress will be reflected in this summer's examination results. You are both experienced enough to know that achieving progress at such a pace is far from easy, particularly in schools that have previously had poor improvement records – and yet this is what is happening.

In bringing about this progress, the efforts of our splendid team of advisers has demonstrated two things in particular: the Welsh education system has massive untapped potential to improve itself; and the Schools Challenge interventions are providing a catalyst for the further strengthening of national school improvement arrangements. This being the case, I suggest that the Challenge can be used to stimulate a new push to bring about systemwide change, focusing in particular on improving outcomes for learners from disadvantaged backgrounds. In taking on this wider role, the models of practice that are being developed in the Pathways to Success schools can provide a stimulus for innovation.

The note went on to conclude:

I believe that, in this way, Wales will become a focus of attention for those in other countries who are seeking to improve their education systems in ways that do not rely on market forces. However, as we know from international research, this will take some years of consistent and persistent action to achieve, particularly if we are to ensure sustainable improvements.

Shortly afterward it was announced that the new Minister would be from a different political party. This came about because the new government did not have an overall majority in the Welsh Assembly. Writing in July 2016 in another letter to the same two civil servants, we argued noted:

You will be pleased to hear that there is growing evidence that the lessons from Schools Challenge Cymru are having an impact across the four consortia, in the way that we all intended. Over the last few months this has become much more apparent through meetings we have held with senior colleagues in each of the regional consortia.

Importantly, these initiatives should ensure continuing support for those of the Pathways to Success schools that remain vulnerable, whilst at the same time widening the impact to other schools facing difficulties. Given the emphasis on school-to-school support, they should also help in strengthening moves towards a self-improving system, with strong school leaders increasing taking on the role of system leaders.

To give you a flavour, here are a few examples:

- Three of our most effective SCC advisers have been asked by one consortium to carry out what sounds like a 'mini challenge programme' with schools in a local authority that is a cause for concern;
- In another region, rapid progress is being made in getting the consortium advisers to adopt bespoke responses of the sort developed by SCC for schools facing challenging circumstances;
- Plans are taking shape in another region to organize two networks of challenging schools (one in the west and the other in the east) that will receive bespoke support from high performing schools, with continuing support from some of our advisers; and
- Another consortium is discussing with some of our advisers about how they can continue to work with schools that need additional support.

In addition, there is now widespread use across the country of the idea of accelerated improvement boards, chaired by headteachers. As you know, these have proved to be a powerful way of achieving local accountability amongst stakeholders and ensuring pace in the improvement of schools.

In taking these initiatives forward, it is also encouraging that all the consortia are exploring ways of retaining our strongest advisers to support the reforms.

Building on such developments, I suggest that we now need a concerted effort over the next few months to maintain this momentum, with strong support from senior colleagues within the Department.

In the three months following these notes, it became apparent that Schools Challenge Cymru was not high on the new Minister's agenda. Indeed, no meetings were held with her until December 2016. Although work with the schools continued, there was a noticeable loss of momentum.

The independent evaluation

The final report of the independent evaluation that had been commissioned by the government was not published until late in July 2017 (Carr, Brown & Morris, 2017), by which time Schools Challenge Cymru had ceased to operate. The study, which had focused only on the first two years of the programme, was concerned with the progress on the Pathways to Success schools but not, unfortunately, with the wider systematic impact. This had been determined by the way in which the contract had been commissioned.

In analysing progress, the evaluation team chose to categorise the schools as follows:

Group A: Schools in which the quality of provision appeared to have been diminishing prior to engagement with the programme and who were at risk of further decline. Eight were identified as Group A schools.

58 Schools Challenge Cymru

Group B: Schools in which the quality of provision appeared stable prior to engagement with the programme but were considered in need of improvement. Sixteen were assessed as Group B schools.

Group C: Schools in which the quality of provision had started to improve prior to engagement with the programme. Fourteen schools were best described as in this group.

As a result of interviews with stakeholders, the evaluators concluded that all the schools, whether in Group A, B or C, now reported a programme of school improvement activities focused on improving teacher quality, reflecting:

- The increased priority interviewees attached to this area;
- Greater confidence amongst senior leaders in being able to implement school-improvement activities;
- A greater emphasis than in 2014/15 on building the capacity of individual teachers already working in the schools, rather than on bringing in new staff;
- Ways of working with partner schools that had improved, with greater emphasis on joint CPD programmes and developing shared solutions to the challenges faced by both schools;
- An early emphasis on the need to improve the quality of self-evaluation and school development planning was less evident as such systems became established; and
- A growing emphasis on improving leadership and management quality, with many schools investing more in the development of middle leaders to ensure that effective practices were cascaded down the school.

Whilst the schools generally performed below the Welsh average in core subjects, they had all made some academic progress in the two years since the implementation of Schools Challenge Cymru. In particular:

- Schools in Group A (where the quality of provision appeared to have been diminishing prior to engagement with SCC) and Group C (where the quality of provision had started to improve prior to engagement with SCC) made more and faster progress than might have been predicted, given their pupil profile.
- Schools in Group B (those in which the quality of provision appeared stable prior to engagement with SCC) made the level of progress that would have been predicted, given their pupil profile.

In addition, the evaluation team reported that external stakeholders thought that improvements had been made to the quality of leadership and management in over 30 of the schools. Where such improvements were not reported, schools were commonly characterised by recent changes within the senior leadership team. The new leadership in these schools were thought to have the potential to deliver the improvements required, but interviewees felt it would take time before they became apparent. Interviewees in most of the schools also believed that gains had been made in improving the quality of self-evaluation. In most cases, too, such improvements were attributed to an improvement in the confidence of leaders to make decisions around school improvement.

It is worth adding here that a factor that was not picked up in the analysis provided by the external evaluators was the variation regarding outcomes between the four regions. In particular, the 16 Pathways to Success schools across the five local authorities in the Central South region stood out in the sense of the positive progress made, even though they included a small number that presented particular challenges, one of which had been described in the media as 'the worst school in Wales.' A factor here may well have been the efforts being made to promote their own regional challenge programme, a detailed account of which is provided in Chapter 4.

Bringing the account up to date, the GCSE results for 2018 confirmed that many of the Pathways to Success schools have continued to prosper, although there are a few that continue to be a cause for concern.[1] We also have anecdotal evidence suggesting that other schools are turning to some of them for advice regarding strategies for improvement. However, the most striking story is of the school referred to in the previous paragraph, the progress of which was reported in an article with the headline *'From rioting pupils to record GCSE results: How a high school turned its fortunes around in four years.'*[2]

The endgame

In 2018, Schools Challenge Cymru was part of the focus of an inquiry by the National Assembly's Children, Young People and Education committee. It heard that the Welsh Government had decided to end the programme after three years and before the results of the government-commissioned performance evaluation were known. It was also noted that critics of this decision had said that Schools Challenge Cymru had ended too soon and that similar models used in other parts of the UK had been given more time to raise standards.

In its evidence to the committee, the Welsh Government said that the regional consortia were now well placed to take over support for Wales' most underperforming schools as part of their functions for overall school improvement. However, the committee commented that it was unclear to what extent the Welsh Government was learning lessons from the Schools Challenge Cymru programme and recommended that, in conjunction with the regional consortia, it should engage with the key players involved in delivering Schools Challenge Cymru. In particular, there was a need to discuss what lessons could be learnt from the programme and other school improvement initiatives, and subsequently apply these more generally across all schools requiring improvement.

The committee noted that the new Cabinet Secretary for Education had inherited the Schools Challenge Cymru programme, which was set up by her predecessor. They were struck by the evidence of the Welsh Government's Schools Challenge Cymru champion, who had explained that it was 'certainly not at the centre of [the new Cabinet Secretary's] agenda' and that the programme rather 'faded out' in its third year. The Committee noted the Cabinet Secretary's position that the programme was time-limited in terms of the funding committed to it but believed that there had been scope for it to be continued if she had felt strongly that it should. It also concluded that the decision to discontinue Schools Challenge Cymru was taken prematurely, without being informed by the independent evaluation report.

In a paper presented to the Committee[3], we offered an analysis of the lessons that had been learnt, plus some suggestions as to what should happen in the future. In it we reported that, in a relatively short time, the schools involved had all, to varying degrees, made significant progress. In some cases, the gains in terms of examination results have been remarkable. This rate of improvement had been faster than the overall progress made across Wales over the same period. A small number of the schools had proved more difficult to move. However, significant progress had been made in strengthening leadership and governance in these schools, such that there were now reasons to be optimistic about their future.

Our paper went on to argue that this progress had been achieved as a result of actions taken by the schools themselves, with bespoke support from the team of highly experienced advisers. This was reflected in comments such as the following from headteachers:

> The Schools Challenge Cymru programme has had a more profoundly positive impact on our school's standards than any other national or regional programme in which the school has participated over the last decade.
>
> Without the support of the programme the rate of progress in raising standards at the school would undoubtedly have been considerably slower.
>
> We really benefited from the School Challenge Cymru programme, and this has been a key driver in our school improvement. The philosophy underpinning the programme was communicated with absolute clarity, complemented by financial and practical help and support.

We argued that the work of Schools Challenge Cymru had shown that schools in Wales had untapped potential that needed to be mobilised in order that they could become more effective in improving themselves. The major contribution of the advisers involved in the programme had been in using their expertise and wide experience to identify and make better use of this latent potential. Importantly, we suggested, they had worked as a team in carrying out this demanding task, meeting regularly to share ideas and sometimes visiting schools together where a second opinion had seemed necessary.

Our analysis of what had happened suggested six interconnected lessons that emerged from the efforts of advisers to move forward schools that had previously been stuck.

Lesson 1: Start by analysing the context

Whilst there were some common factors that had previously prevented progress across the 40 schools, each one had to be analysed in detail. This analysis had involved advisers working alongside school leaders in collecting and engaging with context-specific information related to factors such as culture, capacity and confidence. Whilst this always started with statistical performance data, it required much more in-depth probing, through classroom observations, scrutiny of students' work and discussions with students, staff and governors.

In carrying out an initial review, advisers were able to assess the capacity of the head and senior staff to lead a push for improvement. In some cases, this led to the conclusion that urgent changes in leadership were necessary. Similarly, some situations required changes in the membership of governing bodies. These changes required advisers to work closely with local authority staff and, occasionally, pressure was required to ensure that changes were made. An adviser described what happened following a school being placed in special measures following an inspection:

> An outstanding headteacher was appointed who has now developed a very effective senior team to lead the school. With Schools Challenge funding and support, they have transformed the ethos and aspirations of the school through setting a clear vision and implementing strategies that focus on teaching and learning.

Having seen a massive leap in the school's examination results during less than a year, the adviser added:

> It is now a self-improving school with a motivated staff and a high level of challenge from a very committed governing body that will enable them to become an excellent school providing high-quality education for all the pupils.

Lesson 2: Mobilise leadership from within the school

Contextual analysis had continued throughout the period of Schools Challenge to monitor the impact of the improvement strategies that had been introduced. In this way, barriers to progress were identified and addressed. As a result, strategies had been customised in response to the developing situation in each context, using evidence as a catalyst for change.

Much of the work of advisers had been concentrated on working with senior staff to build confidence and strengthen their leadership skills. So, for example, in a previously failing school that made outstanding progress, the adviser commented:

> All staff at the school have fully embraced the opportunities offered to them through the Schools Challenge Cymru programme, and it has been rewarding working alongside the leadership team and supporting them to raise standards. Teachers at the

> *school now have the necessary drive, resilience and skills to further improve outcomes with a sharp focus on improvement planning and doing things in the right order. The school is built around strong relationships, trust and a sense of community.*

Talking about the impact on schools, another adviser commented:

> *The visible difference in resilience and confidence of leaders at all levels was excellent to see in comparison to where they were three years ago.*

It was also evident that, in many cases, advisers had been able to identify other staff within the schools, including some relatively inexperienced teachers and support staff, with the potential to lead improvement efforts. An important factor here had been to ensure that headteachers and other senior staff encourage and support this process of capacity building.

Additional resources and support had been used tactically to support these developments, as a head explained:

> *The additional funding and wider challenge the school received as part of the Schools Challenge Cymru programme were the catalysts for the accelerated progress made across the main indicators.*

The success of these interventions had strengthened the capacity of the schools to manage change through effective school-based professional development activities. This invites a degree of optimism that these changes will lead to sustainable improvement, as noted by another of the advisers:

> *I was recently reminded by one of the headteachers that, even more significant than the improved pupils' outcomes made in the past two years, is the development of classroom culture and leadership capacity to ensure that these gains will continue to improve year on year.*

Lesson 3: Promote a culture of collaborative learning amongst staff

Across the schools, the progress made had led to changes in expectations regarding what is possible and higher aspirations of what students can achieve. This had promoted cultural change; for example, two heads explained what this had involved in each of their schools:

> *There is a much more collaborative culture, with more effective targeted professional development and a more collegiate approach to school improvement.*
> *The school has moved from quite a hierarchical approach to reviewing teaching and learning to a more collegiate model at the heart of which has been an attempt to ensure that classroom doors are open, that we celebrate the very best classroom practice*

at every opportunity, and develop, support and challenge bespoke programmes where underperformance is evident.

Strategies used to achieve these changes varied from school to school. There were, however, certain overall patterns. So, for example, it was evident at the start of the programme that most of the Pathways to Success schools lacked effective arrangements for tracking student progress in order to target appropriate support. Improving this factor proved to be relatively straightforward, usually by drawing on the expertise of other schools that already have effective mechanisms in place. A head explained:

A significantly improved data tracking system recognises underperformance very quickly and support is directed accordingly.

Another head commented:

Once the student outcomes started to improve, the ambition of younger students increased. This caused a snowball effect as teachers' expectations of the students grew.

There was also a sense of fragmentation within many of the schools, with teachers often working alone to solve the problems they face. With this in mind, efforts had been made in all the schools to promote within-school collaboration through the introduction of participatory, inquiry-based professional development strategies. For example, a head saw the impact in terms of:

significantly enhanced professional development, bespoke high-quality mentoring and coaching from our challenge adviser. The flexibility to allocate resources promptly, all underpinned the change process.

Another head commented:

the development of lead practitioners within the school to provide a coaching model to others has provided sustainability, evidenced in the increasing number of good and excellent lessons and rapidly improved outcomes.

In some schools, the students themselves had also been mobilised to further strengthen the culture of learning. Once again, this points to underused resources within schools that need to be used more effectively.

Lesson 4: Open up schools and connect to relevant external support

We know from research that schools that face challenging circumstances tend to become isolated and inward looking. With this in mind, advisers had placed

64 Schools Challenge Cymru

considerable emphasis on linking the Pathways to Success schools to other schools. A head commented:

> *As a Pathways to Success school we have worked in partnership (with another school) to improve our academic results and refine the school improvement systems that lead to sustainable, stable and improving schooling.*

In many cases, the partnerships built upon the existing local area clusters, a feature that is a strength of some parts of the Welsh education system. In some instances, these groupings had been further strengthened by the development of joint professional development programmes that have enabled the sharing of cross-phase expertise.

In many cases, too, more intensive partnerships had been brokered with other secondary schools. These partnerships, which took many forms, often involved crossing the borders between local authorities. In some cases, they involve two schools, where the strength of one is used to provide support in addressing concerns in another. Other schools had multiple partners for different purposes. As such partnerships developed, advisers continued monitoring what happened because this can sometimes lead to the proliferation of meetings that result in no actions being taken.

Commenting on highly successful partnerships in two of the Pathways to Success schools he supported, an adviser explained:

> *The leadership of both schools see it as a partnership of equals. The headteachers having mutual respect for each other is key. But, just as important, the staff who work with each other across the schools see that it has mutual benefit. Through this work, colleagues have developed their confidence to ask questions of their own practice in order to improve.*

Most notably, we had seen how between-school partnerships led to striking improvements in the performance of schools facing the most challenging circumstances. Commenting on this, an adviser said:

> *The move from the school as an inward-looking organisation to one that has embraced partnerships and contact with other schools, the consortium and other providers, was a critical cultural change and is a significant element in the sustainability of the project.*

It is important to recognise, however, that such collaborations are complex. They therefore need careful brokering and monitoring to ensure they have an impact. Significantly, we have found that, where they are effective, such collaborative arrangements can have a positive impact on the learning of students in all the partner schools.

Lesson 5: Find ways of injecting pace

Moving forward with urgency had been a central emphasis within Schools Challenge Cymru, not least because overall progress within the Welsh education system had been relatively slow over many years. The approach taken by the advisers was vital in this respect. In particular, they were close to the schools – particularly to senior members of staff – through regular visits, supplemented by frequent contacts through phone calls and email. They also established a presence within the schools to connect directly with others who can help to move things forward, including governors. For example, an adviser commented:

> I have just done a support visit to the Maths departments in each of my schools, and it was very pleasing to note the urgency and pace they had all responded to the task ahead of improving outcomes by August. They all have clear action plans and robust high-impact strategies up and running.

Commenting on ways of achieving pace, another adviser argued:

> The significant funds made available, combined with ministerial clout, allowed for quick decision making and the rapid implementation of plans and innovations.

Pace was also encouraged through the involvement of advisers in each school's Accelerated Improvement Board, where those involved held one another to account for carrying out agreed tasks. Crucially, they involved only a small group of key stakeholders, chaired by the headteacher. This reinforces the point that they and their colleagues are responsible for the improvement of their schools. The notes of the monthly meetings of these boards also provided an efficient means of keeping other stakeholders informed in ways that avoided time-wasting reporting arrangements.

Lesson 6: Improve the image of the school within its community and more widely

Within a context where schools are, to varying degrees, in competition with one another, external image is a vital factor. The problem was that many of the Pathways to Success schools had a poor image within their local communities, often going back over many years. As a result, they had found it difficult to attract students, particularly those from more aspirational families. This meant that they often had spare places that were eventually filled by students excluded from other schools. This situation was then made worse by the fact that the schools also had difficulty employing suitably qualified teachers, particularly in those subjects where there is a shortage.

Given these circumstances, emphasis had been placed on promoting the progress made in the Pathways to Success schools in their local communities and,

66 Schools Challenge Cymru

indeed, more widely. This helped to build belief within the schools. Being part of a high-profile national initiative with government backing has helped with this, as noted by one head whose school had a long-term bad image:

> *We never felt a stigma attached to the programme. Rather, the identification that we are amongst a group of schools uniquely placed to make a real difference to young people's lives, including those who are amongst the most disadvantaged.*

Clearly, the rapid progress that many of the schools made in terms of examination results helped in this respect, alongside other achievements related to the arts, sport and outdoor activities. Reports of these developments in the media had been systematically orchestrated, and, as a result, representatives of some of the schools had been invited to make presentations at local and national conferences. Meanwhile, some of the schools were developing as centres of professional development for staff in other schools.

The paper concluded that, in these six ways, as intended, Schools Challenge Cymru was having a ripple effect across the education system by demonstrating what is possible with learners from less advantaged backgrounds and then sharing their expertise with others.

We then went on to argue that as more effective improvement measures were introduced into the Pathways to Success schools, we had experienced various forms of 'turbulence' as taken-for-granted assumptions about what is possible were subject to challenge. This had thrown light on some of the factors that had prevented earlier improvement. Our purpose had been to demonstrate what was possible and, in so doing, find ways of identifying and overcoming barriers that had held back progress in the past.

Our ongoing monitoring of the developments that had occurred suggested that these barriers mainly related to existing ways of working that consumed time and resources and delayed action in the field. They included the following:

- **The over emphasis placed by some local authorities (and consortia staff) on putting schools, particularly those facing challenging circumstances, under increasing pressure.** This tends to demoralise the key agents of change, i.e., the staff in the schools. It also leads to considerable time being wasted on debating and disputing plans and targets. Whilst target setting is helpful, without powerful support strategies it is unlikely to lead to sustainable change.
- **Multiple accountability arrangements.** This means that school leaders are spending too much time preparing reports for different audiences, and attending various review and scrutiny meetings, and being given different (and at times conflicting) advice on the improvements required and how they can be implemented.
- **Lack of effective support for school improvement.** The local advisers working within the consortia were spending far too much time monitoring

and reporting on school progress in relation to national accountability procedures. This left little time for working closely with schools to support authentic improvement processes in the way the Schools Challenge Cymru advisers have been able to do.

- **Actions by local authority and consortia staff that limit the freedom of school leaders to take responsibility for their own improvement.** As a result, this leads to a sense of dependency on outsiders to lead improvement efforts, rather than those within schools taking responsibility and being accountable for improved outcomes.
- **Poor knowledge amongst staff in local authorities about the strengths and weaknesses of the schools with which they work.** Too often their descriptions of schools are expressed in terms of superficial patterns of student performance based on headline figures, rather than detailed understandings of teaching and leadership practices, attitudes, expectations and organisational cultures. As a result, latent potential for leading improvement is too often overlooked.
- **Governors who, in some instances, seem to be unclear about their roles and responsibilities.** These community representatives represent another untapped potential that needs to be mobilised to support the efforts of schools to improve themselves. However, we have found that, in some instances, they are a significant barrier to progress. There are important implications here for local authority relationships' with governing bodies.
- **Local authorities that remain reluctant to make use of their powers of intervention in the case of schools that are a cause for concern.** In some instances, it may be that they believe that their continued use of lesser actions, such as issuing warning notices, is sufficient. Our concern is that, as a result, difficult situations are sometimes allowed to further deteriorate, leading to a collapse of confidence within schools and the communities they serve. Very often, too, this leads to increased union involvement that creates additional barriers.

We added that some of the practices of the national inspection service, Estyn, although often a positive stimulus for change, can also unintentionally act as barriers to progress. For example, we had observed that they can sometimes discourage the efforts of schools by failing to recognise and celebrate the progress being made. The pattern of frequent monitoring visits to some schools can also act as a distraction from their improvement activities. At the same time, the apparent preoccupation with monitoring paperwork as a means of ensuring consistency in the way local authority and consortia staff work tends to encourage an atmosphere of compliance, leading to a satisfaction with mediocrity and a reluctance to explore new responses.

The list of barriers represented a substantive critique of the existing middle tier and had arisen in part because of the low levels of trust between its members, particularly the local authorities and the newly created consortia. The issues to do

68 Schools Challenge Cymru

with a lack of clarity between some local authority and consortia staff about their respective roles and responsibilities had a political edge, as some authorities were reluctant to cede control of their school improvement services to consortia that to varying degrees they had been forced to create by central government. These critiques, we argued, required a rethink of how national education policies were being reconstructed at different levels in the system. This is particularly vital as national efforts are made to develop self-improving school systems, a move that requires radical changes to thinking, practice and relationships at every level in order to give practitioners the space to analyse their particular circumstances and determine priorities accordingly.

Conclusion

Our account of Schools Challenge Cymru has offered further illustrations of the possibilities for researchers to get involved in educational change programmes. At the same time, it has thrown light on some of the difficulties involved, a theme that we return to in Chapter 7. We have also shown how ideas adopted from elsewhere are interpreted and adapted as they are picked up in a different context, but also when they critique established ways of working, or call into question existing power structures, they can also be dismissed and rejected.

Wales proved to be particularly interesting in this respect. It is a country with a rich history of valuing education and a strong ethos of collaboration. However, its recent political complexities seemed to generate continuing tensions regarding educational decision making, all of which are intensified by the strong social networks that exist within such a small country. As we have seen, all of this presents major barriers to efforts to move the system forward.

One Welsh headteacher echoed the views of others when he commented that, in his part of the world, school improvement was like trying to drive more quickly down a road with speed bumps every few yards. As we have explained, many of the 'bumps' relate to existing ways of working, which reflect taken for granted assumptions as to what is possible. Although well intended, these traditions often consume time and resources, and delay action. They include the over-emphasis placed by some local authorities on putting schools, particularly those facing challenging circumstances, under unnecessary pressure to set and achieve narrowly conceived goals. It can also lead to considerable time being wasted on debating and disputing plans and targets. Our experience is that, whilst plans and target setting can be helpful, without powerful support strategies they are unlikely to lead to sustainable change.

Linked to this are actions by some local authority staff that limit the freedom of school leaders to take responsibility for their own improvement. In particular, we found that there were often what seemed to be multiple reporting arrangements, such that school leaders were spending too much time preparing reports for different audiences, attending various review and scrutiny meetings, and being given different (and at times conflicting) advice on the improvements required and how they can be achieved. Despite calls for the empowerment of schools and headteachers, this can lead to a sense of dependency on outsiders to lead improvement efforts, rather than those in schools taking responsibility and being accountable for improved outcomes. In such situations, school leaders can feel undermined and disempowered. As a result, they tend to make poor decisions, and therefore find it more difficult to prioritise their improvement strategies.

In addressing these difficulties, efforts are needed to clarify the respective roles of those at different levels of the system. Specifically, this requires local authority staff to know, trust and support their schools, alongside providing appropriate encouragement to improve. These changes in roles and responsibilities are particularly challenging during periods of transition, whilst more locally led improvement strategies are developing, but they are a matter of urgency in order that rapid progress can be achieved.

There are also barriers related to the uncertainly that exists within national and local government regarding the stance that is needed to support the development of locally driven collaborative improvement. In particular, it must be recognised that the use of the power of collaboration as a means of achieving equity in schools requires an approach to national policy implementation that fosters greater flexibility at the local level, in order for practitioners to have the space to analyse their particular circumstances and determine priorities accordingly.

Finally, a further significant factor in the Welsh story was the way that the aspiration to use Schools Challenge Cymru as a catalyst for system change was lost. It seemed that, despite all our efforts to promote a more sustainable partnership approach, the dominant concern to show short-term gains with regard to improvements in examination scores led to external structures re-asserting control over school leaders. Indeed, as we have seen, this was even apparent in the way the independent evaluation was designed.

As a rather sad epitaph to the story presented in this chapter, one of us recently interviewed the former head of one of the Pathways to Success schools that did well over the three years of the project. He described how members of the regional consortium team arrived shortly after Schools Challenge Cymru ended, imposing accountability requirements and using what he saw as heavy-handed approaches in an attempt to introduce new improvement strategies. A few months later he resigned.

Notes

1 www.walesonline.co.uk/news/education/school-colour-codes-2019-wales-15754205
2 www.walesonline.co.uk/news/education/rioting-pupils-record-gcse-results-15388486
3 http://senedd.assembly.wales/documents/s71219/TF%2009%20Professor%20Mel%20 Ainscow.pdf

4

DEVELOPING A REGIONAL SELF-IMPROVING SCHOOL SYSTEM

Collaboration, competition and transition

A story is told in Wales of a tourist looking at a newly landed bucketful of lobsters on the quayside. As the lobsters writhed around, she asked a fisherman, 'Don't you need to put a lid on the bucket? One of them could easily climb out.' 'Don't you worry about that,' came the reply. 'They are Welsh lobsters, the others will pull it back down.'

Two of us were told different variations of this story at various points during our work in Wales to explain how its tightly knit education community is both supportive and, at the same time, restrictive. It is restrictive in the sense that there is reluctance amongst practitioners to put themselves or their innovatory practises forward for fear that they will be seen as 'getting above themselves.' The solidarity of this tightly knit community can also make it difficult for those within it to break with certain traditions or challenge existing norms without their actions being seen at least, in part, as a criticism or rejection of that community.

The significance of the lobster story is that it illustrates how existing local cultures, into which new systems emerge, effect not only the nature of the existing system's response to the 'new' it, but, crucially, how they will continue to effect its development even after it has become established. The lobster story is a parable of how shared professional identities and collective agency can influence developments within an education system over the longer term, way beyond the tenure of a particular government.

With these themes in mind, in this chapter we describe our involvement in the Central South Wales (CSW) Challenge, a system reform that overlapped with the Schools Challenge Cymru programme described in Chapter 3. As we explain, it involved a fundamental approach to change, and therefore required a much more disruptive transition. Inevitably, this led to difficulties and, as a result, the undoubted progress made remained fragile. This throws further light on the complexities involved in our attempts to build research knowledge and processes into system change strategies.

A disruptive transition

The transition that the CSW Challenge set out to achieve can broadly be characterised as a movement from a bureaucratic and centralised approach to school improvement to a polycentric one led by networks of schools. As we discuss toward the end of this chapter, it has been drawn into attempts within Wales to move away from being a top-down high-stakes accountability system and toward what might be described as a 'low-stakes' collaborative system.

We focus, in particular, on two aspects of the transitional dynamics of the Central South Wales region as it attempted to transform its approach to school improvement to elaborate the lessons we learned from our engagement. First, the change required adoption of a more collaborative approach to emerge within a context marked by a particular mix of partnership working and competition. Although the study of how competition and collaboration can coexist and interact is well established in the private sector (Huxham & Vangen, 2004), within education it is an emergent area of study containing limited empirical research (Muijs & Rumyantseva, 2014).

In the CSW Challenge, the movement from the previous centrally driven and local authority directed system to one that would rely on school-to-school collaboration was carried forward under the banner of the 'self-improving system.' This was a sufficiently broad and vague concept to gather widespread support amongst the existing community of leaders, without appearing to be too direct a criticism of those who positions and interests it might eventually challenge. This led us to pose the question: How does a context marked by a mix of collaboration and competition effect the emergence of a self-improving education system?

Our second area of interest related to a key feature of the development of collaborative improvement initiatives within education systems (NFER, 2007: Claeys et al., 2014 and in the business sector (Asheim, 2002): creation of temporary intermediary structures. These transitory structures are intended to support processes of change by cohering, aligning and developing existing capacities within a locality. The CSW Challenge was a particular form of intermediate structure in that it had to provide a bridge between the 'old' bureaucratic system and the establishment of a 'new' polycentric one (Ostrom, 2010).

As an intermediary structure, the Challenge would facilitate establishment of a new system – one intended to be self-improving. In so doing, it adopted a range of strategies to transition the system. In some instances, there was a rapid whole scale displacement of existing approaches by school-based programmes. Elsewhere, the Challenge adopted a form of 'bricolage' (Koyama, 2014), in which existing elements were combined into new, more collaborative and reciprocal school-to-school approaches. Where the Challenge was not able to dismantle aspects of the local or national accountability structures, it 'layered'

72 A regional self-improving school system

(Mahoney & Thelen, 2009) more collaborative approaches on top of them. All of which led us to focus attention on a second question: What form of intermediary structures and processes can transition an education system to one that is more self-improving?

The Central South Wales Challenge

Since devolution, Welsh education policy has gradually diverged from the other countries in the UK. Its particular approach has been a complex mix of collaboration and partnership working, with aspects of high-stakes accountability. A key turning point in the development of the system was in 2009, when Wales was ranked the lowest of all the countries in the PISA rankings of the UK. As noted in Chapter 3, this resulted in the then Education Minister, Leighton Andrews, initiating a raft of reforms to the education system, including merging the school improvement services of the 22 local authorities into four regional consortia. Representatives of the consortia worked with the central government on the design of a National Model for Regional Working. This was seen as a radical change in that it envisaged a more collaborative partnership-based approach. It was within this changing context that the Central South consortium launched its 'Challenge' in 2014.

The CSW Challenge was instigated by the Directors of Education of the five authorities in the region and received endorsement from local politicians. At the same time, staff of the regional consortium played important roles in supporting its programme of activities. Additional funding and support was provided through Schools Challenge Cymru as part of its capacity building role across the country.

Developed in consultation with representatives of schools in the region, the overall purpose was to transform educational outcomes by improving leadership and teaching, and by finding ways of reducing the impact of poverty on educational outcomes. This was to be achieved, it was argued, by building the capacity of schools to be self-improving. Reference was also made to the development of a culture that embraces innovation and enables teachers and leaders to work together to improve practice in ways that are informed by research and have a positive impact on students' achievement and progress.

Reflecting much of the thinking of City Challenge in England, as described in Chapter 2, the Central South Wales strategy was intended to be 'by schools, for schools.' With this as a guiding principle, activities were planned and coordinated by a headteacher strategy group. At a conference for over 400 headteachers that launched the CSW Challenge in February 2014, one of us talked about lessons that could be learned from research and experiences elsewhere, particularly City Challenge. At the end of the morning, many of the participants expressed their enthusiasm for the rationale presented and the proposed strategies outlined by members of the strategy group. However, a few commented that they had met in the same conference centre on a number of earlier occasions to hear about what seemed like equally impressive plans. Apparently, none of these had led to significant change.

As if that was insufficient as a source of anxiety, the education reporter of a leading national newspaper wrote about what seemed to him to have been a successful conference. However, in commenting on the suggestion that schools would be expected to cooperate across the borders of the five partner local authorities, he wrote:

> [The] desire to blur the boundaries between schools – as well as bordering local authorities – may be wishful thinking. Breaking down age-old barriers between schools of different hues will be no mean feat, and it will be interesting to see whether or not head teachers are willing to play ball.

As we go on to explain, over the following four years, many heads were willing to play ball despite the many obstacles they faced.

The rationale

Applying strategic lessons from City Challenge to Wales required a recognition that the histories and politics of competition and collaboration vary across contexts. In particular, in Wales a broad political rejection of more competitive 'free' market approaches existed, and this was combined with a desire to create a unique 'Welsh approach' to challenging the link between social deprivation and underachievement (Evans, 2015).

The principles that underpinned the CSW Challenge were as follows (Central South Consortium, 2016, p. 3):

- Schools are communities where collaborative enquiry is used to improve practice;
- Groupings of schools engage in joint practice development;
- Where necessary, more intensive partnerships support schools facing difficulties;
- Families and community organisations support the work of schools;
- Coordination of the system is provided by school leaders; and
- Local authorities work together to act as the 'conscience of the system.'

As can be seen, these principles reflected the influence of City Challenge in England, as well as the Welsh government's interpretation of the idea of a self-improving system (see Chapter 3). Importantly, this placed the responsibility for the coordination of the system on the shoulders of school leaders, positioning local authorities as the conscience of the system that would hold them and the consortium to account.

The espoused aim of having current school leaders coordinate the new collaborative system was enacted in practice by the creation of a strategy group,

74 A regional self-improving school system

consisting of headteachers drawn from each of the authorities and all phases of the system. The group itself was not an operational decision-making forum; rather, it set the overall direction of the Challenge. Partnered with staff from the consortium, these heads were mainly seconded from local schools, and they became directly involved in leading collaborative working and setting up new structures. The Challenge was nested within national and local governance structures by the use of various stakeholder and advisory groups, whose roles were framed by the legal agreements that had constituted the consortium.

Gathering evidence

The analysis we go on to develop draws on our 'insider' involvement as researchers employed as advisers within the CSW Challenge, contributing to its design, implementation and formative evaluation. One of us was closely involved in setting up the initiative and chaired the headteacher strategy group during the first couple of years or so; the other author became involved in efforts to develop a more 'self-evaluating' system by injecting processes of inquiry, research utilisation and evaluation into the consortium itself and the programme of activities it developed.

As with all the projects described in this book, our roles point to a rather obvious methodological challenge regarding the analysis we present. As researchers, we were provided with remarkable opportunities to put into practice ideas that had emerged from many years of investigating ways of developing more equitable schools and education systems. At the same time, we were provided with privileged access to information about how decisions were made within the education system. On the other hand, as people who were committed to the success of the project, how far can our interpretations be trusted?

We addressed this methodological challenge by triangulating the evidence we collected from different perspectives, using three sets of strategies:

- **Assessing the impact.** Here the main sources of data were student test scores, teacher self-assessments, school inspection data and responses to an annual survey of leaders, teachers and students. The survey sampled some 20% of schools from across the region, chosen to reflect both school performance and the percentage of students on the role from socially deprived contexts. The staff survey generated over 800 responses from staff concerning their involvement in cross-school working and its effects, and some 3,000 responses from students aged 10 to 16 concerning teaching and learning in their schools.
- **Theories of change.** With our help, each major collaborative strand in the Challenge underwent a theory of change evaluation (Connell & Klem, 2000), based on an initial logic model created by the strand leaders. The model for each strand contained key proxy indicators for the expected impact of the activities upon the individuals and schools involved and on the

A regional self-improving school system 75

local system. Within each strand, a range of evaluative data was collected from participants, including questionnaire surveys and interviews.
- **Case studies.** These involved accounts of particular strands of collaborative activity. This chapter draws primarily on the most recent round of case studies, carried out between 2016 and 2017. The cases were selected based on returns to an annual monitoring process that indicated the scope and depth of their collaborative working.

In addition, we attended many planning meetings, workshops and conferences as participant observers. Drawing on the large amount of data generated over the four years, in what follows we describe and analyse what happened in relation to the two questions we posed at the beginning of this chapter.

Strands of collaborative activity

Within the first 12 months of its existence, the CSW Challenge launched four linked strands of collaborative activity (see Figure 4.1), with all schools in the region engaged in at least one of them. The strands were inclusive in that they

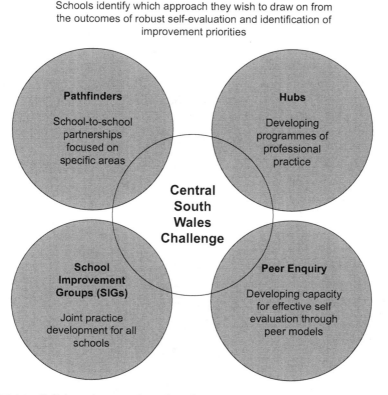

FIGURE 4.1 Collaborative strands within the Central South Wales Challenge.

76 A regional self-improving school system

attempted to focus on and engage different aspects of the system. They varied in the intensity of the collaborative work they entailed, so were open to a range of schools and the degree to which the specific foci of the collaborative work was defined by schools themselves. The four strands are summarised in the following paragraphs.

School improvement groups

Early on, the strategy group took the decision to place all schools into school improvement groups (SIGs). These were designed to create new networks that would break down historical barriers between schools with different local authorities. Up until this point, most school's experience of working in a network had been through their local area clusters. These networks consisted of a number of primary schools and, in the main, the local secondary school that pupils attended. The status of these local clusters varied across the five local authorities: in some they were well regarded structures, whilst in others their major undertaking was statutory requirements, such as the moderation of teacher assessments of pupil progress. Local clusters were disliked by some school leaders because they felt they tended to re-enforce parochial attitudes and were designed more to simplify local authority communication and oversight than to be genuinely supportive.

Being in a SIG was for many school leaders their first experience of being part of a programme of collaborative school improvement in which they were able to select the foci. The groups were consciously configured by the strategic group, rather than school leaders being allowed to select with whom they worked. Each SIG consisted of schools from across at least three local authorities, and attempts were made to ensure that each had a mixture of higher and lower capacity schools and a range of socio-economic intakes. Initially, 33 primary and 8 secondary SIGs were formed, each made up of between 5 and 12 schools. SIGs appointed a convenor, who, in the first instance, tended to be a headteacher. Convenors were provided with training and support to develop programmes of joint practice development based around the identification of shared priorities and existing good practice.

The SIGs were entirely new formal collaborative structures, although they sometimes drew on existing informal headteacher networks. They ran alongside existing local clusters but did not replicate any of their functions. As they drew together schools from across local authority boundaries, they were also a means of managing the dynamics that existed between certain secondary schools serving the same local communities.

Pathfinder partnerships

These pairings involved one school seeking support to improve and another seen as having the right combination of expertise and capacity to help. They were a collaborative addition to the existing school improvement structures brokered and supported by the team of advisers working for the consortium. Traditionally these officers had been central to the school improvement system, not least because they were responsible for the annual categorisation process. This is a process by which all schools are placed into one of four support categories; green, yellow, amber or red, the last being schools requiring the most intensive support. Although there are no school performance league tables in Wales of the sort found in England, a school's categorisation is published annually on the My Local School website. In combination with rolling cycles of inspections by Estyn, the national inspection service, these are all key parts of Wales' high-stakes accountability system, which continues to be a matter of heated debate across the country.

In the previous system, some of the consortium advisers had informally brokered school-to-school support arrangements, but they mainly did so by drawing on their own contacts with schools. The pathfinder partnerships introduced through the Challenge both formalised and expanded the use of collaborative approaches to school improvement for schools requiring extensive support. The significance of these more focused partnerships was twofold: first, they provided evidence of school-to-school collaboration having a positive impact on the learning and achievement of students; and second, they illustrated how careful bricolage – the combination of new collaborative forms of working with the repurposing of existing structures – could support system transition.

Hub schools

Hub schools were relatively high-performing schools that were commissioned by the consortium to provide a wide range of professional learning and school improvement services for local schools. In terms of system reform, their biggest impact was that they replaced the previous professional development offer of the five local authorities.

Some 80 hubs were eventually commissioned to develop programmes for practitioners and school leaders, based on a regional needs analysis drawn up by the consortium. Initially the form of provision they offered mirrored that of the previous local authority programmes in that it was dominated by short, one-day or less courses. However, the content of these activities was mainly based around hub school practices and was led by their staff.

After two years, with our encouragement, the strategy group 'reset' the work of the hub schools. In particular, they were encouraged to making greater use of inquiry and joint practice development, and to bring practitioners into collaborative networks and groups. All of this was intended to shift hubs away from seeing themselves as providers of training and toward the facilitation of forms of joint practice development.

Two years after these changes, budgetary cuts and the requirement to refocus attention on the new national curriculum being developed, the opportunity was taken to reset the work of hubs once again. This led to a reduction in the number of hubs and was controversial in that some schools had begun to view their 'status' as a hub as an indication of the high quality of their provision. Within a high-stakes system, this had the potential to have a negative impact, not only on the reputation of some headteachers but also on the willingness of others schools to take a lead within a collaborative system.

Peer enquiry

This strand of activity grew out of the concerns of Headteachers of high-performing schools about the lack of support on offer to them within the previous school improvement arrangements. As we have seen, high-stakes accountability systems tend to focus their school improvement efforts on the most obviously 'failing' schools. This arises not only because of concerns about the impact these schools have on pupil progress but also because they represent a challenge to the authority and competency of the leaders of local school improvement services and the adequacy of local political oversight. The corollary of this focus is that bureaucratic school improvement systems often define themselves by their ability to 'turn around' failing schools and, in so doing, have little direct engagement with higher-performing schools.

Peer enquiry was initially designed as a systematic process by which senior leaders in higher-achieving schools could support one another through a process of mutual investigation. The process went through several iterations and was gradually expanded to involve many more schools. Indeed, over five years, more than half of the schools within the consortium took part. During this period, the process increasingly came to be seen as a leadership development programme, rather than just a school improvement intervention. As such, the peer enquiry process became the first distinctly new form of leadership development to arise out of a system transitioning into a new collaborative form.

The speed with which the Challenge implemented the four key strands reflected, in part, the effects of the degree of competition between the four regional consortia, which, although officially frowned upon by the Welsh government, had been re-enforced by rounds of external inspections and evaluations. Each consortium had pursued different school improvement strategies, reflecting the various political settlements between local authorities and central government as to their role. As a consequence of these settlements, each consortium varied in its commitment to, and interpretation of, the idea of a self-improving system, particularly the extent to which it was to be self-governing.

The CSW Challenge represented the most highly developed approach in respect of collaborative working and devolved responsibility to school leaders, whilst the other three consortia maintained most of the elements of a more centrally organised system. In this context, maintaining political and professional commitment to the radical approach adopted by the Challenge required its schools to be performing at least as well as the schools supported by the other consortia's more traditional approaches.

Evaluating the impact

At the inception of the CSW Challenge in 2014, overall pupil performance in the region was below the national average. Three years later, this had improved, so that in key stage 4 (students aged 14–16) their performance in national tests (i.e., GCSE exams) was above the national average at the 'Level 2 threshold' (achieved when they gain 5 A*s to C grade qualifications).

This overall trend was driven by improvements in all five authorities, with the two most underperforming improving to the greatest extent and the other three performing above the national average. At the same time, there were encouraging trends in relation to the average progress of pupils eligible for free school meals (an indicator of social deprivation) and other pupils. These positive trends in pupil attainment were matched by similar trends in the reduction of the numbers of schools categorised as requiring additional support as part of national accountability arrangements.

The Central South consortium's position as the most 'improved' region was not formally recognised because comparisons of the relative performance of the consortia were not encouraged by central government, we assume for a fear that this might lead to greater competition. At a system level, the overall improvement data provided a degree of protection for the CSW Challenge from both external and internal criticism as it accelerated the pace of transition.

To evidence the extent to which collaboration was a key factor in the gains made by schools, an annual survey of school leaders and staff was launched in 2016. This revealed that some 43% of primary staff and 35% of secondary staff indicated that they had, over the previous 12 months, been involved in working with other schools (Hadfield & Barnes, 2017). The more senior the respondent's position in the school, the more likely they were to have been involved, with 68% of senior management team members compared to 40% of middle leaders, and just 28% of classroom teachers, working across schools.

The relatively high levels of staff engagement in school-to-school working provided some positive indications that the Challenge's strategy was having an impact across the system. Evidence that the depth of collaborative working had moved beyond the 'come and see what we are doing variety' criticised by Hill (2013) in the initial evaluation of the consortia, was found in the overall profile of staff collaborative activities. Over a third of teachers involved in working collaboratively with other schools had been involved in some form of joint practice development, and approximately a quarter had been involved in inquiry-based approaches to improving teaching and learning.

Evidence of the contribution made by the various strands of the Challenge to the development of the scope and depth of collaborative working in the region was provided by evaluations of four individual strands. The SIGs maintained relatively high levels of school engagement. Indeed, by year four, only 4% of schools had been identified as nonparticipators. Once the SIGs had been established, the focus of their development was on greater depth of collaboration, moving beyond school leaders to encourage classroom practitioners to engage in joint practice development. In the two-year period, 2015–2017, this focus resulted in teacher involvement increasing by around 30% (from 63% in 2015/16, to 91% in 2016/17) and the percentage SIGs that included some form of joint practice development in their work rose to 50%.

Over the four-year period of their operation, the hub schools' annual engagement with other schools rose from just over half (52%) to over two thirds (69%), and following the reset, some 90% of their work was based upon inquiry and joint practice development. In its first three years, the peer enquiry programme increased engagement from just 4% (18) of schools in the region to 23% (93). The effectiveness of this programme in resulting in positive changes in classroom practices is difficult to assess due to the self-selected nature of the sample. However, of the primary schools involved in 2016, some 81% improved their key stage 2 pupil attainment against a regional average of 61%, with 83% of secondary schools improving their key stage 4 student attainment against a regional average of 70%. Meanwhile, the pathfinder partnership strand grew from 11 partnerships to more than 70 over the four years.

Competition and collaboration

We saw how the existing patina of collaboration and competition within the region affected the development of the CSW Challenge at multiple levels. In particular, it constrained leaders' interactions with each strand, preconfigured the approaches eventually adopted in each, and influenced the speed at which they were taken up. It also formed the basis for new professional and organisational networks that had the potential to reconfigure the local system. To analyse the effects of context on the nature of the emerging self-improving system, we adapted the notion of 'practice architecture' (Kemmis & Grootenboer, 2008), applying it to the consortium's attempt to restructure the practice landscape of the local education system.

In so doing, we adopted the idea that an education system consists of the aggregation of individual habitual patterns of practices, dispositions and beliefs: their practice architectures. From this perspective, classroom practices are nested in departmental architectures, whose practices are set within a school's architecture, and so on, through groups of schools, to the education system as a whole. As different architectures are 'nested' one within the other, changes in practice at one level can affect others, and so new practice architectures and educational landscapes are formed. Conversely, it is possible that disruptions to the architecture at one level of the system may have considerable and relatively rapid ripple effects, but over time it may have little impact upon those levels within which it is nested. The key argument that practice architecture puts forward in respect of understanding system change is that the effects of innovation at any given level need to be persistent, and at scale, if they are to reconfigure other levels of the system.

To illustrate how the existing educational landscape affected the Challenge, we focus on its work at two levels: first, the creation of the strategy group, consisting of some 20 or so headteachers, that met monthly to advise on the direction of the Challenge; and, second, the establishment of 40 odd SIGs that would draw over 400 schools into new collaborative structures. Together these two new groupings, along with other aspects of the Challenge, were intended to create new practice architectures. The strategy group was an attempt to reconfigure the landscape at the level at which national and local policy and the consortium's strategy interacted; whilst the SIGs operated at the level of groups of schools and individual classrooms.

The role of the strategy group

The overall implementation strategy adopted by the Challenge was a 'scope to depth' approach (Hadfield, 2017). It initially focused on the widespread mobilisation of school leaders and practitioners in collaborative working and school-to-school support, before gradually deepening the intensity and effectiveness of this way of working. It was also a responsive strategy, reflecting the existing patina of collaboration and competition within the professional context in which the Challenge operated.

The rapidity of the development of the four strands reflected concerns about the degree of fragmentation within various levels of the system, and a lack of trust between different levels, which had suppressed previous attempts to develop collaborative ways of working (Hadfield, 2017). By rapidly expanding the number of schools and practitioners involved, and by replacing existing services, the Challenge hoped to not only increase levels of trust and establish supportive professional norms around collaborative working between schools but also to make it more difficult for other levels in the system to limit, or even roll back, the collaborative agenda.

The expansion of more collaborative working, especially at the level of schools, was made feasible because competition between them as a driver of improvement in Wales was not as significant a policy lever as in other parts of the UK education systems, most notably in England. A combination of the Welsh government's opposition to quasi-market approaches and the particular socio-economic conditions within the country meant that competition to enrol students was restricted to relatively few urban contexts. Existing patterns of competition for resources were, therefore, less likely to be a major influence on schools' willingness to participate in collaborative working.

It was also significant that, due to policy and funding differences, Wales had historically seen lower levels of engagement in school-to-school approaches to improvement and the use inquiry as a school improvement approach when compared with other parts of the UK. This might well have limited the scope of the Challenge if it had initially restricted its collaborative work to processes that required a substantive knowledge of school-based inquiry methods.

82 A regional self-improving school system

This, then, was the context in which the strategy group was formed. It was one in which headteachers were usually treated as acquiescent members of a hierarchical and fragmented system: expected to tow the party line, falling in behind both the requirements of local authorities and the central government. For school leaders to step outside of what this required of them, taking the initiative and working across authority boundaries, had the potential to result in a range of formal and informal sanctions. Indeed, members of the group frequently talked of being 'put on the naughty step' by their local authorities for challenging or subverting aspects of the control they had over them. And it was significant that local authorities exerted considerable influence over both the career development of headteachers and placed considerable effort on constructing professional identities based within 'their' locality.

The Challenge utilised the discourse of the self-improving system as a means of furthering its collaborative approach. In this context, the strategy group was the embodiment of who the 'self' would be in such a system – primarily school leaders. The formation of the group had the potential to be disruptive within different parts of the system, not least because headteachers who were selected were those seen to have a high level of professional status within the existing system. That is to say, they were almost exclusively from high-performing, or 'green' category, schools.

Through their engagement in the main collaborative strands – as leaders of hub schools, acting as SIG convenors, and as originators of peer enquiry, and indirectly through their professional networks and attendance at headteacher meetings within their own local authorities – the strategy group members led the creation of the self-improving system. Indeed, within a relatively short period, they helped to define the system as one created by school leaders for other school leaders; draw up the formal and informal 'rules' of collaboration; and intentionally and unintentionally determine who would be part of it.

During the early stages of the Challenge, the rapidity of these developments led to the formation of a strongly shared identity between the group and the administrative leadership of the consortium. In these ways, they helped determine which innovations and ideas from elsewhere should be brought in; how these needed to be redesigned to fit within the local context; and the process of implementing them at scale. These decisions were made within a fluid environment, marked by a lack of the traditional barriers between policy-makers and practitioners.

As each of the strands developed, the Challenge expanded in terms of both complexity and scope, and the trajectories of strategy group members began to diverge, affecting the group's cohesion and to a degree its connection with the wider system. Some members became more clearly identified with certain aspects of the Challenge than others. Some saw their influence in the local system grow as they became the centre of networks of schools. In addition, many developed a degree of political and financial freedom from local authority control, and in doing so created a platform from which to challenge both local and central government initiatives.

A regional self-improving school system **83**

At times, these leaders found themselves, and their schools, over extended. For example, even a minor falling of a school's performance might trigger criticisms about their sustained engagement in collaborative working, from inside and outside the consortium. The 'competition' generated by high-stakes accountability systems in which individual leaders competency and status is directly linked to changes in their school's performance, no matter how slight, had not been significantly diminished by the Challenge.

In its third year, the Challenge experienced a significant change, as the director of the consortium, who had been closely involved in its initiation, left to take up a post elsewhere. A new director was appointed who had less political room for manoeuvre when the trajectory of positive gains in pupil attainment appeared to temporarily stall. This individual began to redraw the boundaries around organisational decision making in relation to the Challenge and the formal governance structure of the consortium as a whole. The impact of this was that the strategy group became one of many who were to be 'consulted' about major and many minor changes to the Challenge. This 'circuit' of meetings, as it became known, consisted of some four different groupings of elected local politicians, the directors of local education authorities, central government representatives, and an advisory group. Decision making became a protracted process taking weeks, if not months, and it became increasingly unclear who would make the final decision when disagreements around the direction of travel arose.

Faced with a maturing collaborative system, the leadership of the Challenge had to quickly move on from rolling out expansive new developments to more technical issues associated with maintaining and refining a complex new system. In this changed context, the strategy group now had to consider the limitations of a system it was seen to have created as it made decisions as to how it should be further developed. These decisions could have considerable impact upon colleagues, both those in the strategy group and in their wider professional networks. A number of conditions needed to be in place for the strategy group to make these decisions in such a closely knit leadership community. In particular, it required careful facilitation from someone from outside of the community: it needed time to consider how changes might play out in an increasingly complex system; and it had to have access to high-quality data about the functioning of the current system. Unfortunately, these conditions were not in place.

Most significant, the strategy group was increasingly a closed entity in which those of us from outside who had been instrumental in developing its work were no longer involved. Under the previous director, the group had been supported by a range of external experts and facilitators, not least ourselves, bringing in new ideas and challenging group members to review different aspects of their work. During this time, the strategy group was increasingly positioned, and marginalised, as a 'sounding board' that was asked for its views on how the maturing system should be fine-tuned and adapted, but it was less frequently engaged with key strategic issues.

84 A regional self-improving school system

Meanwhile, the consortium as a 'temporary' structure started to suffer from high levels of staff turnover as individuals who had been key to its development left, or returned to the school system. This resulted in a considerable loss of institutional memory at a crucial time, just as the Welsh government started to introduce its own collaborative approach to developing a new curriculum for Wales. The new senior leadership of the consortium had little understanding of the Challenge's existing elements and how they might interact with the new collaborative structures being funded through the Welsh government. When combined with the marginalisation of the strategy group, this lack of leadership understanding resulted in a failure to grapple with new strategic challenges, such as of how to manage the loss of leadership capacity in the new structures and how this might be integrated into the existing strands of the Challenge.

Finally, and decisively, those of us trying to develop the capacity of the Challenge to evaluate its own work had failed to do so rapidly enough to provide the quality of data required to make consistent and transparent decisions about what was working in the current system and what needed to be changed. Feeling frustrated, marginalised, and to a degree overwhelmed by the complexity facing them, the strategy group decided to disband. Its last act was to argue, success-fully, for the expansion of the number of associate headteachers, seconded from their schools a few days per week, to work in close partnership with officers from the consortium on leading key aspects of the Challenge.

The associate headteachers are working to this day, but there is no longer a powerful practitioner voice at the level in the system where policy and strat-egy interact. The demise of the strategy group reflects the complexity of school leaders being rapidly thrust into the role of system leadership. They were system leaders with a capital S, in that they were not 'just' being asked to support other schools or even a network of schools. Rather, they were mandated to develop a strategy for supporting over 400 schools and the allocation of tens of millions of pounds of public money. Unlike the Challenges discussed in other chapters, the funding came from multiple existing streams, with a complex set of outcomes, restrictions, and monitoring and reporting procedures.

The great success of the Challenge's early leadership arrangements were that, if only temporarily, they acted as a buffer, creating a space in which disparate perspectives, interests and sources of funding could be welded into a cohesive strategy, whilst simultaneously attempting to build a new collabo-rative leadership structure. The 'failure' of the Challenge at this level, if we want to construct it as such, was that it was not able to keep this space open long enough to have a permanent impact on this level of the system by build-ing a more permanent leadership structure committed to the idea of a self-improving system.

At a cultural-discursive level, the strategy group had started to define a par-ticular school-led version of a self-improving system, in which school leaders would play a key strategic role in setting policy and strategy. This stance stands in sharp contrast with the more 'school-enabled' model being promulgated by the existing middle tier of the English system. Within a social-political space, it demonstrated the power of a more fluid and dynamic interaction between formal and informal leaders in reshaping power relationships in ways that gave legitimately to a new system leadership structure. Finally, it highlighted the significance of the material-economic space with regard to how managing a rapid system level change, such as the switch of central government funding to a new strand of collaborative working, requires that steps be taken quickly to cohere and realign the available system leadership capacity in line with the growing demands of a new context as it emerges into the existing educational landscape.

School improvement groups

The second level of the system at which the Challenge set out to create radically different types of practice architectures was that of schools and classrooms, primarily by creating 40-plus SIGs, which brought together over 400 schools into new improvement networks. Observing the degree of system change the SIGs have achieved has led us to realise that whilst persistence might be a necessary condition for collaborative networks to effect wider system reform, it is insufficient on its own. If networks of schools are to be the basis of a self-improving system, the lessons drawn from the Challenge indicate that they need to have two key capacities.

First, they need to exhibit the ability to meet individual schools' specific needs in ways that are sensitive to the existing patina of competition and collaboration in the local system. As we have already explained, SIGs were based on groups of schools that had been brought together to cross pre-existing boundaries, with a degree of sensitivity to existing patterns of competition. They were, and still are, mainly phase specific, and how they have evolved to meet their members needs whilst responding to the degree of competition and collaboration in the local system has led to primary and secondary phase SIGs taking very divergent trajectories.

For many primary school headteachers, the SIGs were an opportunity to expand their professional networks from within the confines of local clusters, and this provided them with opportunities to share and develop their visions of teaching and learning. The relative size of primary schools, in comparison with secondary, meant that primary SIGs could quickly engage a high percentage of their leadership directly and indirectly in collaborative working. The trajectory of the primary SIGs was for them to develop quite rapidly their degree of school-to-school working so that it quickly became a significant part of their approach to school improvement. The most recent annual staff survey (Hadfield & Hawkins, 2019) shows the biggest increase in working collaboratively with other schools has been amongst middle leaders in primary schools, the percentage of those who have been frequently engaged each term or more often having increased from 37% in 2016 to 55% in 2018.

86 A regional self-improving school system

The rapid growth in collaborative working amongst primary SIGs was driven by their ability to find 'common cause' with others, as one head explained:

> *We trust each other but need that common cause that you're doing it for the benefit of the children. I think we have all got that common cause, that we want the best learning experience possible for the children however that may be. And I think if you got that as your core concept, as long as that's what you're all trying to do, then you're going to be alright and everything else will fall in to place.*

Such common cause arose from local systems in which there was little or no competition between primary schools in which alternative discourses such as *'belonging to one big school'* could flourish.

Secondary SIGs took much longer to establish themselves as stable structures, and various regrouping took place over the first two years of their existence. Only the more committed secondary leaders persisted in their original SIGs, which, as the level of their school-to-school working increased, gradually grew as they attracted schools from less active groupings. This process of amalgamation resulted in fewer but larger secondary SIGs that increasingly reflected pre-existing patterns of local collaboration and competition.

As the size of SIGs grew, so did their level of collaborative working, in part because of an increase in 'internal competition' between headteachers concerned about not missing out on a possible significant development or opportunity to access the expertise of the high-capacity schools that were often part of the foundational group of more successful SIGs. The largest of the secondary SIGs, which involves some 19 schools, now operates with up to 20 improvement foci at any one time, drawn from individual schools' development plans and areas of expertise. Each foci is taken forward by a smaller, cross-school professional learning group, known as a SIGlet. Schools *'dip in and dip out as we need to'* across the various foci, providing a structural means of managing any potential residual conflicts of interest.

The secondary SIGs were described by one school leader as *'a fantastic forum to share innovative ideas, to have check and balance conversations'* with *'routes of the information* [that] *are a lot tighter and seamless.'* By providing school leaders with pre-warnings of upcoming changes, the SIGs helped them get 'ahead of the game,' providing a 'collaborative advantage' (Huxham, 1996) for their members. In SIGlets, practitioners could share intelligence and existing expertise around new developments, but they rarely resulted in shared responses.

The second key capacity of successful networks was their ability to reconstruct themselves by adding to or reformulating the focus of their collaborative working in response to shifts in the local system. A good example of this was the Welsh-medium network, Cyfleoedd+. In their original formulation, secondary SIGs had distributed amongst them both Welsh-medium secondary schools and special schools. SIGs were in part an attempt to integrate these forms of schools into a more collaborative system, as both had formed long-established but separate networks to meet their specific professional learning and leadership development needs. During the period of SIG amalgamations, schools from both these groups retained their membership of 'mixed' SIGs, but they also took the opportunity to reconstruct themselves within the new collaborative system that was being formed around them.

Cyfleoedd+ is a new network consisting of five schools, which are part of a well-established network of nine Welsh medium schools, and also part of the single largest secondary SIG of 19 secondary schools. Nearly 40% of all secondary schools in the region are bigger than some of the local authorities. Within the new collaborative landscape, Cyfleoedd+ decided to take the idea of the self-improving system to a new level by taking collective responsibility for a key part of the national accountability system, categorisation, and to reconstruct it in a new more collaborative form.

The school leaders of Cyfleoedd+, supported by funding and advice from the consortium, took over the role of school improvement advisers and became responsible for each other's categorisation process. This meant that the headteachers were now involved in determining the support category in which each other's school would be placed. Despite the commitment in terms of time, and the potential strain it might place on their existing relationships, the headteachers were determined that any school support required would be provided by their network, or by drawing from their wider SIG networks. This reconstruction drew on a shared identity and collective responsibility for those in the network that was formed on more than a decade of joint working. It was made possible because the leaders of Cyfleoedd+ have access to the expertise of the wider SIG, giving them confidence to form a self-improving 'subsystem' within a broader collaborative landscape.

The relative success and failures of the various types of SIGs indicated how the emergence of new collaborative forms was influenced by the existing landscapes. At a cultural-discursive level, it showed how important it was, even for primary SIGs, to develop alternatives to the discourse of competition in order to create a collective identity that could sustain collaborative school-to-school working. It also illustrated how such identity-based communities, whether newly formed or long established, could effectively mobilise around shared interests.

At the social-political space, it illustrated how the 'big beasts' of the local system, secondary schools, even though they were most exposed to competitive influences, could under certain conditions appropriate and transform aspects of accountability structures into self-improving subsystems, even if they were not in themselves capable of reconstructing the whole system.

Finally, in the material-economic space, it highlighted the importance of achieving, and sustaining, a critical mass of collaborative working in order for it to influence the collaborative and competitive dynamics of local systems.

Making sense of the process

As we have explained, the work of the CSW Challenge was framed by national policies that had led to the amalgamation of local authority school improvement services into regional consortia and the idea that the system should become increasingly self-improving. At the regional level, the Challenge's efforts to engage school leaders and practitioners in the transition to a more school-led approach drew it, and them, into the political dynamic between central and local government. Particularly in its initial stages, when the Challenge was involved in disassembling the existing structures and recruiting and mobilising local school leaders to develop new structures, it had to operate as much as a leader and coordinator of a professional movement as it did the catalyst for system redesign.

In practical terms, the various strands of the Challenge – the SIGs, hub schools, pathfinders and triads of peer enquirers – each represented a distinct mechanism for establishing a different type of collaborative subsystem. Those coordinating the Challenge had to ensure the operational effectiveness of each mechanism while maintaining a strategic overview of the capacities being generated at an individual, organisational and system level, and the extent to which these met local school improvement needs. They therefore had to identify and learn how to facilitate successful subsystems, and then assimilate and apply this learning to each strand. In terms of its own organisational learning, leading a system level transition placed enormous emphasis upon the Challenge's 'absorptive capacity' (Cohen & Leventhal, 1990; Zahra & George, 2002; Farrell & Coburn, 2017) with respect to how it learned from each strand and applied this to its overall strategy.

The consortium focussed on bringing together existing individual and organisational capacity, and then aligning it around distinct areas of collaborative working, before attempting to deepen the work so that it could generate additional capacity. The simultaneous launch of four different strands of collaborative working was the practical expression of this scale-to-depth approach. The implementation strategy reflected concerns not only about the existing capacity within the system, but also how its development might be affected by tensions in the political and professional contexts from which the Challenge emerged.

The initial strategic aim was to expand the number of practitioners who had experience of working collaboratively across schools, even if initially much of this was at a relatively superficial level. Quickly establishing collaborative working at scale and ensuring that its scope was not restricted to certain types of school improvement work was, in part, driven by the nature of the political and professional contexts from which the Challenge emerged. The political context – particularly the continuing lack of trust between the central government, the consortia and local authorities – meant that there were concerns over the degree of political commitment to a more school-led system. Based on their experience of previous school improvement policies, some school leaders were concerned that moves toward greater collaboration and professional autonomy might be reversed at any point.

As we have explained, the formation of the strategy group was a response to a professional context in which the majority of school leaders had been enculturated into a hierarchical system that required deference to those in 'higher' positions and, when conflict did arise, tended to result in passive rather than active resistance. Being a member of the strategy group was a symbolic rejection of this culture of deference and involved the establishment of a more professionally assertive cohort of school leaders. Quickly normalising collaborative working across a range of areas, from leadership development to professional learning, was seen as key to the mass mobilisation of school leaders across the region – a mobilisation that would make it a professional movement whose momentum would be difficult to disrupt.

Conclusion

There is no doubt that significant progress has been made in developing a self-improving system across the Central South Wales region. It is also clear that our involvement contributed to the progress that was made. In this way, it offers strong evidence of how researchers can influence system change strategies.

However, the developments have remained fragile for a variety of reasons. Key amongst these has been the political failure to establish clarity around roles and responsibilities between those working at different levels of the system, including the Welsh government. What results from this lack of clarity is that, as overlapping and competing interventions play out at different levels of the system, there is no agreement about who is responsible for managing the educational landscape in the longer term.

A striking example of this occurred recently when the Welsh government took the decision to introduce a new national curriculum. With this in mind, the government developed its own networks of schools, called 'pioneers.' Although these schools were supposed to be managed in partnership with the consortia, they found themselves delivering a plan developed centrally.

To ensure that the pioneer schools were able to influence others, the government decided to fund staff in the existing local clusters to take on coordinator roles. The use of local clusters in this way was, we understand, decided upon because they were the only form of network that existed across all four consortia. As a result of these developments, local clusters, which had not been a feature of the CSW Challenge, were quickly added as a fifth strand of collaborative working. However, there was little, if any, planning regarding their relationship with the other strands, and no long-term planning as to how develop their capacity to deliver on this agenda.

The Welsh government then began to fund numerous other local convenors to look after a range of different aspects of the curriculum reform and other interventions in the system. In this way, through its control of funding, central government began to treat the collaborative system developed in the Challenge as a means of developing its own policy agenda directly with schools. And, inevitably, this undermined the developments that had occurred over the previous four years.

90 A regional self-improving school system

Writing about this in a letter to one of us in September 2018, a senior member of staff at the Central South consortium commented on what was shaping the current landscape:

> *Ironically, more and more people in Wales talk about a school-led system but, in reality, they are promoting a school-facilitated system. By that I mean that a centrally recognised need is addressed by schools being paid to do the work on behalf of the consortium and Welsh Government.*

This colleague then went on to list the factors that acted as barriers to what they had been trying to achieve through the CSW Challenge:

- The Government's drive for consortia to work together, watering down our school led model.
- Estyn's continued insistence on impact being demonstrated through simple cause and effect that is too crude to capture what has been achieved.
- Uncertainty about local government organisation, making officers defensive and increasing the need to be seen to 'know their schools' and to be seen to be improving standards within them.
- Continued interference by some local authorities, who see it as their role to sort the schools out, as opposed to trusting consortia to develop their capacity to improve.
- A blame culture when things go wrong.
- Austerity leading to significant cuts and a desire by local authorities to protect 'their staff.'
- Less capacity in schools to release staff to do the school-to-school work.
- National developments, such as the leadership academy, that means that leadership programmes have to be developed by consortia together. Frustratingly few headteachers were significantly involved in this, though now associate headteachers have been employed, though their role is far from clear.

On a more positive note, the colleague noted that the culture in the Central South region remains different to other parts of Wales and that there are many who are still working to ensure that the school-led model is alive and well, before adding:

> *But it's a battle, and I am not convinced it's one we are winning.*

5

THE SCOTTISH ATTAINMENT CHALLENGE

Addressing poverty-related outcomes

Keeping in mind our overall focus on the role of research and researchers in supporting change within education systems, in this chapter we describe and analyse another national initiative with high levels of political commitment, the Scottish Attainment Challenge. Launched in 2015, its overall design was much influenced by the ideas discussed in the chapters on developments in England and Wales, plus some experimentation within Scotland in the two years prior to the launch. At the time of writing, the programme is continuing.

In providing an account of the initiative, we focus on the implementation of the programme within the Scottish context, particularly the factors that have helped and hindered the development of ideas translated and adapted from elsewhere. As we explain, these factors relate to the way policy decisions are made and enacted across the system, not least in schools. Broadly stated, this has involved negotiations between actors at different levels, which have been further stimulated more recently through attempts to create a series of regional collaboratives, similar to those in Wales, that link groups of local authorities around a shared improvement agenda.

We explain how, in the Scottish context, local authorities have retained much more control of the improvement of their schools, leaving school leaders with less influence on decision making than their counterparts in England. This is a factor that has come to the attention of the system, and recent policies have promoted the empowerment of headteachers and a move toward school-led improvements. Reflecting on all of this, we conclude with a consideration of how power relationships, such as these, impact processes of change within an education system.

Education in Scotland

Scotland has a population of approximately 5.3 million people, and there are around 2,500 schools within the education system. More than 95% of the population is educated in publicly funded, local authority managed schools. Since 1999 responsibility for education has been fully devolved to the Scottish government and is administrated through 32 local authorities. Currently, the Scottish National Party leads the national government and also has a third of local council seats. As we explain, it has made improvement of the national education system its top priority.

In 2014, research by the Office for National Statistics concluded that Scotland was the most highly educated country in Europe and among the most well-educated in the world in terms of tertiary education attainment, with nearly 45% of people between 25 and 64 having university degrees or further education qualifications.[1] The school system performs above OECD averages but saw a relative decline in performance in the Programme for International Student Assessment (PISA) in 2016.

Whilst state schools are owned and operated by local authorities, the system is highly centralised, with policy implementation directed, supported and monitored by a government agency, Education Scotland. There is a relatively small number of private schools across the country, although the distribution is uneven, with such schools in 22 of the 32 local authority areas.

Political responsibility for education at all levels is vested in the Scottish Parliament. Inspections and audits of educational standards are conducted by Education Scotland for pre-school, primary, further education and community education. Qualifications at the secondary school and post-secondary level are provided by the Scottish Qualifications Authority, which is the national awarding and accrediting body.

A country review carried out by OECD in 2015 notes that, historically, the people of Scotland have a high regard for education. The report also comments on the inclusiveness of Scottish schools, a feature we also mentioned in relation to Wales. In particular, it noted that Scottish immigrant students achieve at higher levels than their non-immigrant peers, and that the country enjoys one of the smallest proportions of low performers among its immigrant students.

In relation to system change, the OECD report specifically mentions the importance of the introduction of the Curriculum for Excellence, an important reform to put in place a coherent 3-18 curriculum, first introduced in 2010. The report explains that there is widespread engagement with this development and acceptance of its principles by teachers. However, it also notes that implementation is proceeding at varying speeds. This being the case, the review calls for a strengthened 'middle tier,' operating through networks and collaboratives among schools, and in and across local authorities, a factor that also comes up in relation to our account of the implementation of the Attainment Challenge.

It is worth noting, however, that some see this curriculum reform in a less positive light. For example, one teacher writes:

> Once one of the best in the world, Scotland's education system has been steadily marching backwards for the past ten years. From the outside, it seems baffling: why, given that Scottish spending per pupil is among the highest in the world, are things going so wrong? From the inside, it's far easier to understand. You can explain it in three words: Curriculum for Excellence.
>
> (Kearns, 2017)

The current administration is committed to improving the education system in relation to 'excellence and equity' and has placed a major emphasis on improving the attainment of learners from economically poorer backgrounds. With this in mind, in March 2013 the then Cabinet Secretary for Education and Lifelong Learning announced six new policy priorities to tackle educational inequity: school partnerships; class sizes and teacher numbers; use of data to drive improvement; parental involvement; leadership; and innovation. This announcement provided the opportunity to design and implement the national School Improvement Partnership Programme (Chapman et al., 2015, 2016).

As we explain in Chapter 7, the School Improvement Partnership Programme draws on ideas and frameworks developed as a result of our research carried out over a period of more than 20 years. This included lessons that had emerged from the Improving the Quality of Education for All initiative (Clarke, Ainscow & West, 2006; Hopkins, Ainscow & West, 1994), the Extra Mile Programme (Chapman et al., 2011) and a series of studies that had examined what is involved in effective school networks and partnerships (e.g., Chapman, 2015, 2008; Ainscow, 2010; Chapman & Muijs, 2014; Muijs et al., 2011). In addition, the strategic thinking that had emerged from the City Challenge initiatives in England influenced the design and development of collaborative activity within the School Improvement Partnership Programme. These earlier experiences provided a foundation and, indeed, a catalyst for the changes proposed through the Scottish Attainment Challenge.

The Scottish Attainment Challenge

In June 2013, one of us joined a former Chief Inspector and the Executive Director for Education for the Labour-led Glasgow City Council to make the case to senior civil servants for developing a Greater Glasgow Challenge. The aim was to tackle the low levels of pupil attainment amongst the highest concentration of socio-economic deprivation in Scotland. Although this initiative was not taken forward, ideas and examples of practice from London and the other Challenge areas had filtered across the Scottish border. In addition, a series of keynote sessions and presentations that we had been making, plus visits by Scottish civil servants to London to meet with leaders from the London City Challenge, had focused minds on the idea of some form of national initiative.

By the beginning of 2015, the idea of some form of a 'National Challenge' had taken root. Commenting on this, the First Minister stated:

> It is important we learn not just from good practice here in Scotland, but also from elsewhere in the UK and overseas, to find ways of working that have the greatest impact. I have been particularly impressed with the results of the London Challenge in transforming school performance in that city and so, while not all of it will be appropriate to Scottish circumstances, we will draw heavily on it in developing our own Attainment Challenge.[2]

The Scottish Attainment Challenge was launched with high levels of political commitment. Later, in 2016, prior to the Scottish Parliament elections, the First Minister went on to commit her own political reputation to closing and ultimately eliminating the attainment gap, focusing on literacy, numeracy and health and well-being as the key measures.

The programme was backed by a £100m fund to support improvements in attainment over a four-year period in seven 'Challenge authorities.' At the same time, an acknowledgment that not all children in poverty lived in areas of high concentrations of disadvantage led the government to include in the strategy 57 primary schools serving the most disadvantaged children in other authorities. This involved the allocation of another £2.5 million across a further 14 local authorities.

All the Challenge authorities and schools involved in the programme were required to construct annual action plans to access additional resources from the Attainment Fund. These plans were reviewed centrally by staff of Education Scotland and the Scottish government, who either approved or recommended revisions. One of us was also involved in this process, as part of his role as adviser. It is worth noting here that local authorities were not involved in the process, other than those Challenge authorities that submitted plans for review.

The total resource in the fund was increased to £750m and the number of Challenge Authorities extended to nine in August 2016, along with a commitment to support the programme beyond the duration of the current Parliament. In addition, a Pupil Equity Fund was introduced that was used to provide additional funding of £1,200 to every pupil entitled to a free school meal. A Governance Review reinforced the policy intent:

> 'Through the Scottish Attainment Challenge and the new Pupil Equity Fund we are targeting resources to those who need it most'
> (Scottish Government, 2017, p. 13).

These developments were not without controversy. In particular, debate about the use of the place-based indicator of the Scottish Index of Multiple Deprivation as the criteria for inclusion in the programme continues to the present day. For example, Patterson (2018) argues that two-thirds of deprived children are not in deprived areas and that one-quarter of children living in deprived areas are not educationally deprived. Issues have also been raised about entitlement to free school meals as a reliable proxy indicator for poverty and, in particular, the appropriateness of these indicators in rural areas.

The introduction of the Pupil Equity Fund also had a mixed response. Some headteachers welcomed the additional responsibility and autonomy, whereas others have been more sceptical about their own and the system's ability to use the resource wisely, leading to questions about impact and value for money. Within a context of extensive efficiency savings in overall public service funding, particularly to local authorities, some stakeholders view the decision as an attempt to redistribute resources, and, in so doing, both disempower local authorities and move the spend to nearer the front line where, some argue, it is more likely to have more impact. Local authorities have responded in a number of ways, which has created a variation in local practices. For example, in some authorities, the schools' plans for the Pupil Equity Fund are reviewed and 'approved,' thus maintaining local control of the spending. Others have respected the policy intention and taken a much lighter touch approach.

One of us worked part-time as the Senior Academic Adviser to the Challenge between 2015 and 2017. The role was different to that of the Chief Adviser in City Challenge and the Champion in Schools Challenge Cymru in that it did not imply any leadership responsibilities. In terms of the agenda of this book, however, it clearly signalled that the task involved providing an evidence-based perspective on the development of the Challenge, supporting capacity building, and developing understanding and coherence across the system.

More recently, a number of key actors within the system have changed. This has led to new personnel taking on key leadership positions in some local authorities, agencies and government. Many of these people are either newly appointed or have had little previous contact with the programme. Therefore, understanding the history and complexity of the developments that have taken place across the programme has been diluted. There has also been a major recruiting programme within the national agency, Education Scotland, with more than 100 posts being advertised. From our point of view, all of this raises the possibility that the pattern of programme marginalisation that eventually occurred in England and Wales might happen. However, the current strength of political commitment at the national level seems to make this unlikely.

Given these changes, and questions about the direction of travel of the Challenge in various parts of the system, it is encouraging that the government has pledged funding for the Challenge into the first year of the next Parliament. It has also re-established the role of Senior Academic Adviser and one of us has re-joined the programme on a part-time basis for the period 2019–2021. This is a further indication of a commitment to draw in research knowledge and expertise to steer the programme, and to support developments in policy and practice across the system.

In terms of public accountability of the distribution and spend of the Attainment Fund, as yet there is no detailed independent evaluation assessing the impact of the programme. However, the Scottish government has its own

96 The Scottish Attainment Challenge

research strategy and is undertaking an internal evaluation of the programme, which has been supplemented by some small-scale external surveys and interviews conducted by a private company, Research Scotland, whose report is incorporated in the internal evaluation of the first two years of the programme (Scottish Government, 2018). In addition, Audit Scotland intend to review the programme during 2019, and there have been local authority inspections of the Challenge Authorities to assess progress. We return to these later in the chapter.

The story of the Challenge

Implementation of the Scottish Attainment Challenge so far can be thought of in terms of three broad, overlapping phases. In what follows, we consider each of these in turn. In so doing, we throw light on social, cultural and political factors that have helped to shape its development.

Phase 1: Establishing the Challenge (2015–2017)

The Challenge was launched with considerable energy and support. In particular, the First Minister and her colleagues made political mileage out of its announcement. The only disquiet within the system tended to be from the less disadvantaged local authorities and their representative bodies that had been used to the concept of universal funding. In this sense, the Challenge signalled a significant change in thinking. Targeting significant amounts of funding to the most disadvantaged areas meant that the more advantaged areas perceived that they were being treated unfairly. This led to much negotiation amongst key stakeholders during these early stages to establish buy-in and support from across the whole system for the new initiative.

Drawing on the experiences of England and Wales, a team of attainment advisers was appointed to provide support and challenge, either on a full- or part-time basis. Whilst they each worked in a particular local authority, they reported to Education Scotland rather than to that authority. Whilst these Challenge 'type' advisers emerged as a new catalyst for change within the systems, they operate within complex and uncertain settings, where there is no formula, recipe or one-size-fits-all solution. The nature of the role requires highly skilled individuals with a diverse range of experience and a high level of expertise that goes far beyond what has been expected traditionally from local authority support staff.

To support the team, we produced a set of principles that was intended to articulate ways of working and the nature of the role. These principles were developed in conjunction with the attainment advisers and provided a cornerstone for early conversations to develop a shared understanding of their new role in Scotland. They were as follows (Chapman, 2015):

1. **Collaboration**, with advisers working collaboratively, leading their own learning within the team.

The Scottish Attainment Challenge **97**

2. **Use of evidence and data** as a basis for professional dialogue and decision making.
3. **A focus** on a relentless impact on outcomes for young people, working in classrooms, with schools, and in and with local authorities and other partners.
4. **Agility**, with advisers having the power and ability to move people and other resources to areas of greatest need.
5. **Consistency**, such that the team of advisers has a shared understanding of their roles and responsibilities.
6. **A national framework** that provides professional learning and creates coherence.
7. **Alignment and synergy** with other key policies and the work of other networks.
8. **Independence**, with advisers sitting outside of routine reporting and managerial structures.
9. **Allocation of resources** through advisers having their own budget and to allocate this where it is most needed and will have the highest impact.
10. **Leverage** through a direct association with and support from the national and ministerial mandate.
11. **Systemic** from local to national, short term to long term, and tactical to strategic.
12. **Diversity** through a mix of skills, experience and styles and expertise.
13. **Empowerment** in terms of activity and action, with direct accountability for impact.
14. **Flexibility** through constant review and adaptation to arrangements and ways of working.

Early on in the initiative, it was announced that there would be one named attainment adviser for each local authority. At the time of their appointment, one of us reflected that when appointing Challenge advisers in Wales they could only find a handful of people within the country with the capability to undertake this work. This message was conveyed as a cautionary note to signal that the system would be unlikely to find 32 experienced educationalists in Scotland with the capability to undertake this complex role.

Given the nature of the posts, not least the uncertainties regarding their status and roles, it was clear that the newly appointed advisers would require significant investment in their professional development. Therefore, one of our tasks was to support Education Scotland in building capacity within the team in order to develop a cadre of advisers equipped to undertake this new and perhaps most challenging role within education system.

With this in mind, it was decided that a bespoke programme of professional learning needed to be developed, with the ultimate aim of building enough capacity within the team so that they could lead their own learning. Given the complexity and ambiguity they would face in the field, and drawing on some of the lessons from the Challenge advisers in London, Greater Manchester and Wales, it was also decided to ensure there were regular safe spaces to reflect on and discuss the challenges faced during their work in the field. Resources to support this activity were scarce, and some government colleagues seemed to view professional learning as a luxury, and, in one case, as 'naval gazing.' Indeed, the dominant school of thought was that the *attainment advisers should just get on with the job.*

Despite these early reservations, what we saw as a relevant programme of professional learning was developed and put in place to build individual expertise and collective capacity. This involved drawing on expertise from outside the system, including sessions with leading academics in the fields of educational and teacher effectiveness, educational psychology and social and emotional education, improvement, change and participatory methods and collaborative action research. These elements were intended to build the knowledge and expertise of advisers and help increase their confidence and credibility in the field. These insights into research and improvement methods, in particular, equipped the team to support the analysis of a diverse range of datasets, and to monitor change and impact in a more sophisticated way than was the norm across the system. The programme also involved linking with a range of professionals outside of education who could add value to the programme, thus building the advisers' awareness of different approaches and increasing their networks of professional support. These features were all identified as areas of strengths in attainment of advisers' work in the evaluation of the first two years of the programme (Scottish Government, 2019).

In addition, it was argued that the programme should draw on the experience of two of the most successful Challenge advisers from Schools Challenge Cymru, one of whom had also been involved in both the London and Manchester Challenge programmes. After initial reluctance from some parts of the system, the insights of these expert professionals was viewed as invaluable in building a shared understanding of the role and in building the team. Their support for attainment advisers involved seminars and also joint working in the field, where they modelled expectations of the nature of challenge and support that this type of role can offer. The coaching provided in this part of the programme was designed to build advisers' skills in leading challenging conversations in difficult and ambiguous settings. Again, these features were all identified as areas of strength in the evaluation of the first two years of the programme (Scottish Government, 2019).

The two visiting Challenge advisers continue to work with the Scottish System in a variety of ways, and they are often invited to support local authorities in their improvement activities. Interestingly, their early reflections highlighted the high levels of bureaucracy, planning and accountability measures within the Scottish programme compared to the other Challenge settings in which they had worked. Indeed, their initial concern was that this might be a barrier to effective, agile and flexible ways of working that make the adviser role so potent. It is encouraging to report that, as the Challenge has evolved, these early barriers have significantly decreased.

Many of the features of the professional learning programme were admired by the wider Education Scotland team, and, over time, similar opportunities were offered to a wider group of practitioners and some of the practices have subsequently been adopted across the organisation. In this sense, they have had a wider impact on Education Scotland's organisational learning.

Pressures from both national and local government led the attainment advisers to continue to work in ambiguous contexts and, in some cases, with relative isolation within their allocated local authorities, and with varying degrees of access and acceptance within their host authority (Scottish Government, 2018). Furthermore, views about the advisers in the field have been mixed, given their 'outsider position.' Perhaps unsurprisingly, teachers were more positive about their contributions than were local authority colleagues (Scottish Government, 2018). All of which suggests that, despite the inevitable turbulence that has been created, the introduction of these new actors into the system has led to a positive disruption to the status quo. In particular, it seems to have led to increased levels of both challenge and support in relation to the poverty-related attainment gap.

Meanwhile, drawing on the experiences of England and Wales, early advice argued for the appointment of a chief adviser who would have the authority of the Minister to take decisions in the field to stimulate change, cause disruptions and champion the approach. However, these calls largely fell on deaf ears, although tenacity in making the case did lead to such a post being written into a Delivery Plan in 2016: 'Educational leadership of the programme will be extended through a new Chief Adviser role' (Scottish Government, 2016, p. 5).

However, this post was never advertised. Whatever the reason for this, it is certainly the case that educational leadership within the Challenge remains a source of tension and, at times, concern. We return to this later in the chapter.

The early stages of the initiative involved high levels of formal reporting and accountability. For example, the attainment advisers were expected to provide frequent oral reports to a programme board, where they were questioned by senior staff. This was an uncomfortable and, at times, unpleasant process for those involved. There were also unwieldy written reporting mechanisms, with excessive demands placed on both attainment advisers and the Challenge authorities to report on progress. At times, too, this involved duplication, with ambiguity about the nature, purpose and status of the reports that were being produced. All of which echoes the patterns we reported in Wales that tended to act as a brake on rapid progress.

As noted previously, relationships between different stakeholders were sometimes tense during the initiation phase of the programme. However, greater trust has gradually been built, and changes in staffing have meant that, in general, more positive relationships now prevail. These have been encouraged by a number of individuals across the system, ensuring high levels of informal communication and interaction, as well as being constructive in more formal situations. We believe that the Senior Academic Adviser, acting as a critical friend, has played a significant mediating role in these developments, encouraging those involved to step back and consider different points of view.

During the early stages of the Challenge there was also ongoing tension regarding the allocation of resources. This led to the introduction of monitoring

100 The Scottish Attainment Challenge

TABLE 5.1 Allocation and spending in years one and two

	Allocation £ (million)	Actual Spending £ (million)
Year 1 (2015–16)		
Challenge Authorities	£11.7	£5.9
Schools Programme	£2.5	£2.3
Year 2 (2016–17)		
Challenge Authorities	£32.5	£25
Schools Programme	£5.2	£4.0

Source: Scottish Government, 2018, p. 36

procedures to ensure funds were used wisely. At times, ideas and intentions were bold and, but the system did not always have the personnel or capacity to meet these aspirations. In some cases, particularly in some of the Challenge Authorities, this led to significant underspending (see Table 5.1).

In summary, despite the difficulties associated with developing a large-scale change initiative, the first phase of the Challenge provided a 'call to arms' for the system to tackle what was seen as a poverty-related attainment gap. In so doing, it brought the issue of educational inequity to the forefront of political and educational agendas, led to action to shift resources to where they were most needed and intensified action in areas with concentrations of highest poverty. It also introduced new actors into the system with the potential to challenge existing practices and promote new ways of working. As we move on to consider the second phase of the Challenge, we see how further developments led to changes in the scope and scale of its activity.

Phase 2: Embedding and extending the Challenge (2016–2018)

In May 2016, the Attainment Fund was increased for the five years to 2021-22. This involved the programme being extended to 133 secondary schools within nine Challenge Authorities, plus another 28 secondary schools in eleven other authorities. At the same time, this led to increased pressure to provide more direction as to the way it would operate in the field in the form of 'evidence-based' strategies, combined with developing bespoke strategies, designed within particular contexts, which built on the earlier School Improvement Partnership Programme.

Those leading the Challenge were keen to identify evidence-based interventions that would raise attainment in literacy and numeracy and improve health and well-being, as noted in a Delivery Plan in 2016:

> We will launch a new framework of fully evidenced and proven educational interventions and strategies to improve attainment in December 2016. This Framework will inform the decisions schools make to spend the

additional funds and monitor the impact on improving individual children's progress. (p. 6)

An evidence-based framework for interventions was published just before Christmas 2016. This was in the form of a high-level overview of the key areas upon which to focus. Whilst this highlighted what were seen to be sensible areas for investment, it lacked the specificity to provide practical guidance about what might actually be done. Interestingly, this framework can still be seen on the walls of some headteachers' offices across Scotland.

To deliver on this 'what works' agenda, such that schools would adopt 'proven' approaches to tackle the poverty-related attainment gap, the Education Endowment Fund (EEF), an independent charity dedicated to breaking the link between family income and educational achievement, was commissioned.[3] In particular, it was asked to 'Scotify' the Teacher's Toolkit developed for use In England. On reflection, it might have been wiser if the Scottish system had invested in developing its own framework, based on a combination of the best practice emerging from the Challenge, combined with the evidence from international research, an approach that is now beginning to take hold across the system.

In an attempt to develop the narrative beyond 'evidence-based interventions to improve literacy, numeracy and health and well-being,' the rhetoric shifted to what were seen as three key 'levers for change': *excellence in learning and teaching, building leadership capacity*, and *working with families and communities*. These three phrases had the potential to provide some 'glue' to build collective understanding about what needed to be done, rather like the 'Three As' mantra of Access, Aspiration and Achievement used in Greater Manchester. As we have argued, such formulations have the potential to help draw stakeholders together around a common purpose. 'Learning and teaching, leadership, and working families and communities' continues to be used as a galvanising mantra across the system.

The levers narrative found its way into plans and activities in various ways, ranging from formal papers and presentations to conversations between key leaders. For example, as a direct result of a 'Challenge conversation' in one local authority between the Senior Academic Adviser, a senior civil servant and the Director of Education, its plan and priorities were reshaped and reorganised to focus on the three key levers for change. A recent inspection report for the county of Renfrewshire indicated a similar commitment: *'key priority areas being addressed through direct Scottish Attainment funding are: learning and teaching; families and communities and school leadership* (Education Scotland, 2019b, p. 4).

However, as we have implied, the uncritical buy-in of ready-made solutions from elsewhere did not fit well with the overall approach to change being used within the Attainment Challenge, with its emphasis on developing approaches that relate to particular contexts. Another option would have been to turn to external providers from within the Scottish system; for example, the Tapestry Partnership, a well-established national provider of professional learning

102 The Scottish Attainment Challenge

programmes for schools was commissioned to support the Schools Programme between 2015 and 2017.

Gradually, however, another approach that is much more consistent with the ideas developed in this book began to have an impact in the Attainment Challenge programme. This was based on the findings of earlier research carried out at the Robert Owen Centre, University of Glasgow (Chapman et al., 2016). As noted earlier, this had led to the School Improvement Partnership Programme, a networked approach involving collaborative action research and other inquiry techniques. The approach was organised around three phases: building trust and relationships; embedding and extending activity; and building for sustainability.

Over three years, this project had directly involved eight partnerships and over 75 schools across Scotland. However, as the programme brought together different schools and local authorities at learning events, the approach spread to other schools outside the programme and became integrated into the way of working for some local authorities. It was designed to build leadership capacity and impact on student outcomes, specifically for pupils from disadvantaged backgrounds. There is evidence to suggest that the programme made progress in relation to these two goals, which led to considerable interest and support around the system. And, gradually, it became a growing feature of the work of the Attainment Challenge.

So, for example, in 2013 Robert Owen Centre staff worked with one local authority to develop a partnership between two primary schools that used a lesson study approach, a powerful form of school-based professional development adapted from a Japanese model of teacher development. The aim was to explore and refine the teaching of maths. This approach evolved from a couple of trios of teachers to the approach becoming whole school and subsequently local authority wide. Through national learning events for the programme, another local authority became interested in the approach and subsequently incorporated it into its improvement strategy. By 2016, as part of its involvement in the Challenge, this authority based its professional learning and improvement strategy on the School Improvement Partnership Programme, and to this day collaborative action research remains a key driver for improvement.

Another Challenge authority approached the Robert Owen Centre, asking for support in designing a School Improvement Partnership Programme–style intervention. A team of researchers took this into the local authority and one of its neighbours. Initially this involved 12 primary schools but eventually spread to over 30 schools, including some secondary schools. The indications are that it raised teachers' awareness and capability regarding the use of collaborative action research focused on the development of a repertoire of teaching and learning practices.

At its conception in 2013, the School Improvement Partnership Programme was a coordinated national programme of design-based research led by the

Robert Owen Centre, on behalf of Education Scotland, and supported by local authorities. Since 2017, however, it has become a much more organic network, either coordinated locally by the Robert Owen Centre working through Challenge Authorities, or in some cases directly with headteachers as a school-led development. This approach has taken the efforts beyond the search for a perfect evidence-based intervention, to a framework, set of principles and way of working to build leadership capacity, improve learning and teaching, and connect families and communities. Furthermore, groups of schools are now 'clubbing together' without local authority involvement to engage with this way of working. As we will explain, these developments have been stimulated by the introduction of the Pupil Equity Fund and further encouraged by the empowerment agenda of phase three of the Challenge.

Meanwhile, as explained previously, from April 2017 the government provided £1,200 for every child from the most disadvantaged backgrounds (using registration for free school meals as the proxy indicator) in the form of the Pupil Equity Fund. In what was seen as a radical move, this is now allocated directly to schools rather than using the traditional system of allocating resources through local authorities. In practice, this means that some schools serving the most disadvantaged communities are receiving extremely high levels of additional funding. For example, over a four-year period, one primary school in Glasgow will receive approximately one million pounds.

The introduction of these additional funds has injected even more complexity into the Attainment Challenge. The policy intention was for headteachers to decide how this resource would be used to support the progress of their more vulnerable pupils. However, to date, evidence about the effectiveness of this is limited, and the involvement of local authorities in deciding how to use the additional resources is varied. As we will explain, dealing with such complexity whilst maintaining the focus and profile of the Challenge continues to be a priority.

Phase 3: Empowering the Challenge (2017–2019)

The current phase of the Scottish Attainment Challenge has been characterised by an ever-increasing complex educational landscape that has the potential to add further pressures within an education system that struggles to implement changes. In addition to the continuing difficulties of implementing the Challenge, government has put forward a significant set of further educational reforms, including the introduction of a new strategic framework:

> The National Improvement Framework sets a strategic direction for education which aligns with the evidence of the OECD, recognising that both school leadership and teacher professionalism are key drivers of improvement.
>
> (Scottish Government, 2017, p. 13)

In addition to this focus on leadership and teacher professionalism, a National Improvement Framework has heralded the introduction of standardised assessments across primary and secondary schools. This caused fierce debate within educational circles, professional associations, the Scottish Parliament and the media, particularly in relation to the introduction of testing in the first year of primary education. This is ironic in that 28 of the 32 local authorities had already introduced their own form of standardised testing before the introduction of the national programme.

The Scottish government's 'Governance Review: Next Steps' publication in 2017, outlined proposals for the next wave of reform, which includes further radical ideas. These include the introduction of a Scottish Education Council and a Headteachers' Charter designed to give more power and autonomy to school leaders. In addition, the previously independent Scottish College for Educational Leadership was merged into Education Scotland.

The Governance Review also outlined the establishment of six Regional Improvement Collaboratives (RICs). Their role will be to:

- Provide excellent educational improvement support for headteachers, teachers and practitioners through dedicated teams of professionals. These teams will draw on Education Scotland staff, local authority staff and others;
- Provide coherent focus across all partners through delivery of an annual regional plan and associated work programme aligned with the National Improvement Framework; and
- Facilitate collaborative working across the region, including sharing best practice, supporting collaborative networks and pursuing partnership approaches.

(Scottish Government, 2017, p. 7)

These new structures were to be led by a Regional Director, appointed by the Scottish government, who would report to the HM Chief Inspector/Chief Executive of Education Scotland. In practice, each one is now led by a local authority Director of Education, from within their respective RIC.

In establishing the RICs, the government has argued that it was not intending to add another layer of bureaucracy to the system. Rather, it suggested, the aim was to improve performance by increasing coherence, building capacity and providing ways of working that could move knowledge, expertise and practice across local authorities and the wider system. And, of course, such a rationale fits well with the ideas that arose from the developments in England and Wales, with their emphasis on 'moving knowledge around' in the belief that there are untapped resources – especially in schools – that need to be mobilised to strengthen the education system.

Within Scotland, these developments also follow the directions of travel set by the earlier School Improvement Partnership Programme, which called for the establishment of Regional Innovation Hubs (Chapman et al., 2014). They also fit well with the recommendations of the OECD:

> In our view there is need now for a bold approach that moves beyond system management. . . . We call for a strengthened 'middle' operating through networks, within and across local authorities, to create coherent and cohesive cultures of system-wide improvement.
>
> (OECD, 2015, p. 15)

As we have noted, these developments were also informed by the work of the four regional consortia in Wales. As with the government's trips to assess the legacy of London Challenge, visits were made to Cardiff in an attempt to draw out the learning from the Welsh experiences.

The implementation of this policy involves a significant departure from earlier proposals. This was a result of a complex set of arrangements and relationships that was negotiated between local and national government. In particular, it involved discussions regarding arrangement for the line management and accountability for the leaders of the new collaboratives.

In January 2018, the first RIC plans were presented to the Deputy First Minister at the recently formed Scottish Education Council. These plans were prepared within a very short time over the Christmas period and with variable involvement of senior leaders from the local authorities within each of the collaboratives.

To date, progress and commitment is variable, with momentum accelerating in some areas. This has been incentivised by the allocation of additional resources to the regional collaboratives during the summer of 2018 and the preparation of phase two plans in the autumn of 2018. Meanwhile, if things do not go well, the possibility of returning to legislation remains a constant threat. Indeed, in November, during his speech to the 2018 conference of local authority directors, the Deputy First Minister/Cabinet Secretary for Education and Learning reminded delegates that draft legislation exists and that if the system cannot respond positively to the reform agenda then it will be revisited.

This complex agenda for change has significant implications for the government's continuing commitment to create a more equitable and excellent system through the Scottish Attainment Challenge. In particular, the issues raised in the Governance Review have been seen by some stakeholders as an attack on local government. As we have explained, with more resources being allocated directly to schools, rather than through local authorities, and headteachers being more empowered to have greater autonomy and decision-making power, questions about the future status and roles of local authority are raised. Inevitably, this has led some stakeholders to look at the situation in England, where, as we have explained, local authorities have been largely marginalised in respect to the improvement of schools.

106 The Scottish Attainment Challenge

Meanwhile, the teachers' unions have secured a 13% salary increase for teachers, thus avoiding the prospect of industrial action. And, of course, we should not forget that the implementation of the radical changes required by Curriculum for Excellence is still work in progress. As Walter Humes (2019) explains:

> Implementation of CfE has not been straightforward. Although there was broad support for the rhetoric of reform, when it came to the details and practicalities there were many problems. Some ideas, such as 'active' and 'interdisciplinary' learning, were criticised as vague. The quality of programmes of professional development for teachers, intended to prepare for the changes, did not inspire confidence.[4]

This complex context, along with changes in senior leadership within the system, including a change of Director within the Scottish government's learning directorate, means that the profile of the Scottish Attainment Challenge is continually under pressure within an increasingly crowded policy scene. It is still articulated as the government's flagship policy, but the structures and systems of the programme have become routinised and, in our view, there is a need to refresh the narrative and focus its role across the system. There are so many pressing issues across the system that there is the danger that the Challenge machinery trundles on in the shadow of these concerns.

Meanwhile, almost five years on, there remains in place a named attainment adviser for each local authority. Given the distribution and varied nature of the educational challenges within different areas, this decision has continued to be a matter of debate, especially now that local authorities are working more closely together through the establishment of the regional improvement collaboratives. All of this sits within a context of the commitment made in 'Delivering Excellence and Equity in Scottish Education: A Delivery Plan' (Scottish Government, 2016):

> 'We will extend the reach and impact of the Attainment Advisors, through regional alignment to promote collaboration and joint delivery across local authorities from **October 2016**' (p. 5, emphasis in original).

A growing body of inspection evidence highlights the progress that has been made. All of the Challenge Authorities have been inspected within the past year. These inspections report that 'excellent' progress has been made in a number of authorities, such as Glasgow and Renfrewshire. It is also widely recognised that West Dumbartonshire would have likely been featured within this group had it not been the first authority to be inspected in this cycle, whilst it is generally viewed that at least one other authority received a rather generous report. This has raised concerns about the reliability of the inspection process in some circles.

The contrasting fortunes of the inspections are illustrated by the impact of leadership and professional learning opportunities in different authorities. For example in Glasgow, professional learning is seen as being well established:

> Professional learning places a strong emphasis on building practitioner capacity and creating an empowered system. This approach has been successful in creating conditions which allow practitioners, managers and leaders at all levels to make a strong contribution to local and national improvement.
>
> (Education Scotland, 2019a, p. 10)

Whilst in East Ayrshire the inspection reported that professional learning needs have been identified and it is hoped that future activity will have an impact on raising attainment:

> It is hoped that the suite of professional learning opportunities will address the identified need for increased leadership capacity and facilitate greater progress in raising attainment and closing the poverty-related attainment gap.
>
> (Education Scotland, 2019b, p. 7)

These variations highlight the importance of moving knowledge around the system and, again, regional improvement collaboratives provide a significant opportunity to stimulate activity to support this agenda. For example, the University of Glasgow's Policy Scotland unit is using research evidence to support the WEST partnership to make sense of this agenda by creating a 'learning system' across the regional improvement collaborative. This involves providing strategic advice to the governance board, undertaking primary research, including base-lining conditions and capacity across the RIC, and supporting the systematic movement of practice and ideas across the partnership. The Robert Owen Centre also plays a strategic role in supporting Challenge authorities. For example, Renfrewshire's excellent inspection report cites the centre's contribution to the local authority's central team in '*helping to coordinate key workstreams to ensure that they have maximum impact*' (Education Scotland, 2019c, p. 7).

It is also important to note that recent announcements signal that the Attainment Challenge continues to have cross-party support and will be funded into the next political administration and potentially beyond 2022. This is a critical issue for the long-term sustainability of the programme. It seems to us that what is now needed is a re-visioning of the Scottish initiative and its realignment with the broader reforms we have outlined. In this way, it has the potential to act as a coherence building initiative, rather than as an individual programme that cuts across and sometimes competes with other reform efforts.

Looking to the future

Consistent with what we argue in earlier chapters, the approach we are recommending in Scotland is not about the introduction of particular techniques. Rather, it is an overall way of thinking that involves processes of contextual analysis used to develop strategies that fit with particular circumstances. In so doing, the aim must be to make better use of the expertise within those situations and to build capacity to manage change through processes of collaboration and networks. To do this, local barriers will have to be identified and addressed.

In terms of the future direction of the Scottish Attainment Challenge, a series of recent conversations with a range of actors within the system have provided insights into potential ways forward. In particular, a visit to one region pointed to an interesting possibility. This emerged from discussions with colleagues in the then to be announced WEST Partnership, a regional improvement collaborative involving eight local authorities, which serve around 35% of Scotland's children and has the highest percentage of pupils from disadvantaged backgrounds. The region contains five of the Challenge Authorities and the authority with the largest number of schools within the Schools programme. Indeed, it is, in effect, the 'Greater Glasgow Challenge' that was proposed back in 2013, pointing toward the possibility of a future phase being based around the regional improvement collaboratives. In this way the locus of decision making could be moved closer to the action, particularly if school leaders were invited to take on system leadership roles of the sort we described in the other Challenge areas. In our view, such a shift in ownership would have the possibility of enhancing the sustainability of the programme within the wider reform agenda and supporting the policy ambition of empowering headteachers.

Inevitably, the visits triangulated the inspection findings by identifying a few local authorities where, despite the investment, progress appeared to be limited and the pace of change slow. In one case, serious concerns were raised by the team. Despite conversations about the urgent need for peer support and appropriate intervention, over 18 months later government officials still have serious concerns about this local authority, but there has been little attempt to provide additional support or intervention.

For these areas and, indeed, for those schools that seem to be 'stuck,' perhaps some more intensive form of support is required. Some of the ideas that worked well in City Challenge might inform developments. For example, some schools could be identified as the schools with the potential to close the poverty-related attainment gap, leading the way in exploring more effective ways of reaching hard-to-reach learners – a Scottish form of the Keys to Success schools in England. This might also involve some form of accelerated improvement board of the sort that worked so well in Wales. This could bring together a range of stakeholders, such as headteachers, the chair of the parent council, the attainment adviser and a senior inspector working collaboratively on specific issues to drive improvement within an accelerated time frame. Such a group could identify priorities, develop an action plan, agree on milestones and monitor developments on a regular basis. This could be undertaken at the school level but also at the local authority level in partnership with the Association of Directors of Education to accelerate improvements in areas that have struggled to make significant progress.

Ideas such as this suggest that it would now make sense for there to be a rethinking of the role of the Attainment Challenge. It seems to us that this should build on the many strengths that exist, not least being the massive political commitment, the pro-education atmosphere that is a historical feature of the country, and the strong emphasis on inclusion that exists. At the same time, a refined strategy would need to shift the ownership of reform by distributing decision making more widely throughout the education system. This would mean giving teachers and schools greater autonomy, so they can work together and with their local communities to find more effective ways of reaching those young people who are currently being let down. At the same time, local authorities should be given more space to work together in coordinating and monitoring the impact of school-led improvement efforts, stepping in when things are not going well – to borrow a helpful phrase from Wales, acting as 'the conscience of the system.' All of this would allow national policy-makers the opportunity to step back from the action and guide and monitor the overall implementation of national policies.

As we have explained, many of the difficulties regarding the progress of the Attainment Challenge have arisen as a result of struggles regarding control of educational policies and budgets. We have seen, for example, how the amount of reporting and auditing in the early stages was a source of tensions, with information being collected from multiple sources and often in duplication. The signing off of plans and timing releasing resources to local authorities has further hindered progress at times. And, while some of the plans were ambitious, it was common for them not to be realised because they were often contingent on the appointment of new or additional staff, both teaching and additional nonteaching posts. Unfortunately, in many cases these people do not exist within the system. This led to a rationalisation of the ambition and, as we have explained, significant underspending within the programme.

In a sense, all of this is a manifestation of a combination of high levels of social cohesion and social control within a system that supports hierarchical cultures and bureaucratic public service organisations (Chapman, 2019). If the principles of collaboration and moving knowledge around that underpin the Challenge are to be realised, levels of social control will need to be reduced to loosen up the system, whilst at the same time maintaining high levels of social cohesion. Put simply, there is a need to break down hierarchies and build an egalitarian culture (Douglas, 1982) that is underpinned by collaboration. This would involve networks operating in a situation with lower levels of rules and regulation to support the creation of mutualistic, or self-improving, organisations (Hood, 1998).

Such developments are not without risk. We have mentioned the pay negotiations and the reforms designed to give headteachers and schools more autonomy from local authorities and to encourage cross authority collaboration (Scottish Government, 2017). All of this is making some local authority staff and politicians feel nervous and, sometimes, defensive as a result of feeling threatened and disempowered by some of these developments (Chapman, 2019). These policies are testing existing levels of social cohesion and may ultimately lead to fragmentation. Should this be the case, and relationships within the system deteriorate, industrial relations may suffer and a fatalistic culture could emerge as a result of those in the field perceiving the government to be intervening without appropriate consultation or involvement from those responsible for implementing proposed changes.

We have also mentioned the 'draft' Education Bill, which could be interpreted as a fall-back position to control developments through executive power and political management should the system not respond to the challenge of maintaining high levels of social cohesion. Should this legislation be implemented, leading to regulation being increased, the likely effect would be a further reduction of social cohesion within the system leading to a culture where uncertain organisations prevail. It seems likely that, within such a scenario, some stakeholders would look back to the past with nostalgia, viewing the certainty of hierarchy as a safer and better system.

This mosaic of policy developments, involving tensions and dilemmas that combine collaboration and empowerment, may have some unintended consequences that could lead to a more individualised and competitive culture. For example, we have mentioned the impact of the Pupil Equity Fund – the direct payment to schools for their most disadvantaged pupils. This is inadvertently creating a market where a range of public, third and private sector organisations are competing to provide improvement and consultancy services, which traditionally have been provided by the local authority or a national improvement agency. This complex policy landscape is inadvertently opening opportunities for individuals and organisations that did not exist in the past, and the vacuum is there to be filled. For example, there is a growing number of recently retired 'successful' headteachers and local authority personnel offering their services directly to schools, plus a diverse range of providers from south of the border are lining up to offer services. Given the Scottish education system's history, tradition, values and beliefs, this is the worst-case scenario – the creation of a neo-liberal system by default.

Conclusion

The Scottish Attainment Challenge is a significant effort to develop a national education system that is both excellent and equitable. As such it has many of the features that are essential to an effective system change strategy. First and foremost, it has a strong political mandate that, as far as we can see, will continue into the future. This commitment has been matched by an impressive investment of funding that provides the resources to support developments in the field. It also has a clear agenda that addresses concerns largely recognised amongst stakeholders across the country.

As we move into the next phase of the Challenge, there is an opportunity to shift the original focus of the initiative from developing specific interventions to close the poverty-related attainment gap to exploring the relationship between poverty and variations in outcomes in more creative ways. This could involve developing stronger and more coherent mechanisms to draw out the lessons learned, and to move knowledge and practice around the system in a more coherent fashion. There is also an opportunity to build on lessons from elsewhere to develop bespoke ways of injecting pace, challenge and support into those local areas where progress has been limited.

If the current set of reforms are to realise their ambition, however, there needs to be careful consideration of the emerging issues, tensions and dilemmas associated with the direction of travel the Challenge and wider system is taking, and how these reforms play out in practice. In this context, the likely unintended outcomes of miscalculating or unravelling the levels of social cohesion and regulation within the system remain matters of concern. The lessons for Scotland and beyond are therefore clear: not only is system reform a complex and challenging task with many risks, it is also a largely social process where the shaping of cultures must be given primacy over structural change.

Keeping all of this in mind, in Chapter 6 we move back to England to consider how – in the post–City Challenge era dominated by the idea of market forces as a strategy for improvement – the new radical policy context can support or undermine the development of more equitable education systems.

Notes

1 https://www.independent.co.uk/news/education/education-news/scotland-the-best-educated-country-in-europe-claims-ons-report-9497645.html.
2 https://news.govcot/news/smart-money-on-attainment.
3 See https://educationendowmentfoundation.org.uk/.
4 http://sceptical.scot/2019/02/the-parochialism-of-the-present/.

6

NEW CHALLENGES

Managing change in an educational marketplace

Since the period in which the projects we have described so far took place, we have seen new developments that further emphasise competition between schools as the way forward. This is a growing international trend that hardly seems conducive to schools working together. In this chapter, we explore this matter in the context of England, a country where recent national policy has been subject to radical reforms that involve the use of market forces to intensify efforts to 'improve standards.'

With this in mind, we reflect on our more recent experiences of working in this emerging policy context. This leads us to throw light on the challenges involved in achieving system change within a highly competitive education system. At the same time, we draw attention to some promising developments. We begin, however, by setting the context for our analysis, first, in terms of global and national policy developments, and then with regard to relevant research literature.

A global trend

As countries throughout the world seek to improve their national education systems, there is an increasing emphasis on the idea of school autonomy (Meyland-Smith & Evans, 2009). This takes a variety of forms, and the schools involved have different titles, such as charter schools in the USA, free schools in Sweden, independent public schools in parts of Australia and academies in England.

Implicit in these new types of independent state-funded schools is an assumption that greater autonomy will allow space for the development of organisational arrangements, practices and forms of management and leadership that will be more effective in promoting the learning of all of their students, particularly those from economically disadvantaged and minority backgrounds. Salokangas and Ainscow (2017) summarise the steps taken to achieve this overall goal as follows:

- **Making schools more autonomous.** The logic is that giving schools more freedom will put them in a better position to promote the learning of their students. In this way, it is assumed, more decisions need to be made locally, by the people involved in schools, rather than by administrators at the district, local authority or national levels. The matters over which schools became more autonomous varies from one country to another but include, for example, increased decision-making capacity over student admissions, curriculum, classroom practices, finance and regulations concerning staff recruitment and contracts.
- **Bringing new 'actors' into the management, administration and governance of schools.** The criteria concerning who these actors may be has varied from country to country. They have included organisations and individuals who have not traditionally been involved in the management of publicly funded education, such as private, semi-private and charitable organisations, parent groups, religious organisations and wealthy philanthropists. These new actors, it is argued, will bring fresh ideas that will inject new energy and more efficient ways of working into public education. One of the central debates concerning these new actors in school management has been whether or not they will be permitted to make a profit from running autonomous schools. Such for-profit 'edubusinesses' (Hill, 2008) have grown to be big players in the management of charter schools in the United States and free schools in Sweden, but at the time of this writing, they are not permitted to run academies for profit in England.
- **Introducing heavily regulated quality assurance systems.** Here, the aim has been to make the schools' performance transparent for wider audiences. For example, charter school accountability is ensured through charter renewal processes, based on *'results-driven, marketplace-oriented accountability systems to furnish parents, policy makers, and taxpayers and others with information about the school's quality and effectiveness'* (Manno, Chester & Vanourek, 2000, p. 476). In England, students in academies sit the same national tests as those in other state schools and are subject to similar school inspections as others. The results of both are made publicly available. Such narrowly defined measures of effectiveness are used for accountability purposes, not only in autonomous schools but widely in the education systems where autonomous schools operate (Schildkamp, Ehren & Lai, 2012).

The intended outcomes of these reforms are ambitious; autonomous schools are assumed to hold huge potential to address the fundamental problems facing public education. However, this radical global trend is a matter of considerable debate, and views vary regarding the extent to which it is leading to the desired outcomes. In particular, there is a concern that the development of

114 New challenges

education systems based on autonomy, coupled with high-stakes accountability and increased competition between schools will further disadvantage learners from low-income and minority families.

The English policy context

England can be seen as an advanced guard in relation to this type of educational reform. As we explained in Chapter 2, the last 20 years have seen intensive efforts by successive governments to improve the education system. This has involved an emphasis on competition between schools as a means of 'driving up standards' whilst at the same time further reducing the control of local authorities over educational provision. More recently, the emphasis on competition has been intensified as increasing numbers of state schools have been encouraged – and, in some instances, required – to become academies. These schools are funded directly by the national government rather than through a local authority. Moving away from the earlier emphasis on centrally driven strategies, these changes are intended to liberate schools from the bureaucracy of local government influence and, in so doing, establish a form of marketplace. In this way, it is intended that families will have greater choice as to which school their youngsters attend (Adonis, 2012).

As a result of the expanding academies programme, as well as other contributing policies, the education system in England has become increasingly diverse (Chapman, 2015). Furthermore, the introduction of various other types of schools that operate under the academy legislation – such as free schools based on the Swedish model, studio schools and university technical colleges – has contributed to the complexity of the scene.

An independent commission set up to review these developments pointed out that the original aim of academies was 'to address entrenched failure in schools with low performance, most particularly, schools located in the most disadvantaged parts of the country' (Husbands, Gilbert, Francis & Wigdortz, 2013, p. 4). Subsequently, the focus has changed toward increasing the autonomy of all schools and setting up new academies throughout the country. At the same time, there has been a growing emphasis on schools supporting one another, leading to an unusual cocktail of competition and cooperation.

Since election of the Conservative-led coalition government in 2010, followed by the Conservative government in 2015, all of this has become much more central to education policy in England. The basis of the approach was outlined in a White Paper that set out plans to improve the quality of teachers and school leadership through school-to-school support and peer-to-peer learning (Department for Education, 2010). Speaking about these plans in June 2011, the then Secretary of State for Education argued that there is a need to develop a 'culture of collaboration' in order to address the issue of educational underperformance, particular amongst disadvantaged groups of learners. More specifically, he emphasised his intention to develop networks of schools in order to create a 'self-improving system.'

A further feature of the strategy that has subsequently evolved is a national network of 'teaching schools,' a concept that emerged through the City Challenge programme (Matthews & Berwick, 2013). Analogous to teaching hospitals, the intention is that these schools will have a key role to play in leading the training and professional development of teachers and school principals. Some teaching schools work together within an alliance, that is, a group of schools and other partners that is supported by the leadership of the teaching school.

Our earlier research led us to take a positive view of the thinking that guides these developments, particularly the emphasis they place on school-to-school collaboration. However, as we will show, considerable difficulties face those implementing the approach within the new English policy context. We argue that these difficulties arise from policy contradictions, not least in relation to pressures created by accountability procedures. All of this throws further light on the challenges facing efforts to use school-to-school collaboration to foster improvements inside policies that emphasise competition between schools. They also add to the complexities facing engaged researchers who become involved in such developments.

Inevitably, the issue of leadership is an important factor as the system moves toward the idea of a self-improving school system. The government's response to this has been to create a cadre of system leaders. Known as national leaders of education (NLEs), these are successful school leaders who have had the experience of supporting schools in challenging circumstances (Department for Education and Skills, 2014). The policy suggests that they should work alongside teaching schools and other system leaders to provide high-quality support to those schools that need it most.

Alongside the development of teaching schools and the introduction of system leaders, there has been a growing trend toward the formation of academy groups, originally known as chains but usually referred to today as multi-academy trusts (MATs). Adding further complexity is the fact that some MATs are part of teaching school alliances. As we will show, all of this can lead to tensions within the system, with school leaders left uncertain as to where they should position themselves in relation to the structural changes being introduced.

From a legal perspective, MAT's are powerful new governance structures that hold considerable power over the academies they run. Referring to the 2010 Academies Act, Wilkins (2016) explains that, when subsumed within a MAT, a school is no longer managed by the bureau-professionalism of the local authority and its democratic mandate; is not a freestanding legal entity with powers to employ staff, enter into contracts and plan budget spending; is stripped of its assets and any legal entitlement to self-determination; and is subject to the requirements and provisos of the MAT, specifically the board of directors, or trustees, who retain legal powers to shape key policy decisions for all the schools within the cluster or chain. It is worth adding that academies are not allowed to resign from a trust.

116 New challenges

All of this raises questions regarding the local coordination of the system, which is one of the most worrying aspects of the current policy context, with its emphasis on school autonomy, competition and new governance structures that can discourage schools from working with others. A further factor is that recent years have seen a gradual reduction in the power and influence of local authorities that have traditionally taken on this responsibility. This means that no one organisation has the overall picture that would enable them to orchestrate more collaborative ways of working, stepping in when things go wrong.

Meanwhile, in September 2014, eight regional schools commissioners were appointed to oversee the growing number of academies in England. Since taking up this post, their roles have expanded to include decision making in tackling underperformance in local authority maintained schools, and for so-called coasting schools. As a result, they have rapidly become an important and powerful feature of the English education system (Durbin, Wespieser, Bernardinelli & Gee, 2015), although confusion remains in the field regarding their roles, not least in relation to the contributions of local authorities.

The implementation of these massive structural reforms has led to uncertainties and tensions as those involved try to make sense of the complexities they face. At the same time, it is leading to some promising opportunities for building research evidence and processes into the developments that are occurring.

Schools supporting schools

These policy trends can be seen as an opportunity to extend and deepen the tradition of school-to-school cooperation that has been a strong feature of the English education system for many years, following on from earlier initiatives such as the Education Action Zones, Excellence in Cities, and, of course, the City Challenge programme described in Chapter 2. However, Croft (2015) has expressed concern about the lack of hard evidence of its impact on student outcomes. He argues, that with some notable exceptions (e.g., Chapman and Muijs, 2014), much of the research has been dogged by weak methodology. He goes on to suggest that this leads to findings that are of limited use in relation to what actually makes the difference for student progress and attainment.

Having reviewed the literature on the effectiveness of school partnerships, Armstrong (2015) lists what he defines as 'gaps in knowledge.' These gaps include the limited knowledge surrounding the change process and the development and maintenance of relationships when schools enter into collaboration. He also argues that there is a lack of insight into the differential impact of interschool collaboration and how different types of collaborative arrangements might vary in effectiveness, sustainability and the kinds of impact they make. In addition, he argues, little evidence distinguishes the results between short- and long-term collaboration. These themes are picked up later in this chapter.

Notwithstanding these critiques, over the last 15 years or so a growing body of research, including our own, has generated considerable evidence that

New challenges **117**

school-to-school collaboration can strengthen improvement processes by adding to the range of expertise made available (e.g., Ainscow, 2015; Ainscow & West, 2006; Chapman & Hadfield, 2010; Chapman, 2008; Fielding et al., 2005; Hadfield et al., 2006; Muijs et al., 2011). These studies suggest that, under the right conditions, collaboration between schools has a potential for fostering the capacity of education systems to respond to learner diversity. More specifically, they show how such partnerships can help to reduce the polarisation of schools, particularly to the benefit of those students marginalized at the edges of the system and whose performance and attitudes are matters of concern.

However, none of this represents a strategy that will guarantee progress. Indeed, school-to-school collaboration may simply be a fad – an effective approach when led by skilled and enthusiastic advocates in certain types of systems but not scalable or transferable. Concerns have also been expressed that school partnerships can lead to lots of nonproductive time, as members of staff spend periods out of school; schools involved in working collaboratively may collude with one another to reinforce mediocrity and low expectations; those schools that most need help may choose not to get involved; and some headteachers may become 'empire builders' who deter others from getting involved (Ainscow, 2015).

Ainscow and West (2006) outline an escalator of collaborative endeavour, moving from loose and traditional ways of working toward much more sustainable and powerful relationships, as follows:

- *Association* – The traditional pattern of school cooperation, with incidental meetings often initiated through a hierarchy, and little or no sharing of knowledge or resources.
- *Cooperation* – Short-term task-focused activity around a specific issue, and incidental sharing of knowledge or resources on specific issues.
- *Collaboration* – More sustainable ways of working underpinned by a set of common values, and a commitment to share knowledge, resources and practice with some development of new practices.
- *Collegiality* – A longer-term commitment to a shared enterprise, underpinned by a shared long-term vision and set of common values, with a focus on sharing and developing new knowledge, resources and practice.

Linked to this, David Hargreaves (2012) argues that social capital is a key characteristic of mature forms of collaboration. He argues that this is best summed up as involving trust plus reciprocity: 'Reciprocity thrives as long as people can be persuaded to collaborate with one another to improve professional practice. Trust, however, is a more subtle concept and is established more slowly' (p. 13).

Chapman (2019) argues that where social capital is low, collaborative efforts can be undermined to expose a darker side that involves:

- *An illusion of association* – Passive buy-in, creating the illusion of collaboration as a 'sleeping partner';

118 New challenges

- *Fabricated cooperation* – Individuals pursuing their own agendas to enhance power, status or resources, often at the expense of others;
- *Collaboration with the 'enemy'* – Despite intentions, this often turns into collusion, which involves becoming trapped by the dominant discourse; or
- *Contrived collegiality* – False public expressions of value that do not match the behaviours of those involved. This is particularly prevalent where unequal power relationships in bureaucratic hierarchies exist.

Few studies have assessed the ways in which attitudes and practices are evolving on the ground as a result of the radical English policy changes (Greany, 2017). In particular, little is known about how practitioners are reacting to what we referred to earlier as an unusual cocktail of competition and cooperation. Drawing on research from the business world, Muijs and Rumyantseva (2014) have explored how competition and collaboration can sometimes coexist through what they describe as 'coopetition.' They note, however, that there are few studies of this approach in the field of education.

Bearing all of this in mind, we draw on the findings of a study of school leaders who are closely involved in promoting greater cooperation within the new English policy context (see Armstrong & Ainscow, 2018, for a full account). This leads us to pinpoint what seem to be promising developments, as well as barriers to progress.

Gathering the views of insiders

Evidence was generated through in-depth focused interviews with a group of stakeholders who were in a position to offer views 'from the inside.' These data were selected from a larger United Kingdom government-commissioned evaluation of the School to School Support Fund initiative (Armstrong & Ainscow, 2017). This involved funding for which eligible schools applied to support other schools that were underperforming.

Acting as evaluators on behalf of the government gave us privileged access, enabling us to talk with key stakeholders drawn from two regions of the country. These regions included areas where school-to-school support was said by government officials to be at a relatively mature stage and others where this was believed to be less so.

We have drawn on the ideas of system leaders in these regions. In addition, we take account of the views of the coordinators of arrangements for school-to-school support in each region, as well as the team of civil servants closely involved in the further development of national policies related to this agenda.

Promising developments

A key finding was the emergence of new coordination mechanisms through which arrangements for partnerships can be made. These start within schools, where new organisational arrangements have to be made so that key members of staff can be freed to work offsite. They then require new forms of coordination to assess local needs and arrange relevant partnerships between schools. Inevitably, this sometimes leads to tensions, as those with varying priorities have to find ways of addressing their differences. The findings suggest that this problem was being addressed, albeit at a different pace, in each context. These differences relate, at least in part, to historical and geographical factors.

Relevant to our account of City Challenge in Chapter 2, it is significant that one of the areas in the study was Greater Manchester. This provided a particularly strong example of maturity in relation to school collaboration. There, stakeholders have created an overarching learning partnership[1] comprised of representatives from local authorities, teaching schools and the regional schools commissioner. This structure, which grew out of By Schools for Schools set up at the end of City Challenge, has an independent chair.

As part of its remit to coordinate school-led improvement across Greater Manchester, the learning partnership plays a central role in screening which schools require support and are best placed to provide such support. This has been possible because of the willingness of all parties to communicate and share local intelligence and school-level data. It has created a system that not only identifies schools that are categorised as failing, by the nature of their inspection grades and pupil assessment data, but also those that are at risk of falling into this category.

These arrangements illustrate how previous experiences within a locality can provide a sense of optimism regarding what is possible for schools working together. This historical context is important to acknowledge because it is within these previous experiences of partnership work that schools and other educational stakeholders have forged their current relationships and the mutual trust and willingness to work together that underpin their collaborative activity.

Another example of successful partnership work was found in a large rural county. It involved three alliances of system leaders that represent the north, west and south of the county. They each took responsibility for monitoring all the schools in their areas. This then fed directly into discussions surrounding the schools that would be suitable for school-to-school support.

The stakeholders across this particular county had worked hard, we were told, to break down traditional barriers to sharing data and intelligence, and they have moved toward a culture of knowledge mobilisation. However, room for progress remains, and some schools have yet to engage fully.

These two examples highlight the apparent willingness and appetite amongst education stakeholders to mobilise and pool their resources, expertise and knowledge as a means of strengthening and improving their regional and local school systems. Interestingly, although the national educational policy landscape has undoubtedly facilitated and in many ways necessitated such partnership work, much of the activity to which we have referred has been school-led. Furthermore, common to the examples is the key coordinating role of local authorities, which

120 New challenges

remain central to school-to-school support and improvement in these two areas despite national policies.

Barriers to progress

These promising developments offer reason for optimism with regard to the English school system's capacity to collaborate, but there was also evidence of barriers. Confusion over seemingly uncoordinated policy directives and uncertainties over roles and responsibilities have contributed to a lack of coordination at the regional level and to struggles for power over decision making at the local level.

So, for instance, in another rural area some interviewees suggested that schools were being pulled in different directions by various educational policy directives. Many of these issues centred on the competing and conflicting priorities of local authorities, teaching schools and multi-academy trusts, not least regarding the allocation of government funding to facilitate school-to school support. One system leader, who heads up a trust made up of five schools, talked of tensions with her local authority regarding which schools should be targeted for support:

> *It is all controlled by the local authority people. They tell us who should get money to pay for support. You see, they hold the data – this means that the heads don't know which schools are struggling.*

We also heard of tensions created for colleagues involved in the work of teaching school alliances who are increasingly spending their time negotiating the creation of multi-academy trusts. Meanwhile, uncertainties were sometimes created for those working in local authorities by the increasing emphasis on teaching schools as the main source of support for school improvement. For example, the head of a teaching school alliance argued that she now finds herself in direct competition with her local authority, which, she argues, is trying to access funding to support its own central school improvement service.

Many of these issues stem from a lack of clarity regarding the roles and responsibilities of the various stakeholders. In particular, confusions seem to have arisen about the intended role of local authorities and teaching schools within a system where multi-academy trusts are becoming the dominant organisational arrangement for school-to-school cooperation. For example, one school leader explained how the academy he was expecting to assist had been instructed to source support from within its own trust rather than from the teaching school. His view was that the absence of effective coordination in his local area had left a degree of ambiguity regarding this issue. He believed that the newly established regional school commissioners were in a better position to take on this role, although they too are still struggling to define their roles and responsibilities.

Likewise, there remained comparable tensions as different actors jostled for positions, as this system leader explains:

> *We have a half-termly meeting where all the teaching schools and the local authority get together and discuss stuff, but it's not always a useful and productive meeting. . . . I don't think the local authority people really understand the teaching school agenda and therefore they're not sure where they fit.*

Given the relative immaturity of school-to-school activity in areas such as this one, it is perhaps unsurprising that participants cited an absence of trust, collaboration and knowledge mobilisation. Meanwhile, in another county, it was suggested that this problem is a direct result of the local authority choosing to retain its own school improvement service, which is seen to be in direct competition with the teaching schools. It was also argued that funding issues had added to these pressures because the central school improvement service generates income for the local authority. This led the head of a large secondary school to describe himself as being negative about the contributions of local authority staff, although he did admit that their involvement had helped to improve what had previously been a chaotic arrangement for nominating schools for support.

Drawing some lessons

These experiences lead us to draw lessons that might be relevant to those in other contexts where policy is encouraging schools to compete and collaborate. In so doing, we draw on the idea of 'coopetition,' as defined by Muijs and Rumyantseva (2014), and the conditions needed for it to be effective: partners who see *clear and tangible benefits* from collaboration; *trust between partners*, established through the careful development of relationships between key actors; *clear goals and agreements* between partners; and *forms of leadership that are skilful* in managing tensions. Muijs and Rumyantseva go on to argue that these conditions are likely to be hard to achieve in competitive situations.

Bearing this concern in mind, in what follows we consider each of these conditions in turn, whilst also acknowledging that they are interwoven and interdependent.

Clear and tangible benefits

Where there was evidence of progress toward school improvement based on cooperation, it was clear that those involved had recognized the potential benefits. In particular, the colleagues whose schools were providing support frequently spoke of the impact on their own schools. Much of this seemed to be about the professional development opportunities provided by having to support schools facing much more challenging circumstances. Alongside our accounts of the Challenge programmes in England, Scotland and Wales, this pattern is

122 New challenges

important because it offers further evidence of how partnerships can help to strengthen relatively low-performing schools whilst, at the same time, fostering wider improvements in a system.

Those contexts that were more collaboratively mature featured a range of educational stakeholders working together, sharing their individual perspectives and insights to facilitate school-to-school support and improvement across their respective localities. Amongst these stakeholders, the local authority has the potential to play a key role in facilitating this activity. This is noteworthy because the reduced capacity of this tier of government in recent years – a direct consequence of educational policy directives – has handed more responsibility to individuals and networks of schools.

Trust between partners

A willingness to share intelligence and engage in professional dialogue was seen as a strong indication of the growth of trust amongst schools. Although these conversations tended to centre on statistical data regarding student progress and overall school performance, what appeared to be potentially more powerful was the means by which these parties bring their varied experiences and expertise together to scrutinise the data. In this way, they are each confronted with different interpretations of the same set of evidence.

Where this works well, it has the potential to challenge taken for granted assumptions and, in so doing, stimulate creative thinking and problem solving with regard to particular schools and, indeed, the whole education system. In this way, relationships and trust were strengthened. However, there remains the problem of how to get those who are reluctant to join in with processes that they do not see as being to their advantage within the competitive educational marketplace. Indeed, as Muijs and Rumyantseva (2014) point out, any uncertainty regarding the benefits of the partnership serves to weaken the ties between partners. Here the example of the secondary SIGs within Wales, described in Chapter 4, is helpful as it highlights how important it was to achieve a certain scale of collaborative working in order for schools to recognize its benefits. It also allows individual schools choice to pursue those they saw as worthwhile, and in doing so create a form of internal competition that drew others into the network.

Given the complexities surrounding the development of trust within a competitive environment, it is interesting to note the positive influence of the local and regional systems of accountability and evaluation of school-to-school support and improvement that had been established. In these circumstances, participants reported the importance of having a forum through which they could reflect on the work they are undertaking together to support schools and how this process might be improved in building a sense of collective responsibility for an area's improvement. So, whilst they often remained in competition, they were still prepared to work toward a broader aim of educational improvement across the localities within which they are situated.

In those regions where stakeholders have embraced collaboration, by working together and drawing on their respective strengths there is an understanding that the local and regional school systems to which they belong can better meet the needs of the students and the communities they serve. Moreover, in engaging in such collaborative activity and working together to solve issues and address the myriad challenges they face, these local and regional systems are demonstrating characteristics of a self-improving system.

However, it is naïve to ignore the political complexities involved in all of this. In particular, these examples suggest that a need for sensitivity remains with regard to the shift in decision making and influence from local authorities to teaching schools and/or multi-academy trusts. Within some contexts, this transition appears to have been reasonably smooth. But in other areas, there were tensions characteristic of power struggles regarding decision making. Often, too, access to funding was the battleground around which these struggles took place. Schools continue to compete for financial resources, either through the number of students they can attract or other sources of income, and tensions will be present. As Muijs and Rumyantseva (2014) suggest, any ongoing and future prospect of competition between members is likely to be detrimental to the strength and sustainability of their partnership.

Clear goals and agreements

We have drawn attention to a number of promising developments that offer encouragement as to how school systems might harness the capacity of stakeholders as a means of self-improvement. But we have also identified some key issues that are likely to inhibit such progress unless they are addressed. These relate to disputes regarding overall purposes within a policy context that seems to pull stakeholders in different directions. Related to this are disputes over roles and positioning within the system that can lead to confusion amongst stakeholders and, as we have noted, struggles for power.

Areas that were more collaboratively mature were characterized by clarity of purpose amongst members as to the aims and goals of their partnership activity. In these contexts, as the preceding sections suggest, this seems to have been achieved through the establishment of clear and tangible benefits for those involved, and the careful nurturing of trust between all parties. Conversely, these features and the conditions within which they have emerged were largely absent from those contexts that were less collaboratively mature.

As we have discussed, one of the key challenges for stakeholders across all the areas related to the shifting roles of various actors as a result of the ongoing structural reforms within the English system. On one hand, the frantic pace and intensity of such reform is creating an overall climate of innovation; on the other hand, this is leading to some confusion amongst those in the field, not least practitioners, for whom the intensity of daily professional duties leaves limited time for keeping in touch with what is going on.

The danger is that, within this complex policy context, those trying to promote school-to school cooperation can sometimes become marginalised. Furthermore, as the examples we have provided suggest, some of those involved are pulled in different directions. We have reported, for example, tensions created for colleagues involved in the work of teaching school alliances who are increasingly spending their time negotiating the creation of multi-academy trusts. We also heard of the uncertainties being created for those working in local authorities by the increasing emphasis on teaching schools as the main source of support for school improvement. In addition, further complications have arisen where multi-academy trusts are developing their own in-house school improvement arrangements.

This evidence aligns with the findings of Wespieser, Sumner and Bernardinelli (2017) in suggesting that the level of collaborative maturity across the national school system in England varies considerably. Although there are likely to be a multitude of reasons for this, the evidence summarized here suggests that historical factors are particularly important.

In a similar way, establishing goals and agreements is influenced by geography. In this respect, urban contexts clearly have a natural advantage with regard to collaboration because movement between schools tends to be made easier because of shorter distances between schools and greater transport options. As we have noted, there also tend to be much greater numbers of teaching schools in these contexts. On the other hand, there are still vast areas of the country with limited access to support from teaching schools and NLEs. Together, these factors make the development of school-to-school support arrangements much more challenging in these areas.

Skilled leadership

Despite the problems, the evidence we have presented points to encouraging developments within the English education system regarding schools supporting one another. In particular, we have described what appears to be the emergence of a new generation of school leaders who are developing their skills as system leaders. In working with their colleagues – particularly those with longer experience of supporting other schools – they are enhancing their expertise and growing their professional confidence. It occurs to us that, in the future, these individuals can go on to have an even wider impact by supporting other school leaders in following the path that they have laid.

In moving forward, it is important to note that the positive examples of schools collaborating involved shared leadership. In particular, we saw examples of headteachers working together and with other stakeholders to create a new form of middle tier. In these contexts, local authority staff were seen to be taking on new roles, facilitating these new arrangements and bringing to the discussions their wider knowledge of the local education system. Commenting on such a 'leading from the middle' approach, we have argued that this can 'provide a valuable focus for school improvement; be a means for efficient and effective use of research evidence and analysis of data across schools; provide support so schools can respond coherently to multiple external reform demands; and be champions for families and students, making sure everybody gets a fair deal' (Hargreaves & Ainscow, 2015, p. 44).

Another interesting feature of these developments is that, as in the Challenge initiatives describe in earlier chapters, the emerging arrangements for school-to-school support show that the stakeholders themselves have taken the lead in mobilizing their resources and expertise. In so doing, they have established coordinating mechanisms for stakeholder cooperation that provide a formal means of accountability and scrutiny of their collaborative activity.

Of course, national policies do matter and are highly influential. In this respect, the examples we have presented have undoubtedly been facilitated by the overarching structural reforms to the school system in England, resulting in an ongoing period of repositioning amongst the various actors involved. Again, this might be considered symptomatic of a process of decentralization that allowed for the emergence of new structures operating at the middle tier that can help systems transition to being more self improving, as seen in the various Challenges.

Addressing new challenges

The evidence from this study suggests that some schools in England are still willing to support one another, even within a policy context that uses competition as the major driver for improvement. It seems, then, that coopetition is possible, although it is difficult to achieve and, as we have seen, often remains fragile as a result of policy contradictions that pull stakeholders in different directions.

It is also clear that some form of locally led coordination is needed in order to determine needs, engage stakeholders and broker partnerships. The successful examples of this that we have found suggest a possible way forward. They involve shared leadership from within schools, built on previous experience of schools collaborating that had helped to develop relationships and confidence in sharing responsibility. However, our research has also led to what was, for us, a surprise with respect to the significant roles played by local authority staff. In some contexts, their actions acted as barriers to local cooperation, whereas elsewhere they made crucial contributions to its success. This relates to the work of Louis (2013), who notes that district-managed networks in contexts of high accountability may generate high levels of fear and undermine efforts to shift responsibility for accountability to network leaders.

We next look more closely at what all of this involves. We draw on our more recent experiences of trying to foster place-based partnerships using the thinking developed as a result of the developments described in earlier chapters. These developments took place in two English local authorities that are facing particular challenges regarding equity. One of these is a city in the south of the country, and the other is a small urban district in the north.

The particular difficulties the two contexts faced relate to geographical and historical factors. In recent years, however, these have been compounded by pressures created by the greater emphasis on competition and choice introduced by the English national policy for education, not least the move toward school autonomy in the form of academies.

A divided city

The first area is Plymouth, a city in the southwest of England that is divided on socio-economic grounds: one side of the city has a high concentration of low-income families, and relatively better off families are mainly on the other side. The school system largely reflects this sense of social division, particularly at the secondary phase. Amongst the secondary schools are a few grammar schools that select their students at the age of 11 based on performance on tests. The other secondary schools usually reflect the local communities in which they are located. Consequently, students from relatively disadvantaged backgrounds tend to be concentrated in particular schools. As a result, the city has what can be seen as a 'pecking order' of schools, from some that are highly regarded through to others that are much less popular.

The city's education system has been a cause for concern for some years, particular its secondary schools where overall standards are relatively low, as determined by scores on GCSE examinations and OfSTED inspections. Since election of the Conservative-led coalition in 2010, a series of strategies have transformed the profile of its secondary schools. There are now maintained schools, academies, special schools, grammar schools, a studio school, a university technology school and special schools, plus a number of alternative provisions for excluded students. In this sense, the city is a relatively extreme version of the pattern that is developing across the country.

Following an event in 2011 at which the then regional schools commissioner spoke, most of the secondary schools rushed to convert to individual academy status. Gradually, these have been assimilated into various MATs, usually following a period of difficulty. As a result, the system is exceptionally fragmented, and a significant proportion of schools are underperforming. Most of these are concentrated in the area of the city that serve disadvantaged communities. A few are in crisis, and their future existence is uncertain. At the same time, in recent years student exclusions have increased, and the pupil referral unit, which is also an academy, appears to want to expand its numbers.

This apparent crisis led officials from the local authority and the office of the regional school commissioner to instigate a Plymouth Challenge in early 2018. One of us was invited to chair the first year of the project, which was launched at a conference of headteachers and senior staff from the various multi-academy trusts involved in the city. After this event, it was decided that the initial focus should be on the secondary sector, where there was most concern about levels of achievement.

Following the patterns of our earlier projects, particularly the Central South Wales Challenge, a strategy group made up of a group of headteachers was formed, which one of us chaired. Meetings of the group were also attended by senior officers from the regional school commissioner and one from the local authority.

The discussions, which were informed by the ideas presented in the earlier chapters of this book, led to the production of a discussion paper to be shared with other stakeholders. In the paper it was argued that the guiding vision would be of a high-performing system at the forefront of developments to find more effective ways of breaking the link between poverty, low attainment and limited life chances. Central to this vision was the idea of a self-improving system – driven by school leaders and involving practitioners at all levels – that takes collective responsibility for the quality of education across the city.

It was noted in the discussion paper that it would be vital to involve other stakeholders, including businesses, higher education institutes, health and social care professionals, sports and arts organisations, religious groups and the voluntary sector. Informed again by our earlier experiences, this was seen as a recognition that closing the gap in outcomes between those from more and less advantaged backgrounds would only happen when the experience of children outside as well as inside school changes.

Initial discussions within the strategy group emphasised that the project must 'go beyond talk.' It was also recognised that it should not replicate existing initiatives and coordinating arrangements, although these would be built on and, where necessary, strengthened. Rather, it would seek to make a distinctive contribution, adding value to the work that was already ongoing.

The overall focus would be on the challenges associated with equity across the city, recognising that whilst the system works well for many young people a significant proportion are left behind. Many of these young people were at risk of cycles of unemployment, with long-term scarring effects for them as individuals, their families and the wider community. In this respect, it was concluded that doing more of the same, however well, was unlikely to make a difference to this minority of young people.

The intention was to have a long-term sustainable impact on the way the education system does its business. However, the strategy group believed that it was necessary to focus on certain immediate concerns and opportunities to kick-start the process of change. Broadly stated, the initial focus of activities was concerned with ensuring that all young people in Plymouth would have:

- The best start in life, such that they grow up inspired to exceed expectations;
- Access to a suitably varied range of learning pathways; and
- The life skills they will need for the future, as well as the academic and technical qualifications to succeed.

128 New challenges

In addressing this agenda, the strategy group planned to take on the following roles:

- **Contextual analysis.** This would involve having the 'big picture' regarding the current situation in order to determine the barriers preventing the progress of some learners and the resources that can be mobilised to overcome these barriers. It therefore required an analysis of the best available evidence regarding the progress of young people through educational and training across the city.
- **Coordination.** This means ensuring that schools experiencing particular difficulties have access to effective forms of support. It would also involve finding effective ways of joining up services and provision to support and enhance the progress of the most vulnerable groups of learners, including those with special needs. In addition, it would involve providing support for the implementation of externally funded improvement initiatives so they have maximum reach and impact.
- **Collaboration.** The aim was to engage partners, within the city and beyond. in working together to move the system forward with pace. In so doing, it was seen to be essential to ensure that schools do not collude with one another to reinforce mediocrity and low expectations. Efforts would also be made to strengthen links with employers and higher education institutions to broaden curriculum opportunities and ensure that all young people are informed about career opportunities available in the labour market, as well as equipping them with high levels of resilience.
- **Promotion.** The Plymouth Challenge 'brand' opened new possibilities for the creation of an image of the city as an excellent place to live, learn and work. At the same time, there was a need to promote the city as a centre of creativity and innovation in relation to educational equity, such that it will be attractive to well-qualified, ambitious practitioners. With this in mind, efforts would also be made to ensure that there are high-quality opportunities for professional development.

This approach was based on ideas that had emerged from the initiatives described in the earlier chapters; in particular, the belief that education systems have untapped potential capacity for improving the achievement of all young people. The aim, therefore, was to mobilise this potential. This reinforced the argument that educational improvement is a social process that involves practitioners in learning from one another, from their students, and from others involved in the lives of the young people they teach. An engagement with evidence was seen as a powerful catalyst for making this happen.

In moving forward, the strategy group recognised that it would be important to adopt an inclusive approach that draws stakeholders together to shape, implement and evaluate any changes that are introduced. In this context, differences – amongst students, teachers, schools and communities – were seen to be a positive source of stimulation that could encourage new thinking and practices in order to engage hard to reach learners. However, this needed to be developed into a clear set of actions and structures that would galvanise the potential of the city.

As this process of planning developed, discussions were ongoing in the background with local authority and regional school commissioner staff regarding their roles. Some contact was also made with local politicians. These discussions involved a constant struggle to convince colleagues that, although they had important roles to play, decisions regarding the strategy had to be made by the group of headteachers. At the same time, many of the headteachers expressed informal doubts as to the degree of authority they had been given in a way that echoed our experiences in Central South Wales. Further doubts regarding all of this related to the availability of additional funding, which had been provided initially by the regional schools commissioner.

At a meeting in June 2018 of all the secondary heads, plus senior staff from the various multi-academy trusts, representatives of the strategy group presented the approach they were proposing for the following school year. It was evident that this was well received, and the meeting concluded with what appeared to be a consensus that the recommended strategy should be taken forward.

Writing to senior officers of the local authority and regional schools commissioner after this meeting, one of us argued:

> My main concern at present is to maintain the momentum in a context where there is so much potential for things to get side-lined. This is one of the roles that an 'outsider' can take on, providing frameworks to help busy people see possibilities for action and then jockeying things forward. It all sounds rather trivial but my experience is that it is crucial to the success of system-level change.
>
> There is also another vital issue in relation to the politics of all of this. That was partly why I sent you the account of the Welsh experience [an earlier version of Chapter 4 in this book]. As we explain there, the combination of well-intentioned interventions by national government and local authorities created barriers to the development of a school-led system. Independent actors can help with all of this by occupying the spaces between the various levels of decision making.
>
> Let me be clear, bottom-up efforts to promote improvement definitely require a political mandate (as well as additional resources, of course). However, if that mandate appears to involve efforts to impose strategies on practitioners, they will, sooner or later, walk away.

In a letter to all the partners in October 2018, a senior member of staff at the office of the regional schools commissioner wrote that Mel Ainscow had been brought in to share his expertise from past City Challenges, to help facilitate the strategic direction, and to provide a link to wider educational research conversations. Having noted that this had been instrumental to the progress that had been

130 New challenges

made, the letter went on to say that, in going forward, leadership now needed to be driven by individuals who are on the ground in the city each and every day, with an intimate understanding of the local context.

The letter argued that the regional schools commissioner and the local authority were now looking to move to a situation where the overall initiative was driven directly by secondary headteachers, with support from the Department for Education and the local authority. To support day-to-day leadership, it was recognised that capacity was a constraint, and they were trying to identify a local coordinator. In addition, the role of a member of staff of the regional schools commissioner officer would be reshaped to support this initiative. Their office would also ensure that it had a weekly presence in the city.

Gradually it became evident that momentum had been lost. The headteacher strategy group stopped meeting, with the initiative becoming another item on the agenda of occasional meetings of all the secondary heads in the city. Meanwhile, no progress was made on the appointment of a local coordinator. Some weeks later, two senior local politicians contacted us to voice their confusion as to what was happening and, in particular, what their roles were. Although they retained responsibility for the quality of educational arrangements made for all children in the city, they were concerned that they seemed to have no powers to intervene.

Further political activity was reported in the House of Commons Hansard on November 6, 2018,[2] where a local MP argued for additional funding to support the Plymouth Challenge, which he described as 'an example of collaborative action by several educational specialists that are working together to improve educational outcomes across Plymouth.' His main concern was lack of funding to support the initiative.

In reply, the Minister for School Standards is quoted as saying that he too supported the initiative. Commenting on the three strands in the proposed strategy, he took the opportunity to mention his much-quoted personal interest in phonics as 'an essential foundation for teaching children to read' and the importance of the role of multi-academy trusts. Having summarised existing funding already made available to Plymouth, he had nothing to say about the possibility of additional resources. However, he stated that he was keen to work with the MP and headteachers to explore how to support the system, 'allowing schools to be at the forefront of improvement while continuing to challenge standards.'

The sense of different players looking for somebody else to blame was reflected in an article that appeared in a local newspaper in December 2018.[3] In it, the Regional Director of Ofsted is quoted as saying that school and political leaders across the city needed to make more effort. He also suggested that 'parents also need to pull up their socks, with unacceptable numbers of children turning up for their first day at primary school unready to learn. Many are not even toilet-trained by the time they arrive in class.' He then urged parents to 'put your smartphones down and talk to your children.'

All of which provides vivid indications of the lack of an authentic political mandate of the sort we saw in the other initiatives we have described. Meanwhile, the Regional Ofsted Director concluded: 'I am concerned about Plymouth as a local authority and its secondary schools. Thousands of children are going to schools that aren't good enough.'

Collaboration can be a barrier

This second example arises from the work of an education commission set up in 2016 in Knowsley, a small metropolitan borough on the edge of Liverpool in the northwest of England. The local community is predominantly white, and there are high levels of relative poverty. Over many years the area and its education system has been subject to massive negative publicity. Indeed, a recent article in the *New York Times* described part of Knowsley as a striking example of the impact of the UK government's austerity policy.[4]

The education commission was established to drive improved educational outcomes across the borough, building on best practice and providing challenge where needed to address the underlying causes of educational underperformance in local schools. One of us was a member of the group, and the meetings were attended by senior officers from the local authority and the regional schools commissioner.

The council encouraged all local schools to take part, almost 50% of which are faith-based. In addition, a significant minority of schools are members of multi-academy trusts. At the outset, the leader of Knowsley council, said:

> We fully recognise that we need to do everything we can to help to improve educational performance. . . . We know that a different approach is needed. That's why we have invested £1m in order to identify the issues facing our schools and how these can be addressed.

He added:

> We know that our schools are becoming increasingly independent, so we can't do this alone and we can't force them to take part. We have established our Education Commission to bring in the people who can help us drive improvements in education, and I hope that schools across our Borough will take advantage of the opportunity to improve which we are creating for them.

Over a two-year period, the commission carried out a series of initiatives to support local stakeholders in working together to strengthen the education system. Although the impact of some of these was disappointing, they all helped to throw light on the barriers that have previously prevented the progress of some learners. At the same time, they identified what look to be promising pathways for the future.

It became clear that the local authority faces particular challenges in relation to strengthening its school system. These relate, in part, to factors in the wider community, not least of which were the high levels of economic disadvantage that exist. There were also historical factors that seemed to have created an atmosphere of low expectations that pervaded the school system, particularly at the secondary level. Here, the exodus of large numbers of young people to schools outside of the authority at the age of 11 has a major impact on what happened. If that was not enough of a problem, some of these students returned to Knowsley schools at a later stage as a result of their being excluded.

The long-term impact of local and national media attention on the low levels of performance in examinations, plus the legacy of well-intentioned external interventions that have not made a significant difference, had reinforced a feeling that little else can be done to bring about significant change. This was reflected in a tendency for colleagues within the schools to argue that 'we have tried that' to suggestions that are made. There was also evidence of a tendency to be inward looking, a feature that may have resulted from factors such as the size of the authority, the lack of effective regional leadership and negative reactions to a sense of being continually under the spotlight. In addition, some schools have a dependent relationship with the local authority, whilst at the same time blaming it for the lack of progress.

Nevertheless, many positive features could be built upon. In particular, there is a strong loyalty to the Knowsley 'brand,' as evidenced by the continued involvement of senior school staff in meetings and events organised by the local authority. There are also resources in the local area that can be mobilised, not least through the contributions of school governors. In addition, the continuing commitment to three long-established area collaboratives is evidence of a sense of 'togetherness,' particularly in the primary sector. The commission had some success in getting the three collaboratives to learn from one another. However, despite this progress, the work of these groupings appeared to remain largely at a superficial level, with schools taking part in their activities but unwilling to explore deeper forms of cooperation that would involve a much greater emphasis on mutual challenge. The programmes of the collaboratives also continued to take the form of rather traditional conferences and workshops that tend to have low leverage in respect to change.

Over two years the commission was able to encourage a more outward looking approach. This led to schools making links beyond the local authority with other schools and organisations that can support improvement efforts, including teaching schools, and through the MATS and faith-based partnerships.

Two developments proved to be particularly positive and upon which future strategies in Knowsley can be built. First, a school improvement project was instigated. Funding through the DfE's Strategic School Improvement Fund, referred to earlier in this chapter and ongoing at the time of writing, focused on 26 primary schools and four secondary schools. Based on the strategy used in City Challenge and Schools Challenge Cymru, these schools are designated as the Pathways to Success. That is to say, it is anticipated that their accelerated progress will generate a 'ripple effect' leading to sustainable improvements across the system.

The strategy is designed to make use of the best available knowledge and evidence to bring about rapid improvements, focusing specifically on raising standards in literacy across both the primary and secondary phases. This is expected to produce significant improvements in local schools, as reflected in teacher confidence and expertise; and improved performance in national tests and examinations, at both the primary and secondary levels. Three main approaches are being used to effect change: intensive work in classrooms to improve practice and its impact on learning in years 6, 7 and 8; improvements in teaching quality encouraged through powerful forms of professional development; and bespoke support provided by schools with demonstrable expertise and outstanding practitioners from within the local authority and beyond.

As with our earlier projects, support for these developments is provided by a team of highly experienced advisers with strong track records of success in challenging contexts. An emphasis on pace is being achieved through each school's Accelerated Improvement Board, which meets monthly in a similar way to those in the Welsh schools.

Second, a strategic partnership board made up of headteachers and local authority staff was established to add value to what each partner is already doing to provide an effective education for every child and young person in the area. The board's work is guided by a vision of a high-performing system at the forefront of developments to find more effective ways of breaking the link between poverty, low attainment and limited life chances. Once again, a central feature is the idea of a self-improving local system that is driven by school leaders and involving practitioners at all levels in taking collective responsibility for the quality of education across the authority. Importantly, the board has set out to involve all maintained schools, voluntary aided schools and academies with multi-academy trusts and teaching schools, mobilising support from both within and outside the authority. In this way it is attempting to create a new type of partnership-based middle tier that can coordinate an increasingly complex map of networks and support possibilities. There is also an intention to continue commissioning challenge-type advisers to support schools experiencing difficulties.

These two initiatives provide the basis of what could become a new, more powerful strategy for educational improvement. Together, they offer a more challenging strategy for supporting schools that will make better use of the available expertise, plus an overall mechanism for coordinating and monitoring the use of this strategy. However, as the period of the Knowsley commission came to an end in 2018, there was considerable uncertainty as to how such a strategy might be taken forward, not least because of the existence of a well-established collaborative culture that, perversely, tends to act as a barrier to change. This reminds us that whilst strengthened collaboration is essential to effective change, without other conditions it is insufficient as a strategy (Ainscow, 2016a). In this context, the sorts of interim arrangements that occurred in Central South Wales would be valuable in moving the system forward.

134 New challenges

Conclusion

Despite the worrying trends that have emerged from the recent reforms in England, we believe that greater autonomy for schools still makes sense, particularly if it provides space for practitioners to innovate. However, as we have seen, other policies based on competition between schools have sometimes prevented this from happening. Rather, they have led to a search for one-size-fits-all strategies for improving examination and test scores that can be imposed on teachers.

This leads us to recommend three actions to make school autonomy more effective in promoting equity within the English education system. First, there needs to be a fundamental rethink of national accountability systems, not least the ways in which student progress and the outcomes of school inspections are reported, so that there is a focus on a much broader range of outcomes. Second, more resources should be aimed at the improvement of teaching and learning through teachers' continuous professional development. This is a recognition that well-supported staff, who are encouraged to continue developing their practices, are in the best position to create inclusive learning experiences for students. And third, incentives need to be provided that encourage greater collaboration within schools and between schools, so successful practices are made available to more students. This emphasis on collaboration then needs to move beyond the school gate, with schools drawing on the energy and resources that exist within families and local communities.

Given the dangers associated with school isolation, some form of local coordination is necessary. Unfortunately, as we have explained, in many parts of England no one organization has the overall picture that would enable them to orchestrate more collaborative ways of working. With this in mind, we argue that reformed local authorities should be involved in monitoring and challenging schools, including academies, and headteachers and their colleagues should share responsibility for the overall leadership of improvement efforts. In this respect, it is encouraging to see the recent emergence in various parts of England of new forms of partnership arrangements (Gilbert, 2018).

All of this has significant implications for national policy-makers. To make use of the potential of autonomy and minimise the potential risks involved, they need to foster greater flexibility at the local level so practitioners have the space to analyze their particular circumstances and determine priorities accordingly. This means that policy-makers must recognize that the details of policy implementation are not amenable to central regulation. Rather, these should be dealt with by those who are close to and, therefore, in a better position to understand local contexts.

There is a crucial role here for governments. They must provide a strong sense of direction regarding the principles that are intended to steer locally led developments. Linked to this, there is a need to ensure that national accountability systems reflect these principles. This involves a recognition that, within education systems, 'what gets measured gets done' (Ainscow, 2005). So, for example, the education systems discussed in this book all collect far more statistical data on schools than ever before in order to determine their effectiveness. However, this narrow view of education has led to significant pressures, as those guiding national policies in many countries have become preoccupied with comparing their progress with that of other countries through systems such as the Programme for International Student Assessment (PISA).

This trend to measure learning through test scores is widely recognized as a double-edged sword precisely because it is such a potent lever for change (Ainscow, 2005). On one hand, data are required to monitor the progress of learners, evaluate the teaching and learning, review policies and processes, plan new initiatives, and so on. In these senses, data can, justifiably, be seen as the life-blood of educational decision making. On the other hand, if effectiveness is evaluated on the basis of narrow, even inappropriate, performance indicators, then the impact can be deeply damaging. While appearing to promote accountability and transparency, data can in practice be used to conceal more than it reveals; invite misinterpretations; and, worst of all, have a perverse effect on the behaviour of professionals to teach to the test, such that their efforts to include vulnerable children are not valued and recognized by schools and policy-makers.

The challenge, therefore, is to focus on a broader range of data, where progress is determined not just in terms of scores on learning outcomes, but where information on progress regarding equity is incorporated into the analysis. This suggests that care needs to be exercised in deciding what evidence is collected and, indeed, how it is analysed and used. Put simply, we need to 'measure what we value' rather than, as is so often the case, 'valuing what we can measure.'

Notes

1 http://www.gmlp.org.uk/
2 https://hansard.parliament.uk/commons/2018-11-06/debates/6102EAD2-3776-4176-A54D-93CB3FB69031/PlymouthChallengeForSchools
3 https://www.plymouthherald.co.uk/news/plymouth-news/ofsted-boss-raises-serious-concerns-2294834
4 https://www.nytimes.com/2018/05/28/world/europe/uk-austerity-poverty.html

7

ADDRESSING BARRIERS TO CHANGE

This book does not provide a toolkit of techniques for promoting educational change that can be moved from place to place. Rather, it describes and explains a way of thinking that should be used flexibly in response to local circumstances. We argue, too, that this approach has the potential to create the conditions within which researchers can contribute directly to system change.

Putting ideas from research into such developments, however, remains difficult because of certain sorts of contextual barriers. Broadly stated, these relate to *social factors*, including the extent to which relationships exist that encourage sharing expertise though mutual support and challenge; *political factors*, due to the impact of the attitudes and preferences of key partners; and *cultural factors*, related to local traditions and the expectations of those involved concerning what is possible. It is important to note, too, that these different types of barrier interconnect.

In this chapter we draw on a series of further studies that have involved collaboration with networks of schools to consider how these barriers can be addressed. This leads us to move closer to the action in order to consider ways of changing practices, schools and leadership. In so doing, we suggest a strategic model that sets out to clarify the positions and relationships between practitioners and policy-makers on one hand, and researchers wishing to adopt an engaging stance on the other. We begin, however, by describing the sorts of barriers we have experienced.

Making sense of the barriers

A common feature of the various large-scale initiatives we describe in the earlier chapters is the emphasis that they place on bottom-up leadership within a context of top-down political mandate. As we have seen, evidence from research was used to inform these developments to varied degrees. However, we found that injecting ideas from research into such developments is sometimes difficult because of certain forms of interconnected barriers. In what follows, we reflect on our involvement in the projects further in order to make sense of these barriers, some of which draw attention to the role of what is sometimes called 'the middle tier,' that is, the structures that bridge between schools and the central government.

Social factors

The education systems we have described have varied capacities for change. In particular, some have low levels of social capital: that is, few social networks and the norms of reciprocity and trustworthiness that arise from them. In reflecting on his work with schools serving disadvantaged communities in the United States, Payne (2008) argues that contexts characterised by low levels of social capital have difficulty making use of additional financial resources. They also are likely to reject expertise coming from elsewhere.

The contexts we have mentioned had a varied capacity in this respect. We have described, for example, our involvement in contexts that are characterised by relatively high levels of cooperation. However, this can also create social barriers, as we found in Wales, where its tightly knit educational community can be both supportive and, at the same time, restrictive. So much so, that it can sometimes lead to a reluctance amongst practitioners to put their ideas forward. We have also found that a tightly knit community may make it difficult for those within it to break with certain traditions or challenge existing norms without their actions being seen, at least in part, as a criticism or rejection of that community. We saw something similar in Knowsley, where a long history of collaboration amongst schools sometimes seemed to limit innovation.

Thinking further about these experiences, it strikes us, too, that 'size matters.' To take another example, one of us contributed to planning in a very small rural district that had concerns about poor standards in the schools. From the point of view of an outsider with lots of urban experience, the closeness of the links between headteachers in this community seemed to be a positive feature in terms of the encouragement of greater collaboration.

In line with the thinking developed in this book, we encouraged a restructuring that would enable existing good practices within local schools to be made available to more students and encourage joint practice development. This was to be achieved through strengthening various forms of cooperation between the schools. With this in mind, we consulted with all the heads within the authority. As a result, a new momentum for change quickly emerged in the primary sector, where a group of five relatively successful headteachers took the initiative in moving things forward.

In discussing their roles, these heads commented on the social complexities they faced in getting colleagues to cooperate. In particular, they explained the

138 Addressing barriers to change

implications of the fact that amongst schools in a small community 'everybody knows one another.' They commented, too, that relationships were usually warm and cordial, something that we certainly experienced. However, it was also apparent that this closeness between colleagues had the potential to create barriers to genuine collaboration between schools. One headteacher summed this when she said, 'we don't bare our souls around here.' In other words, if you have a problem in your school, you keep it to yourself. Clearly, such a social climate makes it difficult for colleagues to support one another. It also means that the external researcher who is there to support and advise faces barriers in trying to understand these subtle dynamics, the local causality of the local school system.

To us, there also seems to be something important about the size of the national systems in which we have been working. We have mentioned the tightness of certain education communities and the effect this can have. In Scotland and Wales, key players often know each other, and many players wear 'several hats,' playing a range of roles. This can be an advantage when there is a shared vision and a collective will to pursue a joint agenda. However, without these features, differences of opinion can lead to horse trading and negotiation, which often leads to fudged outcomes that lack the radical action required to move a system forward. At best this can lead to a regression to the mean that maintains the status quo and, at worst, to deliberately undermining developments that have been made. For example, one senior local authority officer committed to raising expectations amongst children was astonished at the behaviour of a union representative who claimed that it was impossible to raise the outcomes for young people and that you just had to 'drive around the streets to see this.' Challenging such deeply held assumptions is difficult, and it seems to us that they can be more easily reinforced and amplified in smaller jurisdictions.

An implication of all of this is that system change strategies have to include persistent efforts to engage stakeholders. This was why it was so helpful in the English and Welsh Challenge programmes that ministers and other senior government officials carried out school visits. Apart from signalling the importance of the programmes from the point of view of the participating schools, they were also opportunities to inform local media of the Challenge programme. Visits usually included a short tour of the school, orchestrated by the headteacher, discussions with groups of students and meetings with parents. Finally, there was a meeting with senior representatives of the local authority, including politicians, to share ideas about how the Challenge should proceed.

Political factors

The most striking evidence of the political nature of large-scale system change projects occurred in two of the countries following national elections. As we explained in earlier chapters, this led to new ministers being appointed and, as a result, the Challenge projects losing much of their political mandate. The projects did continue, however, although with less power to make things happen. Having said that, in the case of the Greater Manchester Challenge (see Chapter 6), we have presented more recent empirical evidence of the continuing impact of its legacy seven years later, most strikingly in terms of partnerships and networks, and system level coordination. We have anecdotal evidence, too, of a similar legacy in London.

The three national Challenge programmes emerged during an unprecedented period of change within their education systems, not least in terms of decision making regarding education policy. The ways in which decisions were made regarding changes varied across the three countries. As we have noted, England was in the process of giving schools much greater autonomy, not least regarding the use of financial resources and the appointment of staff members. This was also leading to a much greater role for headteachers as system leaders, working together to coordinate collaborative improvement efforts. In this context, the role of the local authority in relation to the management of the school system was massively reduced and, as explained in Chapter 6, tensions have emerged between the new structures that are being developed.

Meanwhile, Wales and Scotland have both continued in a much more centralized way, with decisions mainly shared between the national government and local authority levels, albeit with stated aspirations to empower headteachers. However, as we have documented, there is evidence of continuing tensions between these two levels. All of this provides further difficulties for researchers as they navigate the system, trying to position themselves and advise on policy developments.

During the setting up phases of the three national Challenge programmes, much use was made by government officials of the terms 'partnership' and 'collaboration' in describing what was to happen. We sensed that for some local authority colleagues this was a source of irritation because the decisions to have the initiatives were largely imposed by national government in what were clearly seen as processes of intervention in areas of concern. Another source of irritation for some local authority colleagues is the extent to which the agendas and action were perceived to be driven by political rather than educational imperatives. So, for example, at times this involved ministers using the Challenge programmes to reaffirm their own status and power within their systems, at the expense of professional voices.

Further factors behind these tensions were to do with different views about the priorities and time scales for change, with government officials often being largely concerned to achieve a rapid impact on student progress, as measured by test and examination results. This, in turn, influenced decision making regarding setting targets, which often seemed to be a preoccupation of civil servants, and the allocation of resources to support change efforts. Meanwhile, our own major preoccupation tended to be with wider, longer-term goals and sustainable change.

140 Addressing barriers to change

The pressures on civil servants who become involved in field-based improvement projects is also worth noting. Inevitably their priority is to deliver positive outcomes for their minister, within time scales influenced by the pattern of national elections. In these contexts, we also have to be conscious that civil servants are competing with one another for promotion within a hierarchical structure.

Further tensions were apparent regarding what needed to happen to improve these education systems; put simply, there was a difference between those who believed in locally led developments and others who continued to adopt a centralizing perspective. For example, the latter view was starkly expressed in an email note sent to colleagues within the DfES in London during the City Challenge period, which stated that, as far as improving attainment amongst disadvantaged students was concerned, 'the strategy must be exactly the same, whether it is in Plymouth (*in the southwest of England*), or in Sunderland (*in the far northeast*).' Meanwhile, in Scotland we saw how frustration amongst government officials about lack of early pace led them to seek 'what works' strategies that could be imposed across the education system.

This instinct to direct from the centre kept surfacing at meetings of challenge advisers, when civil servant colleagues took opportunities to brief the groups on the latest proposals from central government. In general, the teams found these inputs helpful in the sense that they made them feel ahead of the game regarding policy decisions. However, our concern was that, too often, they gave the wrong message in respect to the theory of change we had adopted, with its emphasis on encouraging the development of locally relevant solutions.

A striking example of this that created a significant distraction was in Greater Manchester as a result of the publication of a White Paper about the reform of the national education system. The civil servant who led on this initiative as far as primary schools was concerned became particularly dogged in her efforts to impose a centrally determined strategy on the schools. With this in mind, for some months she guided the agenda of the team of primary advisers in a direction that, from our point of view, represented a significant deviation from the rationale we had developed together. During this phase, our own involvement in decision making was clearly marginalized.

The history of large-scale, heavily funded improvement projects is that, even when they are seen to be initially successful, the impact gradually fades once the additional resources are taken away (Ainscow, 2015). Sustainability is, therefore, a major concern. One way of addressing this problem is to strengthen the so-called middle tier – the administrative arrangements intended to coordinate the development of education provision within a local area. In Wales, for example, this means that the 22 local authorities are grouped together in four regional consortia to support school improvement efforts. As we have explained, Scotland, with its 32 local authorities and six regional improvement collaboratives, is moving in a similar direction. In England, the recently introduced regional schools commissioners can be seen as taking a similar coordination role, although, as we have explained, considerable uncertainties remain regarding their roles and status in relation to other players.

There are, however, potential barriers to making such regional partnerships work, including the large geographical areas that they sometimes cover and the potential conflicts amongst partners regarding decision making regarding priorities and use of resources. This might be seen as leading to an illusion of cooperation rather than to meaningful work that can impact schools, classrooms and ultimately pupils.

As we have seen, within national systems that continue to emphasise top-down accountability, the responses of local authorities can also, at times, act as a barrier to school-level innovation. For example, one very experienced headteacher in Wales, appointed to turn around a school in difficulty, talked about local authority officers frequently commenting negatively regarding the ways he deals with minor administrative matters.

Cultural factors

The concept of organisational culture is complex and difficult to define, particularly when we are thinking about its role with regard to whole education system reform. Schein (1985) suggests that it is about the deeper levels of basic assumptions and beliefs that are shared by members of an organisation, operating unconsciously to define an organisation's view of itself and its environment. This manifests itself in norms that suggest to people what they should do and how. In a similar way, Hargreaves (1995) argues that cultures can be seen as having a reality-defining function, enabling those within an organisation to make sense of themselves, their actions and their environment. A current reality-defining function of culture, he suggests, is often a problem-solving function inherited from the past. In this way, today's cultural form created to solve an emergent problem often becomes tomorrow's taken-for-granted recipe for dealing with matters shorn of their novelty. Hargreaves concludes that by examining the reality-defining aspects of a culture it should be possible to gain an understanding of the routines the organisation has developed in response to the tasks it faces.

An inevitable historical dimension is always present when, as outsiders, we become involved in a new context. These are most evident in our accounts of Scotland and Wales, but we can assume that they are there in any context. As both Hargreaves and Schein imply, the problem is that they may not be articulated because they are largely taken for granted by those involved. Making sense of it from an outsider perspective is, therefore, a major problem.

An illustrative example of this in relation to Scotland is provided by Walter Humes of the University of Stirling, who draws on what Bantock calls 'the parochialism of the present', a condition that focuses on current preoccupations alone and fails to consider what might be learned from past experience (Humes, 2019). Focusing on the major curriculum changes being introduced in Scotland, Humes argues that if those responsible for directing the reform had paid more

142 Addressing barriers to change

attention to the lessons of history, things might have been different. Previous reforms, he suggests, although more modest in scale, had all encountered difficulties and had taken longer to implement than had been hoped. Moreover, these reforms had been centrally directed, with limited scope for teacher involvement. Quoting Lawrence Stenhouse, Humes explains that there can be no successful curriculum development without teacher development.

Humes goes on to explain how historical factors can influence reactions of stakeholders – teachers, school leaders and local administrators – to proposals for change of the sort we have described. In so doing, he suggests that expressing views that may not accord with official policy can carry significant risks. In some schools and local authorities, he argues, this may lead to a climate of fear. And, of course, such feelings may be well below the service, influencing what happens in subtle ways.

Such arguments represent a significant cause for concern as we try to make sense of how cultural factors, shaped by earlier experiences, have influenced what happened within the Challenge programmes we have described. We recall, for example, the story in Chapter 4 of headteachers at the launch of the Central South Wales Challenge who, having expressed their enthusiasm for the rationale presented, commented that they had met in the same conference centre on a number of earlier occasions to hear about what seemed like equally impressive plans, none of which had led to significant change.

In all three countries, the efforts to inject greater pace into the improvement of schools drew attention to the untapped potential that exists within schools. To varying degrees, the Challenge programmes were successful in mobilising this potential. However, our accounts of what happened have also thrown light on cultural factors that have limited the impact of previous efforts to mobilise this potential. Our monitoring suggests that these barriers often relate to existing ways of working that, although well intended, consume time and resources and delay action in the field. We noted earlier how one secondary headteacher in Wales commented that this like trying to drive more quickly down a road with speed bumps every few yards.

As we have seen, the experience of the various programmes suggests that many of the 'bumps' relate to taken-for-granted assumptions as to what is possible. They include, for example, the overemphasis placed by local authorities on putting schools, particularly those facing challenging circumstances, under unnecessary pressure. This tends to demoralise the key agents of change, i.e., the staff in the schools. It can also lead to considerable time being wasted debating and disputing plans and targets. Target setting can be helpful, but our experience is that it is unlikely to lead to sustainable change without powerful support strategies.

Linked to this, we report in earlier chapters how actions by local authority staff limited the freedom of school leaders to take responsibility for their own improvement. In particular, we found that there were often what seemed to be multiple reporting arrangements, such that school leaders were spending too much time preparing reports for different audiences, attending various review and scrutiny meetings, and being given different (and at times conflicting) advice on the improvements required and how they can be implemented. This can lead to a sense of dependency on outsiders to lead improvement efforts rather than those in schools taking responsibility and being accountable for improved outcomes. In such situations, school leaders can feel undermined and disempowered. As a result, they tend to make poor decisions and find it more difficult to prioritise their improvement strategies.

In addressing these barriers, efforts are needed to clarify the respective roles of local authorities. Specifically, this requires local authority staff to know, trust and support their schools, alongside providing appropriate encouragement to improve. These changes in roles and responsibilities are likely to be particularly challenging during periods of transition, whilst more locally led improvement strategies are developing, but they are a matter of urgency in order that rapid progress can be achieved. The story of developments in Central South Wales in Chapter 4 and the account of schools working together to pool their Pupil Equity Funding in Scotland in order to work with a university are particularly helpful in this respect. However, in Chapter 5 we described how local authorities can support developments by brokering and facilitating improvement efforts. What works would seem to depend on local capacity and leadership rather than on simplistic notions of school or local authority-led change.

Within these contexts are barriers related to the uncertainly that exists within governments regarding the stance needed to support the development of locally driven collaborative improvement. This was particularly apparent in Scotland and Wales, with their more centralised approach to policy development. We argue that using the power of collaboration as a means of achieving both excellence and equity in schools requires an approach to national policy implementation that fosters greater flexibility at the local level. Practitioners must have the space to analyse their particular circumstances and determine priorities accordingly. This means that policy-makers must understand that the details of policy implementation are not amenable to central regulation. Rather, these have to be dealt with by those who are close to and, therefore, in a better position to understand local contexts. This implies a renegotiation of how strategic decisions are made.

Influencing decision making

The examples we provide in this book illustrate the sorts of struggles regarding decision making that occur when a politically high-profile system improvement intervention is attempted, particularly if it is instigated from outside. They also show how researchers can, sometimes at least, help local stakeholders resolve the arguments that are generated. This involves them using their ambiguous positions and knowledge of research to frame debates and suggest ways of resolving disputes. As we have seen, this is sensitive work that leads researchers to face

144 Addressing barriers to change

many dilemmas that usually have to be addressed immediately when they occur in the field.

Whilst the details of what this involves vary from place to place, certain patterns are evident. Broadly stated, they involve interruptions to the normal ways in which decisions are made. As a result, they are likely to disturb existing relationships amongst national policy-makers and civil servants, local authority politicians and administrators, and senior staff within schools. It should be noted that this can lead to difficulties that cut across the distinctions we have made between social, political and cultural barriers.

An important interruption in all the programmes has involved attempts to create new structures to develop new strategies and innovations 'outside' the confines of existing organisations, and their associated cultural norms. These structures often take the form of a temporary additional layer between national/local administrations and schools. As the title implies, the structures are not intended to be permanent; rather, they are interim arrangements to get things moving. However, in some instances they have led to the establishment of longer-term structures depending on their relevance in the new system they help emerge from the old.

In the case of City Challenge, the new structure involved the teams of advisers working closely with small groups of assigned civil servants. In both London and Greater Manchester, this led to tensions with local authority staff that had to be resolved. In these contexts, the Chief Advisers had key negotiation roles, which was helped by the mandate they were given by their respective ministers. Gradually these arrangements were replaced by headteacher-led groups, both of which are still in operation some eight years later, albeit in new forms. A sense of this is provided by the study of school-to-school support in Chapter 6, where progress in one of the City Challenge areas is contrasted with parts of the country that had not participated in the project. At the same time, we have shown how contradictory policy initiatives are creating new barriers to such developments.

In a similar way, the coordination of Schools Challenge Cymru was delegated to a team of advisers and champions, again with support from a dedicated group of civil servants. During the first two years of the programme this arrangement had a strong mandate from the minister, who occasionally joined meetings of the group. In the third year, however, all of this faded as a new minister was seen to take much less interest. At the same time, senior staff of the regional consortia, who, to varying degrees, had felt marginalized during the first two years, re-established their influence under the overall headline of 'learning lessons from Schools Challenge Cymru.' Meanwhile, as the system slipped back into its traditional ways of doing business, tensions between the central government and local authorities regarding control of the educational improvement agenda re-emerged. As we have highlighted, this was also a potential risk for those involved in the Scottish Attainment Challenge.

In the context of Scotland, no temporary structure was developed initially, either nationally or at the local level. Rather, during phase one of the Attainment

Challenge, key decisions were concentrated with officers of the central government and the improvement agency in ways that appeared to sometimes leave other stakeholders feeling marginalized and, therefore, largely unenthusiastic about what was, undoubtedly, a well-resourced national improvement effort. More recent phases, plus the introduction of the Pupil Equity Fund, has loosened up the system a little. Furthermore, recent moves to create regional improvement collaboratives open up few possibilities to move forward in a more delegated way. However, this would represent a radical change to an overall approach that has deep cultural roots, and it will require senior leaders to adopt new leadership behaviours and practices that move beyond relying on power and positionality to manage change.

Moving on to the other initiatives we have described, we once again see creation of temporary structures, bringing policy and strategy much nearer to the action going on in the field. The Central South Wales Challenge was the most developed of these projects. Sadly, it is also illustrative of how effective arrangements can quickly fade if they are seen to be too challenging of the status quo.

For us, the key factor in making progress toward the creation of a self-improving system in Central South Wales was establishment of the headteacher strategy group. Working with this group on a regular basis, our main task was to use evidence from elsewhere to stimulate their strategic thinking. At the same time, we had a crucial role in negotiating the space for them to make decisions, something that frequently disturbed the status quo. This involved us in endless discussions with national and local politicians and administrators to assure them that what was happening was in line with their overall policy aspirations. Despite the progress made over the four-year period, more recently we saw the abolition of the headteachers strategy group, leaving a vacuum that has now been filled by local authority and consortium staff, who mainly share a rather traditional view of how education systems can be helped to improve.

We see a similar pattern of development in our account of developments in Plymouth in Chapter 6, during a period of less than a year. There, once again, a headteacher strategy group was formed. One of us attended all of its meetings to advise on possible ways forward. In this context, much use was made of ideas and approaches used in Central South Wales. The group designed what was, from our point of view, a splendid strategy, which was well received by all of the heads in the authority, including senior representatives of the various multi-academy trusts involved. Unfortunately, after a relatively short period, actions by local and regional officers – or, more accurately, no actions – led to momentum quickly disappearing.

Meanwhile, as we also explain in Chapter 6, developments in Knowsley involved a rather different approach to the creation of a temporary structure: the establishment for two years of an education commission, set up by the local authority to instigate a new impetus for improvement. However, changes of key local staff meant that the commission struggled to stay as a priority on the authority's overall education agenda. As a result, the sustainability of its actions

146 Addressing barriers to change

remains uncertain, not least because of the existence of a highly collaborative local culture that, perversely, tends to act as a barrier to change.

One way of explaining all of this is to see it in terms of what has been called the maintenance/development dilemma (Hopkins et al., 1994). This arises because, in times of significant changes, education systems, like other social organisations, face a dilemma: they cannot remain as they now are if they are to respond to new challenges but at the same time they also need to maintain some continuity between their present and their previous practices. As we have seen, sooner or later the need for education systems to ensure maintenance means that initiatives for change are likely to be drawn back, particularly if they are seen to disrupt what exists in ways that challenge the status quo.

That said, there remain spaces where practitioners can work together in developing more effective practices, even in the most centralised education systems (Constantinou & Ainscow, 2018). This is part of the explanation of why changing education systems can be so difficult. As we have argued, as far as education is concerned, policy is made at all levels, not least at the level of schools.

In these contexts, we have found ourselves struggling to define an appropriate stance when working as 'engaged researchers.' Our ideal position is one that gets us 'at the table' when important decisions are being made, so we are able to make contributions that challenge taken-for-granted assumptions as to what is possible. However, this can be a difficult stance to maintain. It leads to two potential risks: one is that of colluding with ideas that feel uncomfortable in order to continue being involved; the other is to take a strong position that may lead to some form of exclusion from the decision-making process. In this sense, managing these tensions and dilemmas requires us, as researchers, to draw on the qualities of reticulists (see Chapter 1).

Keeping these difficulties in mind, we next describe and analyse some further experiences of working with colleagues in the field, using research to encourage locally led improvement initiatives. These experiences, which took us much closer to action at the level of schools, led us to develop and refine a strategic model that is intended to help researchers who get involved in such activities. Central to the model are processes of collaborative inquiry, carried out by practitioners with support from university-based researchers. As we explain, this creates further dilemmas as a result of the coming together of the different purposes of practitioners and researchers.

Collaborative inquiry

The strategic model we describe was developed through a series of change projects carried out since the 1990s. Whilst each of these had its own context and agenda for change, the common feature was a process of collaborative inquiry involving networks of schools supported by teams of academic researchers and guided by a broad commitment to equity. Significantly, the studies were conducted within policy contexts that did not appeared to be conducive to school collaboration. In particular, research has pointed to the challenges involved when introducing such approaches within national policy contexts that emphasise increased school autonomy, competition between schools and accountability as central strategies for improving schools (e.g., Ingram, Louis & Schroeder, 2004; Gallimore, Ermeling, Saunders & Goldenberg, 2009).

The projects illustrate the complexities involved when researchers attempt to create collaborative partnerships that cross borders between actors who have different professional experiences and ways of seeing the world. At the same time, they show how such an involvement can provide privileged access to information regarding the way decisions are made within an education system and the pressures that impact these decisions.

We refer to the overall approach used in the projects as collaborative inquiry. This can be seen as being part of a 'family' of approaches within the overall tradition of action research (Reason & Bradbury, 2001) that has developed out of the action research tradition of Kurt Lewin (1946) and the work other academics over many years (e.g., Cochran-Smith & Lytle, 2009; Elliott, 1991; Kemmis & McTaggart, 1988; Schön, 1983; Stenhouse,1975). It emphasises an engagement in inquiry to inform and improve practice, and intentionally combines knowing and doing to achieve positive social change (Kemmis, 2010).

What distinguishes this approach from more traditional research is that it involves a commitment to forms of inquiry that have the following characteristics:

- *An engagement with the views of different stakeholders*, in the belief that bringing together the expertise of practitioners (and, sometimes, students) and academic researchers can challenge taken-for-granted assumptions, not least in respect to vulnerable groups of learners, stimulate new thinking and encourage experimentation with new ways of working (Ainscow, Dyson, Goldrick, & West, 2012a; Deppeler, 2013; Messiou & Ainscow, 2015).
- *The improvement of practice within schools* through the sharing of expertise and forms of collaborative action that stimulate efforts to find more effective ways of engaging students who are seen to be 'hard-to-reach' (Harris et al., 2017; Lo, Yan, & Pakey, 2005; Messiou, 2018).
- *Collaboration and networking within and across classrooms, schools and systems* to move expertise around within education systems (Ainscow, 2015; Muijs, West & Ainscow, 2010; Chapman et al., 2016; Louis & Lee, 2016; Rincón-Gallardo & Fullan, 2016).
- *The development of local capacity for sustaining change through linking the efforts of schools to wider resources.* This requires the use of more holistic strategies that seek to connect schools, communities and external political and economic institutions (e.g., Kerr, Dyson & Raffo, 2014; Chapman, 2013; Lipman, 2004).
- *The simultaneous pursuit of technical, practical and emancipatory understandings of practice.* Inquiry is a reflective process that explores both the ends and means of educational practices. It requires those involved to not only consider how to achieve technical improvement in their teaching but also to

148 Addressing barriers to change

understand different interpretations of what constitutes 'education' in order to generate mutual understanding and collaborative action. It also requires them to emancipate themselves, and others, from seemingly 'natural' constraints. Each interest draws on a distinct type of knowledge about the social world, and the pursuit of each defines the nature of the inquiry process (Hadfield, 2012).

The development of this approach began with our involvement in the Improving the Quality of Education for All (IQEA) project in the early 1990s. Initially it involved researchers at the University of Cambridge working with schools in and around London. Subsequently, IQEA led to developments in other parts of the world (see Ainscow, 1999; Clarke et al., 2006; Hopkins, 2007; Hopkins et al., 1994, and West & Ainscow, 2010, for more detailed accounts of some of these projects). All of these activities involved teams of researchers working in partnership with colleagues from schools to identify ways the learning of all members of the school community – students, parents and staff – could be enhanced.

Work with schools in the IQEA projects was based on a contract that attempted to define the parameters for our involvement, and the obligations those involved owed to one another. It emphasised that all staff be consulted; that an in-school team of coordinators be appointed to carry the work forward; that a critical mass of staff were to be actively involved; and that sufficient time would be made available for necessary classroom and staff development activities. Meanwhile, we committed ourselves to supporting the school's developments, usually for one year. Often the arrangement continued, however, and, in some instances, we were involved for periods as long as seven years. We provided training for the school coordinators, made regular school visits and contributed to school-based staff development activities. In addition, we attempted to work with the schools in recording and analysing their experiences in a way that also provided data relevant to our own ongoing research agendas.

As a result of our engagements with schools involved in the IQEA project, we evolved a style of collaboration that we referred to as 'working with, rather than working on' (Ainscow & Southworth, 1996). This phrase attempted to sum up an approach that deliberately allowed each project school considerable autonomy to determine its own priorities for development and, indeed, its methods for achieving these priorities. In attempting to work in this way, we found ourselves confronted with staggering complexity, and by a bewildering array of policy and strategy options. It was our belief that only through a regular engagement with these complexities could a greater understanding of school change be achieved.

These experiences also shaped our ideas regarding what needs to happen for a school to make progress in relation to equity. This led us to formulate a series of 'organisational conditions' – distributed leadership, high levels of staff and student involvement, joint planning, a commitment to inquiry and so on – that promote collaboration and problem solving amongst staff, and that, therefore, produce more inclusive responses to diversity (Hopkins, Ainscow & West, 1994).

Changing practices

Lessons that emerged from IQEA influenced the design of another project, *Understanding and Developing Inclusive Practices in Schools*. This initiative, which took the form of a collaborative action research study, occurred between 2000 and 2004, and involved 25 urban schools in three local education authorities and three partner universities (i.e., Canterbury Christ Church, Manchester and Newcastle). It was funded by the Economic and Social Research Council (ESRC) as part of its Teaching and Learning research programme.

In designing the study, we saw inclusion as a principle and set of practices about which something was already known. Moreover, as established authors and researchers in the field, we had played our part in generating this prior knowledge. From our own work and from others in this field, we also knew that acceptance of the values and practices of inclusion were frequently resisted by practitioners who saw themselves as having other priorities and as working within constraints that made inclusive practice impossible. This was particularly the case within the then English policy context, where a relentless focus on 'raising standards' was being imposed on schools by the Labour Government.

We therefore needed a means of releasing practitioners from the constraints of national policy and enabling them to change their value positions and assumptions. We saw the use of research evidence as offering this means. Furthermore, we made an assumption that when practitioners were confronted by evidence about their practices they would – with appropriate encouragement from their critical friends – begin to recognise the noninclusive elements of those practices and would find ways of making them more inclusive. Fortunately, this is what most often happened, as reported in a series of publications (Ainscow, Booth & Dyson 2004, 2006; Dyson, Gallannaugh & Millward, 2003; Howes et al., 2004, 2005).

Within the network schools, we saw how the use of evidence to study teaching can help to foster the development of more inclusive teaching. Specifically, it can help create space for reappraisal and rethinking by interrupting existing discourses, and by focusing attention on overlooked possibilities for moving practice forward. Particularly powerful techniques in this respect involved the use of mutual observation, sometimes through video recordings, and evidence collected from students about teaching and learning arrangements within a school. Under certain conditions, these approaches provide *interruptions* that help to make the familiar unfamiliar in ways that stimulate self-questioning, creativity and action. In so doing, they can sometimes lead to a reframing of perceived problems that, in turn, draws the teacher's attention to overlooked possibilities for addressing barriers to participation and learning.

In almost all of the schools in the study, there was strong evidence that attempts to foster inclusive practices were associated with significant improvements in terms of the presence, participation and achievement of students. At the same time, involvement encouraged a broadening in the concept of outcomes

150 Addressing barriers to change

beyond the confines of the so-called standards agenda. There was also evidence that a culture of critical reflection had developed in many of the schools. It was noted, for example, that during the course of school-to-school visits questions from other teachers helped to foster a commitment to self-questioning. As a result, many teachers in the schools became more enthusiastic and confident in the value of asking questions about outcomes, and in being actively involved in working out how their school can be organised better with respect of their learning and the learning of their students.

The research suggested that some elements of the then national reform agenda, with its emphasis on raising narrowly defined standards, were exacerbating difficulties through the effects of the accountability culture and fragmentation caused by competing priorities. Nevertheless, many of the teachers involved talked in terms of the values that sustained their commitment to change in this context. For them, increasing the learning and participation of all learners was seen to require more wide-ranging and ambitious change. In these contexts, the national policy agenda's emphasis on the attainment of *all* learners did appear to open possibilities for moving schools in a more inclusive direction.

The involvement of so many partners in the study presented many organisational challenges. In particular, there was a need to ensure that the work in the 25 schools, in three different parts of the country, followed a similar pattern, whilst at the same time allowing discretion in order to relate activities to local circumstances. Similarly, we needed to have a means by which the three university teams generated data in relation to a common research agenda.

With these challenges in mind, a strategic model was designed. Its purpose was to clarify the positions and relationships within the partnerships we were establishing between practitioners and local policy-makers on one hand and researchers on the other (see Figure 7.1). We saw these as involving two interlinked strands of research carried out by practitioners and researchers.

The first of these strands was driven by the agendas of the partner schools. It set out to use existing knowledge within these contexts, supplemented by further research evidence, as the means of fostering developments in the field. The second strand attempted to scrutinise these developments in order to address the overall agenda of the network, using existing theory and previous research as a basis for pursuing deeper understandings. Between the two strands was a set of 'boundaries' that had to be crossed to synchronise the two driving agendas.

Throughout the study, we learned much about the difficulties that can occur as researchers attempt to negotiate these boundaries with practitioners. However, the major omission in our initial model was not detail about the practicalities of managing researcher-practitioner relationships but a failure to think through the nature of the knowledge each possessed and the ways in which such knowledge might be shared and used by each group. The matter was particularly confused because we encouraged practitioners to undertake their own research, while we as researchers sometimes involved ourselves in discussions about the detail of practice and policy.

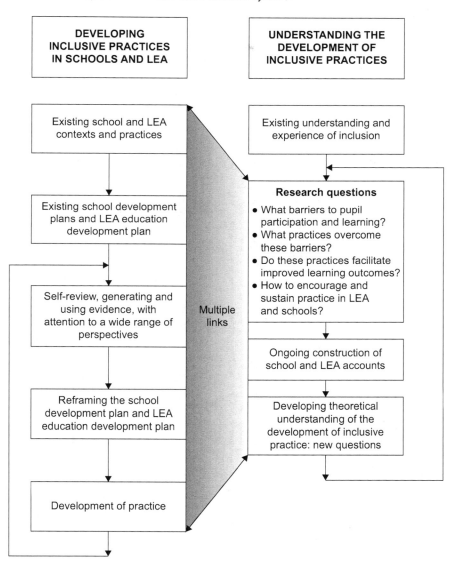

FIGURE 7.1 The strategic model: first iteration (Ainscow et al., 2006).

Our perspective on inclusive development proved to be helpful in clarifying these issues. This does not differentiate between research-based and practice-based knowledge, much less between researcher and practitioner knowledge. It does, however, differentiate between the sorts of 'understandings' that sustain ongoing practice and the 'interruptions' that can 'disturb' such understandings. Moreover, it became clear that, somehow, the interruptions have to come from

152 Addressing barriers to change

'outside' current understandings: not in the sense that they must be generated beyond the classroom or school, but that they must start from different assumptions. We saw how interruptions in this sense can take many forms – encounters with students who do not respond well to established approaches to teaching and learning, or with teachers who do things differently, or with schools with varied value systems.

We also saw how research evidence can sometimes create the capacity for practitioners to step outside their current understandings. This is not because research-based knowledge is in some sense superior to practice-based knowledge – and certainly not because researchers somehow know more than practitioners. Rather, it is because research-based knowledge and practice-based knowledge are built from different assumptions and according to different rules. There is always the potential, therefore, that they will lead to different understandings. In many cases, it seems likely and proper that research will aim at providing evidence *for* practice and policy. In other words, the understandings generated by each will be similar and the findings of research will readily become practitioner knowledge. However, we found that research-based and practice-based knowledge can sometimes stand in a critical relationship to each other.

Changing schools

Reflecting further on what had happened within the inclusion study, it was possible to discern the different ways in which each of the three university teams positioned themselves in relation to the two strands of the strategic model. One team continued to adopt what might be seen as a traditional stance. That is to say, they chose not to get too involved in the practitioner action research. Rather, they mainly visited the schools occasionally to collect data through formal interviews and informal conversations, seeing little need to observe for themselves what was happening in the classrooms. In this way, they were able to build detailed and credible accounts, albeit from a relatively detached perspective.

Another team decided to position themselves alongside the staff research groups, contributing to decision making regarding practice and sharing responsibility for actions taken. In this way, they felt able to experience the challenges of practitioner action research from an insider perspective. However, in some instances this led to tensions as teachers felt that the ideas of the university researchers were being imposed upon them. There is also the question of whether this stance allows researchers to maintain a detached, critical view of the action that takes place.

The third team attempted to take a middle road, crossing back and forth between the two strands in the model. This involved them being occasional contributors to the schools' action research; for example, helping to collect data through surveys, classroom observations and student focus groups. At the same time, they carried out occasional formal interviews to help in the development of accounts of practice that were then negotiated with colleagues in the schools.

We found that a potential problem associated with this way of working is that confusion regarding roles may develop.

Between 2006 and 2011 we had a chance to explore these issues regarding the use of the strategic model in more detail through our involvement in another network of schools in England (see Ainscow et al., 2012a and 2012b for detailed accounts of this study). This initiative was located in a district characterised by socio-economic disadvantage and social and ethnic segregation. The district's secondary school system comprised a hierarchy of 16 schools, some selective on the basis of attainment or religious faith, and others nonselective and described as comprehensive schools.

The network grew out of an existing partnership of four secondary schools, with 10 other schools joining in at various stages over the five-year period. Whilst the four headteachers involved had developed very good working relationships, and this had led to some collaborative activities, they felt that the impact had been limited. Consequently, they decided that there was a need to develop ways of working that would challenge practices, assumptions and beliefs of staff, and that would help to create a stimulus for further sustainable improvement. With this in mind, they approached us to support and facilitate the use of research to strengthen their network. The schools agreed to fund our involvement.

Through discussions involving the four headteachers, it was agreed that equity was a central issue facing each of the partner schools. It soon became evident, however, that what this meant was different in each context, not least in respect to the groups of learners who seemed to be missing out within existing arrangements. As a result, it was agreed that the work of the network should take account of these differences by adopting a broad set of research questions to focus its activities, within which each school would determine its own particular focus. These questions were as follows:

- Which of our learners are most vulnerable to underachievement, marginal-isation or exclusion?
- What changes in policy and practice need to be made in order to reach out to these students?
- How can these changes be introduced effectively and evaluated in respect to student outcomes?

In taking the strategic decision to focus attention on groups of learners thought to be missing out within existing arrangements, we were anxious that this might lead to narrowly focused efforts to 'fix' students seen as being in some sense inadequate. We found, however, that collecting evidence about these groups usually led to a refocusing of attention around contextual factors that were acting as barriers to their participation and learning. Where such changes took place, we saw them as resulting from an 'interruption' to continuing practice that brings about a transformation from 'single-loop' to 'double-loop' learning (Argyris & Schon, 1996 1996); that is, from learning that enables

154 Addressing barriers to change

practice to be improved incrementally to learning that shifts the assumptions on which practice is based.

As with the various earlier projects, staff inquiry groups were set up, usually consisting of five or six members representing different perspectives within their school communities. These groups took part in introductory workshops at which we discussed with them an initial analysis we had made of the local area. Our analysis was based on a consideration of various documents, statistics and interviews with a selection of stakeholders, including headteachers, local authority staff, community group representatives and politicians.

Following on from this contextual analysis, we took the staff teams through a process of planning the investigations they intended to carry out. In so doing, we kept in mind the theory that access to knowledge and activities is socially mediated by the members of a 'community of practice' and is central to the way relative newcomers learn to be members, and to see themselves as members (Wenger, 1998). This supports the conclusion that teachers' practices are always partly socially constructed, even though they are usually individually performed.

Our involvement in these social processes was intended to help the staff inquiry groups develop a clearer focus and plan the procedures they would follow. Subsequently, each school team set out to gather evidence about students identified as losing out in some way, the aim being to develop better insights regarding their experiences in the schools. The groups also shared their findings with their colleagues in the partner schools. In these ways, the intention was to deepen understandings of practices, beliefs, assumptions and organisational processes, both within and across the schools in the network.

Taking place over a period of five years of further intense government activity to improve educational outcomes – or at least raise the annually reported attainment levels – this was a time of multiple policy initiatives and interventions to drive up standards. Consequently, it is not easy to disentangle particular effects and attribute them to the work of the project teams rather than to the pressures imposed generally on schools over this period of time. Nonetheless, the evidence we collected showed that teachers in the schools themselves felt able to identify changes and to trace these to their involvement in the project. It can also be asserted that these schools contributed to what were seen as significant improvements in examination results recorded in the particular local authority during this period (Ainscow et al., 2012a).

Our analysis of what happened in this network led us to formulate what we defined as an 'ecology of equity' (Ainscow et al., 2012b). By this we mean that the extent to which students' experiences and outcomes are equitable is not dependent only on the educational practices of their teachers, or even their schools. Instead, it depends on a whole range of interacting processes that reach into the school from outside. These include the demographics of the areas served by schools, the histories and cultures of the populations who send (or fail to send) their children to the school, and the economic realities faced by those populations. Beyond this, they involve the underlying socio-economic processes that make some areas poor and others affluent, and that draw migrant groups into some places rather than others. They are also influenced by the wider politics of the teaching profession, of decision making at the district level, and of national policy-making, and the impacts of schools on one another over issues such as exclusion and parental choice. In addition, they reflect new models of school governance, the ways in which local school hierarchies are established and maintained, and the ways in which school actions are constrained and enabled by their positions in those hierarchies.

Looked at in this way, it is clear that individual schools can do a lot to tackle issues within their organisations, and that such actions are likely to have a profound impact on student experiences, and perhaps have some influence on inequities arising elsewhere. However, it is equally clear that these strategies do not lead to schools tackling between- and beyond-school issues directly. No school strategy can, for example, make a poor area more affluent, or increase the resources available to students' families, any more than it could create a stable student population, or tackle the global processes underlying migration patterns.

Drawing lessons from this study led us to further refine our thinking regarding our strategic model. In particular, we recognised that we had not embarked with a pre-defined set of methods, nor yet with fully elaborated theoretical propositions. Rather, we had begun with 'hunches,' lessons from past experience, and disparate theoretical resources. We were then setting out to enable people with different assumptions, experiences and backgrounds, who happened to be engaged in the same sites of practice, to talk and debate together in order to develop sufficient shared understanding for them to be able to act in a coordinated manner. However, we were also seeking to create a situation in which any consensus at which they arrived could be problematised by the diversity of views and experiences within the group of actors, by evidence about their practices, which they collected, and by the provocations from university researchers acting as critical friends. We anticipated that practitioners' shared 'single-loop learning' about 'how to do the same things better' would be complemented by 'double-loop learning', which questions the aims of and assumptions underpinning current practice.

As a result of this study, we came to see the use of the strategic model as a process of knowledge-generation. This occurs when researcher and practitioner knowledge meet in particular sites and is aimed at producing new knowledge about ways in which broad values might better be realised in future practice. This has significant implications for the relationship between researchers and practitioners. The coming together of their different kinds of knowledge has to be embodied in real encounters between these groups. This may involve close engagement, as in the sorts of networks we created in these projects, or it may involve more distant encounters. In either event, it requires new forms of relationship between practitioners and researchers, in the way that is outlined helpfully by Hiebert, Gallimore and Stigler (2002). They suggest that fruitful forms of collaboration require a reorientation of values and goals amongst both groups.

156 Addressing barriers to change

So, they argue, teachers need to move away from the dominant view that teaching is a 'personal and private activity.' Rather, teachers have to adopt the 'more risky view' that it is an activity that can be continuously improved, provided it is made public and examined openly. At the same time, they argue that researchers must stop undervaluing the knowledge teachers acquire in their own classrooms. In this way researchers are able to recognize the potential of personal knowledge as it becomes transformed into professional knowledge.

Changing leadership

Building on the lessons from these earlier studies in England, a further opportunity was provided to explore the use of the strategic model in a very different context, that of the state of Queensland in Australia, where equity is a long-standing and seemingly intractable challenge. The study involved a research network comprising six schools, spread across what is a large state, and a team of eight university researchers who, together, explored how ethical leadership could promote ways of interpreting and using various forms of evidence to promote learning and equity. It was funded by the Australian Research Council (see Harris et al., 2017, 2019; and Spina et al., 2019, for accounts of the study).

The schools were all involved broadly in the same process of inquiry over a period of three years. They usually started this by exploring how the interpretation of publicly available performance data developed for the purpose of accountability might prompt discussions about possible new ways of reaching out to all of their students. Given the emphasis this places on contextual analysis and decision making within each organisation, it was inevitable that the approaches and forms of interventions adopted varied from school to school. What was striking, however, was the influence of local circumstances on the ways that these schools engaged with the study.

The design of the study was adapted from our earlier projects in England. In particular, it used the idea of an ecology of equity. As explained previously, this focuses attention on *within-school* factors that arise from existing policies and practices; *between-school* factors that reflect the characteristics of local school systems; and *beyond-schools* factors, including the wider policy context, family processes and resources, and the demographics, economics, cultures and histories of local areas.

The study also built on the varied interests and expertise of the team of university researchers. Together they provided extensive expertise in educational leadership, data analysis, collaborative inquiry, school change, assessment, and inclusion. Their diverse interests and areas of expertise supported the overall design of the research and the development of locally relevant approaches in each of the network schools.

As illustrated in Figure 7.2, the study involved a refined version of the strategic model used in the two earlier projects, with its parallel strands of activity. The first of these builds on the ongoing development of knowledge within each

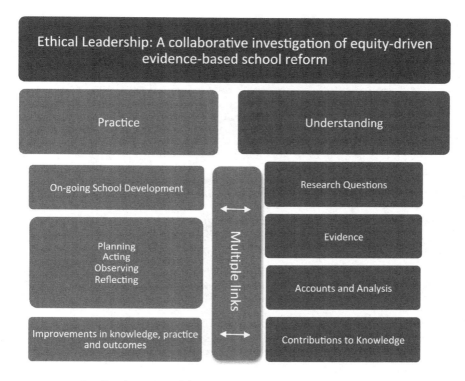

FIGURE 7.2 A refined version of the strategic model (Harris et al., 2017).

school, drawing on various forms of evidence and using processes of collaborative inquiry – planning, acting, observing and reflecting – led by groups of staff and supported by the university research team. Based on our earlier work, the assumption was that the interpretation of data and engagement in collaborative inquiry would lead to changes in practice that would support more equitable schooling.

The second strand of inquiry was central to the concerns of the university research team. It focused on these four research questions, which were developed beforehand:

- How can an evidence-based inquiry approach be used to support efforts to achieve equity within schools?
- What forms of leadership are needed to support such developments?
- How can networking allow educators to examine expectations and achievement, and take action to improve student learning?
- How can all of this be achieved in the context of high-stakes accountability policies?

These four research questions formed the foundation of the 'understanding' strand of the research design. This involved a more traditional research stance, which involved the collection of evidence through a range of methods, including observation, interviews, data analysis and preparation of accounts of practice. Here, an intended outcome was to make contributions to knowledge about equity in education, social justice and ethical leadership in a policy context dominated by accountability and managerialism.

Taking lessons from the earlier studies, a key feature was the ways in which the two strands interconnect. As noted earlier, we viewed these multiple interactions as a process of knowledge-generation, occurring when researchers' and practitioners' knowledge meet in particular sites. In this way, our aim, once again, was to produce new knowledge about ways in which broad values might be better realised in future practice.

This socially complex approach employed iterative cycles of action research to build inquiring communities, which were informed by Kemmis and McTaggart's (1988) summary of action research as a form of collaborative, self-reflective inquiry. It involved participants in making efforts to improve the rationality and justice of their own practices, and their understanding of these practices and the situations in which they are carried out. More specifically, to use the words of Garth Boomer (1985), it required teachers 'to seek out knowledge and test it in action' (p. 123).

Initially, we worked mainly with school leadership teams, usually consisting of principals, deputy principals and heads of departments, to engage in intensive reviews of publicly available data, plus the collection and analysis of statistical data from within their schools. In working with school leaders and the school-based research teams, we tried to stimulate critical reflection on current practices, starting particularly with discussions about data and equity. Our expectation was that the situational analyses using publicly available data, alongside insider knowledge, would point to potential 'levers for change' (Ainscow, 2005). Within these contexts, the task of the team from the university was to help school staff interpret and reflect upon school data, and plan strategies to improve the learning of all of their students.

The schools then established one or more staff research teams to design and carry out plans for investigating and managing change as part of their engagement in the collaborative inquiry process. The range of inquiries was diverse and included the collection and analysis of multiple forms of evidence, involving school leaders, teachers, students, and members of the broader community. These initiatives focused on issues such as assessment practices and use of data to support equitable school-based systems and procedures; challenging deficit views about students; the development of a coaching model for implementing school change; developing new approaches to feedback for senior school students; strategies to engage students as active agents in writing; and interventions for enhancing student engagement. At least two university researchers worked with each of the schools, acting as critical friends throughout the three years, supporting and collecting evidence in order to report the inquiry processes.

Meanwhile, to address the research questions in the 'understanding' strand of the strategic model, school leaders were interviewed regarding their understandings of ethical leadership in the context of high-stakes accountability (Ehrich et al., 2015). In total, three sets of semi-structured interviews were conducted by members of the research team with each of the school leaders to analyse the challenges of being an ethical leader in their particular context. In addition, during occasional research network meetings, discussions were facilitated by university researchers to gauge their collective thoughts regarding ethical leadership as experienced by the leaders, and to learn more about ethical dilemmas that they experienced and worked to resolve in their schools.

We were particularly interested in the impact of accountability data on all of this, not least the pressures this placed on school leaders in relation to the performance of their schools. Whilst not dismissing the dangers associated with such policies, it did seem that they could be turned to advantage when practitioners are driven by a commitment to inclusion and fairness. Such a conclusion echoes the conclusions of the earlier studies in England. As we explained, they had both taken place in the context of government efforts to improve standards in public education, as measured by test and examination scores. This involved the creation of an educational 'marketplace' coupled with an emphasis on policies fostering greater diversity between types of schools.

Within the Queensland study, research network meetings, as well as workshops organised for the participating schools by the university researchers, helped to strengthen the partnerships between all those involved. In particular, they provided contexts in which expertise was shared with the aim of helping schools to develop locally relevant strategies for improving outcomes for all of their students. In these ways, knowledge was generated both within schools and in the emergent understanding of how the research network schools were all working toward quality and equity, whilst at the same time addressing their own contextual challenges.

Leaders from the schools were also involved in occasional meetings with the university research team, where the focus was on examining the challenges involved in leading their school teams in cycles of inquiry to support equity. They gave examples of professional conversations that promoted reflection and provided opportunities for engagement with an ethic of critique as 'moral dialogue' (Shields, 2004). Collaborative inquiry processes challenged each of these leaders to adopt an 'inquiry stance' (Cochran-Smith & Lytle, 2009) in examining practices within their school. Gradually these shared experiences helped to cultivate a context of openness and trust in which school leaders could challenge ideas and share their experiences.

In these contexts, the role of the university team as critical friends was complex. While offering advice and challenging current approaches and thinking, there were opportunities, too, where the engagement in this project facilitated more open communication and understanding around the new structures the schools had implemented. We also grew to appreciate the role of collaborative

160 Addressing barriers to change

inquiry in helping teachers and leaders develop a discerning eye regarding current (in)equitable practices, and to take appropriate action following further exploration and analysis. Detailed explanations in Harris et al. (2017, 2019). provide descriptions of the processes involved, including the relationships within the network, between schools and the team of researchers, and the strategies used to collect data in order to draw lessons from the study.

The experiences of the schools in the Queensland study illustrated how collaborative inquiry does not always involve a smooth, rapid or assured path to more equitable school development. In fact, in some instances, we saw how collaboration can be the means by which progress is blocked, leading stakeholders to collude with one another in resisting change. Efforts to develop opportunities for collaboration can also be hampered by a range of barriers of the sorts described earlier in this chapter, including varied levels of support from school leaders, different understandings of the purpose of the research, as well as time pressure in schools. We also saw evidence of what Hargreaves (2000) refers to as 'contrived collegiality,' i.e., artificial arrangements that may lead to ineffective collaborative relationships.

In addressing these challenges, the fact that the university team involved members with very different expertise, stances, methodological preferences and, indeed, nationalities, proved to be a particular strength. At the same time, our varied ideas occasionally led to moments of dispute and tension, with different viewpoints having to be resolved in order to determine next steps. During these periods of uncertainty, each of us was further challenged in our thinking. Fortunately, our partnership helped us cope with these disturbances, and they often became critical incidents that led to the development of new ideas. We explored the outer limits of collaboration in ways that proved to be both productive and enriching.

Conclusion

In this chapter we have argued that putting ideas from research into practice is difficult because of a range of contextual barriers. These relate to *social factors*, including the extent to which relationships exist that encourage the sharing of expertise though mutual support and challenge; *political factors*, due to the impact of the attitudes, agendas and preferences of key partners; and *cultural factors*, related to local traditions and the expectations of those involved regarding what is possible.

In thinking about how to overcome these barriers, we have drawn on our experiences of working with networks of schools, using collaborative inquiry to promote equity. The overall purpose of these studies was to carry out research that makes a difference in two interrelated senses. First, the aim was to contribute directly to thinking and practice in the participating schools, within the particular policy and local contexts they were facing. Second, we hoped to develop explanations of what happened that would have wider relevance to practitioners, policy-makers and other researchers interested in the idea of promoting equity within education systems.

Addressing barriers to change **161**

Through these studies, a strategic model was developed that is intended to help researchers who become involved in such activities. Having used it in varied contexts, we feel confident in commending it for the consideration of others involved in collaborative research partnerships. As we have explained, it offers a helpful means of clarifying purposes and roles within such partnerships, as well as providing a way of identifying and addressing problems as they occur. It can also help build relationships within which barriers to progress can be discussed and addressed.

The use of the model has significant implications for the relationship between researchers and practitioners. Our own experience suggests that successful partnerships involve a complex social process within which colleagues with very different experiences, beliefs and methodological assumptions learn how to live with one another's differences and, even more difficult, learn how to learn from these differences. This is why it is important to be clear that, in these projects, the members of the research teams both conducted research and were the subjects of research, as their thinking and practices were examined by themselves and others. As we engaged with data about the work of practitioners, we too were constantly challenged to think through our own practices as researchers.

8

A RESEARCH-BASED APPROACH

The hit musical *Hamilton*, which is about the founding fathers of the United States, includes a song called *The Room Where It Happened* that describes the way political decisions are made behind closed doors. We tried to be in 'the room where it happens' in the projects we have described. We also explained the dilemmas we experienced as we made contributions that sometimes required us to challenge existing assumptions regarding how to proceed. And, of course, we also described how, sometimes, this led to us being excluded from the room.

Reflecting on these developments stimulated us to formulate a series of propositions that can be used to promote change within education systems. Together they are the basis of a research-based approach that has the potential to create new spaces within which academic researchers can become partners in the process of development, adding their expertise to that which exists within an education system.

In this final chapter, we summarise these propositions before going on to contrast them with the perspective regarding the use of research in education that is increasingly influencing thinking, practice and investment, in our own country and internationally.

Propositions

In thinking about the complexities we have experienced in the various contexts referred to in this book, we are occasionally reminded of Karl Weick's argument that educational organizations should be understood as being 'loosely coupled.' That is, they consist of units and individuals that tend to operate in isolation from one another. Weick (1985) illustrates this by describing an unconventional soccer match in which the field is round and has several goals scattered haphazardly around. He explains that players enter and leave the game whenever they want, saying 'that's my goal,' as many times as they want. He adds that the entire game takes place on a sloped field and is played as if it makes sense.

Bearing this complexity in mind, we propose a way of thinking about system change that offers opportunities to make use of research processes and findings. This involves a series of interconnected propositions that point to a need for:

- **A shared understanding of overall purposes.** Many of the difficulties we have reported had their origins in a lack of agreement about what should be the intended outcomes. Given that change requires coordinated efforts across the different levels of an education system, an agreed and clear purpose is an essential condition. Reaching the required degree of clarity is both a cultural and political process in which certain voices might be excluded, whilst others are overprivileged, and in which underpinning assumptions need to be challenged.

- **Ongoing contextual analysis of a system's existing capacity for improvement.** As we have shown, this has to be capable of providing a deeper analysis of the barriers that are limiting progress. At the same time, it should identify areas of promising practice, drawing out key learning and applying this to the development of the necessary human and social capital to support system-level improvement efforts. It is important that this analysis continues at different levels of the system.

- **Brokerage that crosses professional and social boundaries, within schools and across networks.** This increases exposure to various sources of expertise and innovative practice. It requires the orchestration of different forms of individual and organisational networks into integrated subsystems capable of fostering system-level improvements, even in challenging circumstances.

- **The development of capacity for leadership at all levels of a system.** This must be capable of leading collaborative learning within and between schools, and with the wider community. It requires the micro-mobilisation of successful senior staff members to take on system leadership roles, in combination with the macro-mobilisation of sufficient school leaders at all levels to create a professional movement with sufficient momentum to overcome internal and external resistance.

- **The creation and maintenance of a strong political mandate at the national and local levels.** This is necessary to create the conditions within the education system that are supportive of collaborative local action. It requires new thinking, attitudes and relationships across education systems. It also means that inequalities of power between elements of the system are addressed.

What connects these propositions in a way that makes them coherent is the way they focus attention on the importance of managing and interconnecting individual, organisational and system level learning, within complex transitional

164 A research-based approach

dynamics. These learning processes help to make the familiar unfamiliar in ways that challenge expectations as to what is possible, whilst, at the same time, drawing attention to examples of different ways of working that can act as the focus of joint practice development. In these contexts, engaged researchers can make significant contributions, such as acting as critical friends, drawing attention to relevant research evidence from elsewhere, and advising how processes of inquiry can be built into strategies that are trialled.

Effective change requires coordinated efforts at all levels of an education system, and these propositions have implications for the various key stakeholders within education systems. In particular, it requires teachers, especially those in senior positions, to see themselves as having a wider responsibility for all children and young people, not just those who attend their own schools. It means that those who administer district school systems have to adjust their priorities and ways of working in response to improvement efforts that are led from within schools. And it requires that what schools do must be aligned in a coherent strategy with the efforts of other local players, including employers, community groups, universities, public services and so on.

This argument is consistent with what has been called 'leading from the middle,' which was defined by Fullan (2015) as *'a deliberate strategy that increases the capacity and internal coherence of the middle as it becomes a more effective partner upward to the state and downward to its schools and communities, in pursuit of greater system performance'* (p. 24). The goal of this approach, Fullan argues, is to develop greater overall system coherence by strengthening the focus of the middle tier in relation to system goals and local needs. Fullan goes on to argue that this is powerful because it mobilises networks of schools in the way that we have described.

There are important implications here for the contributions of engaged researchers. In each of the projects, we had some success in using our knowledge of research to inform decision making. These experiences confirm for us the comment of Jane Tinkler (2012), referred to in Chapter 1, that policy makers look for *'the result of experience and expertise built up over an academic's career, rather than just the findings from a particular piece of research.'* This means that research-informed interventions involve on-the-hoof decisions as to when to make contributions and how far these should challenge existing assumptions. In order to do this, researchers have to find ways of establishing their credibility with other stakeholders. Here, the literature we cite in Chapter 1 gives helpful leads, not least being Sullivan and Skelcher's (2002) notion of 'reticulists,' i.e., researchers who build capacity and collaborative practices to enhance their influence.

It is also important to bear in mind that, unlike consultants, engaged researchers have two related but separate purposes. First, they have to contribute to the success of the projects in which they are involved. Second, they have to draw lessons from these experiences in a critical and systematic way for wider audiences, including policy-makers, practitioners and, of course, others in the research community interested in similar themes. The model we present in Chapter 7 is a helpful way of thinking about the complexities and the dilemmas this presents for researchers.

A research-based approach **165**

Finally, of course, all of this has significant implications for national policy-makers. To create the conditions within which this form of research-based change can occur, they need to foster greater flexibility at the local level so practitioners, community partners and researchers have the space to work together. This means that policy-makers must recognize that the details of policy implementation are not amenable to central regulation. As we have stressed, these have to be dealt with by those who are close to and, therefore, in a better position to understand local contexts.

What works

The approach we have presented involves social learning, bringing together different types of expertise to address challenges faced in particular contexts. Making this happen often requires structural and cultural changes. And, as we have seen, there are many barriers that make this approach difficult, not least because the changes that are necessary are likely to challenge the status quo.

A very different approach to the use of research knowledge in education is becoming dominant in an increasing number of countries, however, not least within the United Kingdom. Sometimes referred to as 'what works,' the approach is based on very different assumptions regarding how to use research knowledge to inform improvement efforts. In this way of thinking, the task of researchers is to convince practitioners to change their practices in light of evidence from elsewhere. The implication is that policy-makers and practitioners are there to 'deliver' practices that have been designed and evaluated by researchers – this means that those in the field are characterised as users of expert knowledge, not as creators.

In an earlier era, this approach involved systematic reviews of research findings that were expected to facilitate evidence-based policy-making and practice. Institutional moves were made to increase the production of such reviews; for example, the Evidence for Policy and Practice Information Coordinating Centre established at the Institute for Education, University of London; and, internationally, the Campbell Collaboration, in parallel with the Cochrane Collaboration, which produces systematic reviews in the field of medicine.

Commenting on these developments, Hammersley (2001) expresses concerns about the rather instrumental model they present of the relationship between research and practice. He also argues that there are serious questions about whether research can deliver on all of this effectively, and about the effects of trying to make it fulfill this function. Specifically, it is not proven that providing solutions to practical problems, or evaluating them, is the most important contribution research can make to policy-making and practice. Furthermore, he argues, it involves a search for technical solutions to what may well be political or social problems. This evidence-based practice movement also tends to adopt a view about the role of educational research that undermines practitioners' expertise because it privileges research evidence over evidence from other sources.

More recently, a massive investment has taken place in England using similar thinking through the Education Endowment Foundation (EEF), an independent charity 'dedicated to breaking the link between family income and educational achievement, ensuring that children from all backgrounds can fulfil their potential and make the most of their talents.'[1] Since its launch in 2011, the EEF has awarded £80 million to 133 projects working with over 850,000 pupils in more than 8,300 schools across England. Some moves have also been made to export the outcomes of these projects to other parts of the world.

The overall aim of the EEF is to raise the attainment of children from disadvantaged backgrounds by:

- Identifying promising educational innovations that address the needs of disadvantaged children in primary and secondary schools;
- Evaluating these innovations to extend and secure the evidence on what works and can be made to work at scale; and
- Encouraging schools, government, charities, and others to apply evidence and adopt innovations found to be effective.

Most of the studies commissioned by EEF involve randomised controlled trials. The children are separated into different groups so the impact of a specific programme or teaching method can be compared with the progress of their peers who do not experience it.

Within the research community there is considerable debate about the appropriateness and effectiveness of these research designs (e.g., Connolly, Keenan & Urbanska, 2018; Siddiqui, Gorard & See, 2018). They can work well, it is argued, for interventions with a simple causal model and where there is good reason to believe that any improvements can be directly attributed to the intervention – for instance, because it is tightly defined, with easily measured outcomes, specified target groups, and implemented in controlled contexts. Such evaluations are, however, ill-suited to more complex interventions that seek to address 'wicked problems.' As with the projects described in this book, these may involve complex, evolving and iterative causal pathways, requiring multiple partners working together to improve multiple, interrelated outcomes, in open and changing environments, over extended time scales.

A recent study that analysed 82 randomised control trials commissioned by the EEF found that 55% produced results that were inconclusive, even though the authors recognise the extremely high methodological standards involved (Lortie-Forgues & Ingles, 2019). This led the EEF, which spends about £500,000 on each trial, to comment that, even if its trials did not provide conclusive evidence, they have still helped to expose programmes that falsely claim to boost results.[2]

Reflecting on their analysis of the impact of these developments in the field, Kerr and Ainscow (2017) present a series of concerns. First, they argue that the approach has created a situation that favours simple, short-term, single-issue interventions and encourages a narrowly classroom-focused approach – even though barriers to learning originating beyond the school gates are known to be even more influential in shaping outcomes. The approach also involves an expectation that simple solutions can easily be imported into schools.

Kerr and Ainscow go on to explain that, as a result of these developments, government funding in England is being channelled into evaluations that use experimental designs, whether these are suitable or not. Furthermore, they suggest, considerable sums are being spent evaluating interventions that appear not to 'work,' although it is rarely clear why – whether because of weaknesses in intervention design, implementation, evaluation design other contextual factors, or some combination of these. Finally, even if an intervention is found to 'work,' they argue that there is often no guarantee it will continue to work once scaled up and left to schools in differing settings to implement in less than ideal conditions, without support.

None of this is to argue against the value of experimental designs per se. When applied appropriately, they undoubtedly have a role to play in supporting schools to improve outcomes. However, the worry is that the pervasive and narrowly formulated understanding of 'what works' is limiting the system's capacity for development, particularly in relation to the challenge of equity. We experienced a vivid example of this during a project planning meeting of school leaders. Following a suggestion that the group might consider using lesson study, a highly regarded professional development model used widely in Japan and other Asian countries, one participant put an end to the discussion by stating, 'EEF says it doesn't work.'

Searching for solutions

A related concern for us is that the challenges involved in promoting equity within unequal societies becomes reduced to a search for more effective technical responses. In this way, it becomes relatively easy to blame schools and teachers for failing their students. In so doing, this distracts attention away from wider community issues that need to be addressed, not least of which is the impact of poverty, as well as the resources within those communities. At the same time, this also overlooks the expertise that is already there within any education system, which must surely be the starting point for professional learning and organisational development.

As we saw in the Scottish Attainment Challenge, it is understandable that the works approach is appealing to policy-makers, who are looking for clear guidance for investing in reform efforts. However, we have also seen how this can distort the use of financial resources, not least because politicians are often attracted to what seem like ready-made, quick-fix answers to the complex challenges they face. In England, this has led to the promotion by government of lists of preferred 'providers' of training and support who are presented as having exceptional expertise in relation to those approaches recommended by EEF. So, for example, in the project referred to in Chapter 6, government funding was won for an initiative focused on 26 primary schools and four secondary schools.

168 A research-based approach

Based on the successful strategy used in City Challenge, these schools were designated as the 'pathways to success.' It was anticipated that their accelerated progress would generate a 'ripple effect,' leading to sustainable improvements across the local education system.

The strategy was designed to make use of the best available local knowledge, alongside external expertise, to bring about rapid improvements, focusing specifically on raising standards in literacy across both the primary and secondary phases. However, in applying for this additional funding, we were tipped off by a person close to government to ensure that we mention particular strategies approved by EEF. It was also recommended that there should be the involvement of a well-known national organisation that provides school improvement support in relation to the introduction of these approaches.

Reflecting similar thinking, more recently we have seen the introduction in England of a series of Opportunity Areas.[3] The aim is to improve the attainment of children and young people through targeted funding in 12 areas facing the biggest challenges to social mobility. The programme, which is seen as involving a place-based approach, is supported by local delivery teams made up of DfE staff. In addition, each area has a partnership board that has strategic direction and oversight, alongside the DfE local delivery team.

Our impression is that despite the claims that the Opportunity Areas projects are place-based, in practice they are largely driven by ideas very different from the propositions presented at the beginning of this chapter. They largely involve the introduction of externally determined strategies, with little emphasis placed on understanding context, limited use is made of local expertise, and few links are made with what else is going on across the borders of the particular local authorities. Summing this up, a research report commissioned by the DfE reports that some stakeholders observed that sometimes the partnership board in their area felt too led by DfE and not driven enough by a representative selection of stakeholders (Easton et al., 2018).

Final thoughts

The examples we provide in this book are almost all set in parts of the United Kingdom, but we believe the ideas we present about educational change are relevant to other countries, not least because of the emphasis we place on the importance of contextual analysis. At a time when countries around the world are seeking to address issues related to inclusion and equity raised by the UNESCO Education 2030 Framework for Action, our recommendations seem particularly pertinent. Indeed, they have been incorporated into a recent guidance document that is now being used internationally.[4]

Meanwhile, the sorts of barriers that we have described continue to have an impact on efforts to use research knowledge to guide educational change in both the developed and developing worlds (Ainscow, 2015). The implication is that changes have to be made in the way education systems operate to create the organisational conditions within which new thinking based on formal research can be accommodated. Without this, even the most sophisticated ideas and strategies are likely to be ignored or dismissed.

The accounts of our involvement in the projects described point to the nature of the conditions that need to be encouraged. They also illustrate the relationships that have to be created amongst practitioners, policy-makers and academic researchers. By and large, these are not based on a technical-rational process through which research-based knowledge is presented to practitioners in the hope that this will then be used to guide decision making and action. Rather, they involve a rather messy social learning process, within which researchers' expertise and perspectives are brought together with the knowledge of colleagues in the field. As we have shown, where this works, it can lead to the development of new, context-specific knowledge that supports change processes.

The implication is that successful change requires the coming together of different perspectives and experiences in a process of social learning and knowledge creation within particular settings. Researchers involved in these processes must expect to face many difficulties and dilemmas. Consequently, they have to develop new skills in creating collaborative partnerships that cross borders between actors who have different professional experiences. They also need to mobilise personal support in dealing with the pressures this involves.

We have also illustrated how the different roles and socio-cultural contexts of policy-makers/practitioners and academics create a complex set of power relations that have to be factored into the process of introducing ideas from research. This reveals how those who work in the field derive their power from being primary actors: they can cause things to happen or to cease to happen in a way that is denied to academics. Meanwhile, researchers derive their power from standing at a distance: they can problematise the actions of practitioners and policy-makers.

At their most productive, these power relationships lead to dialogue in which the academics' views are informed by the realities of practice, and practitioners' views change in response to 'outsider' critique. At their least productive, academics mistake their distant position for superiority and claim moral and intellectual authority over practitioners; and practitioners dismiss academics as being unworldly and resist their critiques. Managing these relationships is crucial to the success of attempts to use research knowledge to guide the improvement of policy and practice in the field.

Notes

1 See https://educationendowmentfoundation.org.uk/
2 https://schoolsweek.co.uk/most-eef-trials-dont-tell-us-anything-say-researchers/
3 https://www.gov.uk/government/news/education-secretary-announces-6-new-opportunity-areas
4 http://www.unesco.org/new/en/media-services/single-view/news/a_guide_for_ensuring_inclusion_and_equity_in_education/

REFERENCES

Adonis, A. (2012). *Education, education, education, reforming England's schools*. London: Biteback Publishing.

Ainscow, M. (1999). *Understanding the development of inclusive schools*. London, UK: Routledge.

Ainscow, M. (2005). Developing inclusive education systems: what are the levers for change? *Journal of Educational Change* 6: 109–124.

Ainscow, M. (2010). Achieving excellence and equity: reflections on the development of practices in one local district over 10 years. *School Effectiveness and School Improvement* 21(1): 75–91.

Ainscow, M. (2012). Moving knowledge around: strategies for fostering equity within educational systems. *Journal of Educational Change* 13(3): 289–310.

Ainscow, M. (2015). *Towards self-improving school systems: lessons from a city challenge*. London: Routledge.

Ainscow, M. (2016a). Collaboration as a strategy for promoting equity in education: possibilities and barriers. *Journal of Professional Capital and Community* 1(2): 159–172.

Ainscow, M. (2016b). Schools Challenge Cymru: a catalyst for change? *Wales Journal of Education* 1(1): 6–22.

Ainscow, M., Booth, T., & Dyson, A. (2004). Understanding and developing inclusive practices in schools: A collaborative action research network. *International Journal of Inclusive Education* 8(2), 125–140.

Ainscow, M., Booth, T., Dyson, A., Farrell, P., Frankham, J., Gallannaugh, F., Howes, A., & Smith, R. (2006). *Improving schools, developing inclusion*. London: Routledge.

Ainscow, M., Dyson, A., Goldrick, S., & West, M. (2012a). *Developing equitable education systems*. London: Routledge.

Ainscow, M., Dyson, A., Goldrick, S., & West, M. (2012b). Making schools effective for all: rethinking the task. *School Leadership & Management* 32(3): 197–213.

Ainscow, M., Hargreaves, D. H., & Hopkins, D. (1995). Mapping the process of change in schools: the development of six new research techniques. *Evaluation and Research in Education* 9(2): 75–89.

Ainscow, M., & Howes, A. (2007). Working together to improve urban secondary schools: a study of practice in one city. *School Leadership and Management* 27(3): 285–300.

References 171

Ainscow, M., Muijs, D., & West, M. (2006). Collaboration as a strategy for improving schools in challenging circumstances. *Improving Schools* 9(3): 192–202.

Ainscow, M., & Southworth, G. (1996). School improvement: a study of the roles of leaders and external consultants. *School Effectiveness and School Improvement* 7(3): 229–251.

Ainscow, M., & West, M. (Eds.). (2006). *Improving urban schools: leadership and collaboration*. London: Open University Press.

Apple, M. W. (2004). Creating difference: neo-liberalism, neo-conservatism and the politics of educational reform. *Educational Policy* 18(1): 12–44.

Argyris, C., & Schon, D.A. (1996). *Organisational learning II: theory, method and practice*. Reading, MA: Addison-Wesley.

Armstrong, P. (2015). *School partnerships and collaboration: a review of the evidence*. London: Department for Education.

Armstrong, P., & Ainscow, M. (2017). *The school to school support fund: promising developments and barriers to progress* (Final Report). London: Department for Education.

Armstrong, P., & Ainscow, M. (2018). School-to-school support within a competitive education system: views from the inside. *School Effectiveness, School Improvement* 29(4): 614–633.

Asheim, B. T. (2002). Temporary organisations and spatial embeddedness of learning and knowledge creation. *Geografiska Annaler: Series B, Human Geography* 84(2): 111–124.

Barrs, S., Bernardes, E., Elwick, A., Malortie, A., McAleavy, T., McInerney, L., Menzies, L., & Rigall, A. (2014). *Lessons from London schools: investigating the success*. Reading: CfBT Trust.

Benn, M., & Millar, F. (2006). *A comprehensive future: quality and equality for all of our children*. London: Compass.

Blanden, J., Greaves, E., Gregg, P., Macmillan, L., & Sibieta, L. (2015). *Understanding the improved performance of disadvantaged pupils in London* (Working Paper 21). London: Centre for Analysis of Social Exclusion.

Boomer, G. (1985). *Fair dinkum teaching and learning: reflections on literacy and power*. Upper Montclair, NJ: Boynton/Cook.

Brighouse, T. (2007). The London Challenge – a personal view. In T. Brighouse & L. Fullick (Eds.), *Education in a global city*. London: Institute of Education Bedford Way Papers.

Brighouse, T. (2013). The importance of collaboration: creating 'families of schools'. In J. Clifton (Ed.) *Excellence and equity: tackling educational disadvantage in English secondary schools*. London: Institute for Public Policy Research.

Burgess, S. (2014). *Understanding the success of London's schools*. (Working Paper No.14/333). Bristol: CMPO.

Carr, C., Brown, S., & Morris, M. (2017). *Assessing the contribution of Schools Challenge Cymru to outcomes achieved by Pathways to Success schools*. Cardiff: Welsh Government.

Chapman, C. (2008). Towards a framework for school-to-school networking in challenging circumstances. *Educational Research* 50(4): 403–420.

Chapman, C. (2013). Academy federations, chains and teaching schools in England: reflections on leadership, policy and practice. *Journal of School Choice: International Research and Reform*, 7(3), pp. 334–352.

Chapman, C. (2019). *Making sense of education reform: where next for Scottish education?* Manchester, UK: Association of Directors of Education in Scotland/The Staff College.

Chapman, C., Ainscow, M., Bragg, J., Gunter, H., Mongon, D., Muijs, D., & West, M. (2008). *New models of school leadership: emerging patterns of practice*. Nottingham: National College of School Leadership.

Chapman, C., & Hadfield, M. (2010). Supporting the middle tier to engage with school-based networks: change strategies for influencing and cohering. *Journal of Educational Change* 11(3): 221–240.

172 References

Chapman, C., Mongon, D., Muijs, D., & Williams, J. (2011). *A National Evaluation of the Extra Mile*. Project Report. Department for Education, London.

Chapman, C., & Muijs, D. (2014). Does school-to-school collaboration promote school improvement? a study of the impact of school federations on student outcomes. *School Effectiveness and School Improvement* 25(3): 351–393.

Chapman, C., Lowden, K., Chestnutt, H. R., Hall, S., McKinney, S., Hulme, M., & Friel, N. (2014). *The School Improvement Partnership Programme: using collaboration and inquiry to tackle educational inequity* (Report to Education Scotland). Livingston: Education Scotland.

Chapman, C., Lowden, K., Chestnutt, H. R., Hall, S., McKinney, S., & Friel, N. (2015). *The School Improvement Partnership Programme: using collaboration and inquiry to tackle educational inequity* (Report to Education Scotland). Livingston: Education Scotland.

Chapman, C., Chestnutt, H., Friel, N., Hall, S., & Lowden, K. (2016). Professional capital and collaborative inquiry networks for educational equity and improvement? *Journal of Professional Capital and Community* 1(3): 178–197.

Claeys, A., Kempton, J., & Paterson, C. (2014). *Regional challenges: a collaborative approach to improving education*. London: Centre Forum.

Clarke, P., Ainscow, M., & West, M. (2006). Learning from difference: some reflections on school improvement projects in three countries. In A. Harris & J. H. Crispeels (Eds.), *Improving schools and education systems* (pp. 77–89). London: Routledge.

Cochran-Smith, M., & Lytle, S. L. (2009). *Inquiry as stance: practitioner research for the next generation*. New York, NY: Teachers College Press.

Cohen, D. K. (1995). What is the system in systemic reform? *Educational Researcher* 24(9): 11–31.

Cohen, M., & Leventhal, D. (1990). Absorptive capacity: a new perspective on learning and innovation. *Administrative Science Quarterly* 3(1): 128–152.

Connell, J. & Klem, A.M. (2000). You can get there from here: using a theory of change approach to plan urban education reform, *Journal of Educational and Psychological Consulting*, 11(1), 93–120.

Connolly, P., Keenan, C., & Urbanska, K. (2018). The trials of evidence-based practice in education: a systematic review of randomised controlled trials in education research 1980–2016. *Educational Research* 60(3): 272–291.

Constantinou, E., & Ainscow, M. (2018). Using action research to achieve school-led change within a centralised education system: perspectives from the inside. *Educational Action Research*. https://doi.org/10.1080/09650792.2018.1564686

Croft, J. (2015). *Collaborative overreach: why collaboration probably isn't key to the next phase of school reform* (Research Report 7). London: Centre for the Study of Market Reform of Education.

Department for Education. (2010). *The importance of teaching (The schools White Paper)*. London: Department for Education.

Department for Education and Skills. (2013). *The future delivery of education services in Wales: Consultation document*. Cardiff: Welsh Assembly.

Department for Education and Skills. (2014). *Qualified for life: an education improvement plan*. Cardiff: Welsh Government.

Deppeler, J. (2013). Developing equitable practices in schools: professional collaboration in research. In P. Jones (Ed.), *Bringing insider perspectives into inclusive teacher learning: potentials and challenges for educational professionals* (pp. 178–188). New York, NY: Routledge.

Dixon, P. (2016). *Testing times: success, failure and fiasco in Welsh Education Policy Since Devolution*. Cardiff: Welsh Academic Press.

Douglas, M. (1982). *In the active voice*. London: Routledge & Kegan Paul.

References 173

Durbin, B., Wespieser, K., Bernardinelli, D., & Gee, G. (2015). *A guide to regional schools commissioners.* Slough: NFER.

Dyson, A., Gallannaugh, F., & Millward, A. (2003). Making space in the standards agenda: developing inclusive practices in schools. *European Educational Research Journal* 2(2): 228–244.

Earl, L., & Katz, S. (2007). Leadership in networked learning communities: defining the terrain. *School Leadership and Management* 27(3): 239–258.

Easton, C., McCrone, T., Smith R., Harland, J., & Sims, D. (2018). *Implementation of opportunity areas; an independent evaluation.* London: DfE.

Education Scotland. (2019a). *Inspection of local authorities: how well is Glasgow City Council improving learning, raising attainment and closing the poverty-related attainment gap?* Livingston: Education Scotland.

Education Scotland. (2019b). *Inspection of local authorities: how well is East Ayrshire Council improving learning, raising attainment and closing the poverty-related attainment gap?* Livingston: Education Scotland.

Education Scotland. (2019c). *Inspection of local authorities: how well is Renfrewshire Council improving learning, raising attainment and closing the poverty-related attainment gap?* Livingston: Education Scotland.

Ehrich, L. S., Harris, J., Klenowski, V., Smeed, J., & Ainscow, M. (2015). Ethical leadership in a time of increasing accountability. *Leading & Managing* 21(1): 22–35.

Elliott, J. (1991). *Action research for educational change.* Buckingham, UK: Open University Press.

Elmore, R. F., & McLaughlin, M. W. (1988). *Steady work, policy, practice, and the reform of American education.* Santa Monica, CA: Rand Corporation.

Estyn. (2015). *Improving schools through regional education consortia.* Cardiff: Estyn.

Evans, G. (2015). *A class apart: learning the lessons of education in post-devolution Wales.* Cardiff: Welsh Academic Press.

Farrell, C., & Coburn, C. (2017). Absorptive capacity: a conceptual framework for understanding district central office learning. *Journal of Educational Change* 18(2): 135–159.

Fielding, M., Bragg, S., Craig, J., Cunningham, I., Eraut, M., Gillinson, S., Horne, M., Robinson, C., & Thorp, J. (2005). *Factors influencing the transfer of good practice.* Nottingham: DfES Publications.

Fishman, B. J., Penuel, W. R., Allen, A.-R., Cheng, B. H., & Sabelli, N. (2013). Design-based implementation research: an emerging model for transforming the relationship of research and practice. *National Society for the Study of Education* 112(2): 136–156.

Forrester, J. P., & Adams, G. B. (1997). Budgetary reform through organizational learning – toward an organizational theory of budgeting. *Administration & Society* 28(4): 466–488.

Fullan, M. (2009). Large-scale reform comes of age. *Journal of Educational Change* 10: 101–113.

Fullan, M. (2015). *Leadership from the middle: a system strategy.* North York, Ontario: Education Canada.

Fullan, M., Rincon-Gallardo, S., & Hargreaves, A. (2015). Professional capital as accountability. *Education Policy Analysis Archives* 23(15). doi: http://dx.doi.org/10.14507/epaa.v23.1998.

Gallimore, B., Ermeling, W. S., & Goldenberg, C. (2009). Moving the Learning of Teaching Closer to Practice: Teacher Education Implications of School-Based Inquiry. *The Elementary School Journal,* Vol. 109, 5, 537–553.

Gilbert, C. (2018). *Optimism of the will: the development of local area-based education partnerships (A think-piece).* London: UCL Institute of Education.

Gorrard, S. (2008). Who is missing from higher education? *Cambridge Journal of Education* 38(3): 421–437.

174 References

Gray, J. (2010). Probing the limits of systemic reform: the English case. In A. Hargreaves, A. Lieberman, M. Fullan, & D. Hopkins (Eds.), *Second international of educational change* (pp. 15–34). Dordrecht: Springer.

Greany, T. (2017). Collaboration, partnership and system leadership across schools. In P. Earley & T. Greany (Eds.), *School leadership and education system reform* (pp. 56–65). London: Bloomsbury Academic.

Greaves, E., Macmillan, L., & Sibieta, L. (2014). *Lessons from London schools for attainment gaps and social mobility*. London: the Social Mobility and Child Poverty Commission.

Gruenewald, D. A., & Smith, G. A. (2014). *Place-based education in the global age: local diversity*. London: Routledge.

Hadfield, M. (2012). Becoming critical again: reconnecting critical social theory with the practice of action research. *Educational Action Research* 20(4): 571–585.

Hadfield, M. (2017). Decentralisation, localism and the role of PLCs in supporting school collaborations in Wales in Harris, A. Jones, M., & Huffman, J. (Eds) *Teachers Leading Educational Reform: The Power of Professional Learning Communities* Routledge: London.

Hadfield, M., Jopling, M., Noden, C., O'Leary, D., & Stott, A. (2006). *What does the existing knowledge base tell us about the impact of networking and collaboration?* Networked Learning Group. National College for School Leadership. Nottingham.

Hadfield, M., & Barnes, Y. (2017). *Annual staff survey*. Ty Dysgu: Central South Consortium.

Hadfield, M., & Jopling, M. (2018). Case study as a means of evaluating the impact of early years leaders: steps, paths and routes. *Evaluation and Program Planning* 67: 167–176.

Hadfield, M., & Hawkins, J. (2019). *Annual staff survey*. Ty Dysgu: Central South Consortium.

Hammersley, M. (2001). On 'systematic' reviews of research literatures: a 'narrative' response to Evans & Bene. *British Educational Research Journal* 27(5): 543–554.

Hargreaves, A. (2000). Contrived collegiality: the micropolitics of teacher collaboration. In S. J. Ball (Ed.), *Sociology of education: major themes* (vol. 3; pp. 1481–1503). London: Psychology Press.

Hargreaves, A., & Ainscow, M. (2015). The top and bottom of leadership and change. *Phi Delta Kappan* 97(3): 42–48.

Hargreaves, D. H. (1995). School culture, school effectiveness and school improvement. *School Effectiveness and School Improvement* 6(1): 23–27.

Hargreaves, D. H. (2003). *Leadership for transformation within the London Challenge*. Annual lecture at the London Leadership Centre, May 19. London.

Hargreaves, D. H. (2010). *Creating a self-improving school system*. Nottingham: National College for Leadership of Schools and Children's Services.

Hargreaves, D. H. (2012). *A self-improving school system: towards maturity*. Nottingham: National College for School Leadership.

Harris, A., Chapman, C., Muijs, D., & Reynolds, R. (2013). Getting lost in translation: the problem of the limited international take-up of educational effectiveness research (EER). *Teacher Effectiveness Research (TER) and School/System Improvement Research (SSIR) by Practitioners and Policy Makers School Leadership and Management* 33(1): 3–20.

Harris, J., Ainscow, M., Carrington, S., & Kimber, M. (2019). Developing inclusive school cultures through ethical practices. In L. J. Graham (Ed.), *Inclusive education in the 21st century: theory, policy and practice (chap. 10)*. Sydney: Allen & Unwin.

Harris, J., Carrington, S., & Ainscow, M., with Comber, B., Ehrich, L., Klenowski, V., Smeed, J., & Spina, J. (2017). *Promoting equity in schools: collaboration, inquiry and ethical leadership*. London: Routledge.

Hiebert, J., Gallimore, R., & Stigler, J. W. (2002). A knowledge base for the teaching profession. *Educational Researcher* 31(5): 3–15.

Hill, R. (2008). *Achieving more together: adding value through partnership*. Leicester: ASCL.

References **175**

Hill, R. (2013). *The future delivery of education services in Wales*. Cardiff, UK: Welsh Government.

Hingston, J. (2018). *The impact of school autonomy reform on secondary principals* (PhD dissertation). School of Education, University of Newcastle. Newcastle, New South Wales.

Honig, M., & Hatch, T. (2004). Crafting coherence: how schools strategically manage multiple, conflicting demands. *Educational Researcher* 33(8): 16–30.

Hood, C. (1998). *The art of the state, culture rhetoric and public management*. Oxford: Clarenden Press.

Hopkins, D. (2007). *Every school a great school: realizing the potential of system leadership*. Maidenhead: Open University Press.

Hopkins, D., Ainscow, M., & West, M. (1994). *School improvement in an era of change*. London: Cassell.

House of Commons Education Committee (2013). *School partnerships and cooperation*. London: House of Commons.

Howes, A., Booth, T., Dyson, A., & Frankham, J. (2005). Teacher learning and the development of inclusive practices and policies: framing and context. *Research Papers in Education* 20(2): 133–148.

Howes, A., Frankham J., Ainscow, M., & Farrell, P. (2004). The action in action research: mediating and developing inclusive intentions. *Educational Action Research* 12(2): 239–258.

Humes, W. (2019). The parochialism of the present. *Sceptical Scot*, February 15.

Husbands, C., Gilbert, C., Francis, B., & Wigdortz, B. (2013). *Unleashing greatness: getting the best from an academised system. The Report of the Academies Commission*. London: RSA/Pearson.

Hutchings, M., Hollingworth, S., Mansaray, A., Rose, R., & Greenwood, C. (2012). *Research report DFE-RR215: Evaluation of the City Challenge programme*. London: Department for Education.

Hutchings, M. and Mansaray, A. (2013). *A review of the impact of the London Challenge (2003-08) and the City Challenge (2008-11)*. London: Ofsted.

Huxham, C. (1996). *Creating collaborative advantage*. London: Sage.

Huxham, C., & Vangen, S. (2004). Doing things collaboratively: realizing the advantage or succumbing to inertia. *Organizational Dynamics* 33(2): 190–201.

Ingram, D., Louis, K. S., & Schroeder, R. G. (2004). Accountability policies and teacher decision making: barriers to the use of data to improve practice. *Teachers College Record* 106(6): 1258–1287.

Innvaer, S., Vist, G., Trommald, M., & Oxman, A. (2002). Health policymakers' perceptions of their use of evidence: a systematic review. *Journal of Health Services Research and Policy* 7(4): 239–244.

Junge, E. R. (2014). Charter school path paved with choice, compromise, common sense. *Phi Delta Kappan* 95(5): 13–17.

Kearns, M. (2017). Scotland used to have the best schools system in the world then devolution happened. *The Spectator*, November 4.

Kemmis, S. (2010). Research for praxis: knowing doing. *Pedagogy, Culture & Society* 18: 9–27.

Kemmis, S., & Grootenboer, P. (2008). Situating praxis in practice: practice architectures and the cultural, social and material conditions for practice. In P. S. Petri Salo & S. Kemmis (Eds.), *Enabling praxis* (pp. 37–62). Rotterdam: Sense Publishers.

Kemmis, S., & McTaggart, R. (1988). *The action research planner* (3rd ed.). Geelong, Australia: Deakin University Press.

Kerr, K., & Ainscow, M. (2017). *Equity in Education: Time to stop and think. A report on the state of equity in the English education system*. Manchester: The University of Manchester.

Kerr, K., & West, M. (Eds.). (2010). *Social inequality: can schools narrow the gap?* Macclesfield: British Education Research Association.

176 References

Kerr, K., Dyson, A., & Raffo, C. (2014). *Education, disadvantage and place: making the local matter.* Bristol: Policy Press.

Kidson, M., & Norris, E. (2014). *Implementing the London Challenge.* London: Joseph Rowntree Foundation.

Kingdon, J. W. (1995). *Agendas, alternatives, and public policies* (2nd ed.). New York: Harper Collins.

Koyama, J. (2014). Principals as bricoleurs making sense and making do in an era of accountability. *Educational Administration Quarterly* 50(2): 279–304.

Levin, B. (2011). Mobilising research knowledge in education. *London Review of Education* 9(1): 15–26.

Lewin, K. (1946). Action research and minority problems. *Journal of Social Issues* 2(4): 34–46.

Lima, J. A. (2008). Thinking more deeply about networks in education. *Journal of Educational Change* 11(1): 1–21.

Lipman, P. (2004). *High stakes education: inequality, globalisation and urban school reform.* New York: Routledge.

Lo, M. L., Yan, P. W., & Pakey, C. P. M. (Eds.). (2005). *For each and everyone: catering for individual differences through learning studies.* Hong Kong: Hong Kong University Press.

Lortie-Forgues, H., & Inglis, M. (2019). Most rigorous large-scale educational RCTs are uninformative: should we be concerned? *Educational Researcher* 48(3): 158–166.

Louis, K. S. (1998). A light feeling of chaos: educational reform and policy in the United States. *Daedalus* 127(4): 13–40.

Louis, K. S. (2013). Districts, local education authorities, and the context of policy analysis. *Journal of Educational Administration* 51(4): 550–555.

Louis, K. S., & Lee M. (2016). Teachers' capacity for organizational learning: the effects of school culture and context. *School Effectiveness and School Improvement* 27(4): 534–556.

Lowe, J. (2015). The London schools revolution: something remarkable has happened in the capital's schools. *Prospect*, January 22.

Mahoney, J., & Thelen, K. (Eds.). (2009). *Explaining institutional change: ambiguity, agency, and power.* Cambridge, UK: Cambridge University Press.

Manno, B. V., Chester E. F., & Vanourek, G. (2000). Charter school accountability: problems and prospects. *Educational Policy* 14(4): 473–493.

Matthews, P., & Berwick, G. (2013). *Teaching schools: first among equals?* Nottingham: National College for Teaching and Leadership.

Meadows, S., Herrick, D., & Feiler, A. (2007). Improvements in national test reading scores at Key Stage 1: grade inflation or better achievement? *British Educational Research Journal* 33(1): 47–59.

Messiou, K. (2018). Collaborative action research: facilitating inclusion in schools. *Educational Action Research* 27(2): 1–13. doi: 10.1080/09650792.2018.1436081

Messiou, K., & Ainscow, M. (2015). Engaging with the views of students: a catalyst for powerful teacher development? *Teacher and Teacher Education Teaching and Teacher Education* 51(2): 246–255.

Meyland-Smith, D., & Evans, N. (2009). *A guide to school choice reforms.* London: Policy Exchange.

Mitton, C., Adair, C. E., McKenzie, E., Patten, S. B., & Perry, B. W. (2007). Knowledge transfer and exchange: review and synthesis of the literature. *Milbank Quarterly* 85(4): 729–768.

Mourshed, M., Chijioke, C., & Barber, M. (2010). *How the world's most improved school systems keep getting better.* London: McKinsey & Company.

Muijs, D., Ainscow, M., Chapman, C., & West, M. (2011). *Collaboration and networking in education.* London: Springer.

Muijs, D., & Rumyantseva, N. (2014). Coopetition in education: collaborating in a competitive environment. *Journal of Educational Change* 15(1): 1–18.

Muijs, D., West, M., & Ainscow, M. (2010). Why network? theoretical perspectives on networking. *School Effectiveness and School Improvement* 21(1): 5–26.

Mulford, B. (2007). Building social capital in professional learning communities: importance, challenges and a way forward. In L. Stoll & K. Seashore Louis (Eds.), *Professional learning communities: divergence, depth and dilemmas* (pp. 167–180). London: Open University Press.

NFER. (2007). *Inter-school collaboration: a literature review.* Slough: NFER.

OECD. (2007). *No more failures: ten steps to equity in education.* Paris: OECD Publishing.

OECD. (2012). *Equity and quality in education: supporting disadvantaged students and schools.* Paris: OECD Publishing.

OECD. (2014). *Improving schools in Wales: an OECD perspective.* Paris: OECD Publishing.

OECD. (2015). *Improving schools in Scotland: an OECD perspective.* Paris: OECD Publishing.

OECD. (2018). *Education at a glance 2018: OECD indicators.* Paris: OECD Publishing.

Office for Standards in Education (2010). *London Challenge.* London: Ofsted

Opertti, R., Walker, Z., & Zhang, Y. (2014). Inclusive education: from targeting groups and schools to achieving quality education as the core of EFA. In L. Florian (Ed.), *The SAGE handbook of special education* (2nd rev. ed.). London: SAGE.

Osborne, S. P. (2006). The new public governance? *Public Management Review* 8(3): 377–387. doi:10.1080/14719030600853022

Ostrom, E. (1999). Institutional rational choice: an assessment of the institutional analysis and development framework. In P. A. Sabatier (Ed.), *Theories of the policy process* (pp. 21–64). Boulder, CO: Westview Press.

Ostrom, E. (2010). Beyond markets and states: polycentric governance of complex economic systems. *Transnational Corporations Review* 2(2): 1–12.

Patterson, S. (2018). *Scottish education policy: why statistics matter.* Public Lecture at Moray House School of Education in Honour of Professor David Raffe, March 26.

Payne, C. M. (2008). *So much reform, so little change: the persistence of failure in urban schools.* Cambridge: Harvard Education Press.

Pickett, K., & Vanderbloemen, L. (2015). *Mind the gap: tackling social and educational inequality.* York: Cambridge Primary Review Trust.

Pocklington, K., & Wallace, M. (2014). *Managing complex educational change: large scale reorganisation of schools.* London: Routledge.

Putnam, R. D. (2000). *Bowling alone.* New York: Simon & Schuster.

Reason, P., & Bradbury, H. (Eds.). (2001). *Handbook of action research: participative inquiry and practice.* London: SAGE.

Reimers, F., & McGinn, N. F. (1997). *Informed dialogue: using research to shape education policy around the world.* Westport, CT: Greenwood.

Rinehart, R. M. (2017). *Intergroup dynamics in education reform: how identity, power, and emotions hinder systemic reform.* Paper presented at the Academy of Management Proceedings.

Rincón-Gallardo, S., & Fullan, M. (2016). Essential features of effective networks in education. *Journal of Professional Capital and Community* 1(1): 5–22.

Rittel, H., & Webber, M. (1973). Dilemmas in a general theory of planning. *Policy Sciences* 4(2): 155–169.

Robson, B., Deas, I., & Lymperopoulou, K. (2009). *Schools and pupil performance in Greater Manchester: a key driver of social polarization.* Manchester: Manchester Independent Economic Review.

Salokangas, M., & Ainscow, M. (2017). *Inside the autonomous school: making sense of a global educational trend.* London: Routledge.

Sammons, P. (2007). *School effectiveness and equity: making connections.* Reading: CfBT.

178 References

Schein, E. (1985). *Organisational culture and leadership*. San Francisco, CA: Jossey-Bass.

Schildkamp, K., Ehren, M., & Kuin Lai, M. K. (2012). Editorial article for the special issue on data-based decision making around the world: from policy to practice to results. *School Effectiveness and School Improvement* 23(2): 123–131.

Schleicher, A. (2018). *World class: how to build a 21st-century school system*. Paris: OECD Publishing.

Schön, D. (1983). *The reflective practitioner: how professionals think in action*. New York: Basic Books.

Scottish Government (2016). *Delivering Excellence and Equity on Scottish Education: A delivery plan for Scotland*, Edinburgh: Scottish Government/APS Group.

Scottish Government (2019). *Evaluation of Attainment Fund Scotland: Interim Report (Year 3)*, Edinburgh: Scottish Government/APS Group.

Schrum, L., & Levin, B. B. (2009). *Leading 21st-century schools: harnessing technology for engagement and achievement*. Thousand Oaks, CA: Corwin Press.

Scottish Government. (2018). *Evaluation of the Attainment Scotland Fund – interim report (Years 1 and 2)*. (Accessed April 10, 2019). https://dera.ioe.ac.uk/31284/1/00532725.pdf

Scottish Government. (2017). *Education governance: next steps* Edinburgh: Scottish Government.

Scottish Government. (2016). *Delivering excellence and equity in education governance: next steps*. Edinburgh: Scottish Government.

Shields, C. M. (2004). Dialogic leadership for social justice: overcoming pathologies of silence. *Educational Administration Quarterly* 40(1): 109–132.

Siddiqui, N., Gorard, S., & See, B. H. (2018). The importance of process evaluation for randomised control trials in education. *Educational Research* 60(3): 357–370.

Simon, H. (1978). Rationality as process and as product of thought. *The American Economic Review* 68(2): 1–16.

Smith, K. (2013). *Beyond evidence-based policy in public health: the interplay of ideas*. Basingstoke: PalgraveMacmillan.

Spina, N., Harris, J., Carrington, S., & Ainscow, M. (2019). Resisting governance by numbers. *In Re-imagining Education for Democracy*, edited by Stewart Riddle, Michael W. Apple. London: Routledge.

Stenhouse, L. (1975). *An introduction to curriculum research and development*. London: Heinemann.

Stoll, L., & Louis, K. S. (2007). *Professional learning communities: divergence, depth and dilemmas*. New York: McGraw Hill.

Sullivan, H., & Skelcher, C. (2002). *Collaborating across boundaries*. London: Palgrave.

Tinkler, J. (2012). The REF doesn't capture what government wants from academics or how academic impact on policymaking takes place. http://blogs.lse.ac.uk/impacto fsocialsciences/2012/03/27/ref-doesnt-capture-impact-policymaking/

Tripney, J., Gough, D., Sharples, J., Lester, S., & Bristow, D. (2018). *Promoting teacher engagement with research evidence*. Cardiff: Wales Centre for Public Policy.

Tymms, P. (2004). Are standards rising in British primary schools? *British Educational Research Journal* 30(4): 477–494.

UNESCO. (2010). *EFA global monitoring report: reaching the marginalized*. Paris: UNESCO/ Oxford University Press.

UNESCO. (2015). *Education for all 2000–2015: achievements and challenges*. Paris: UNESCO.

UNICEF Office of Research. (2018). *An unfair start: inequality in children's education in rich countries*. Innocenti Report Card 15. Florence: UNICEF Office of Research – Innocenti.

Wallace, M. (2003). Managing the unmanageable? coping with complex educational change. *Educational Management and Administration* 31(1): 9–29.

Weatherly, R., & Lipsky, M. (1977). Street level bureaucrats and institutional innovation: implementing special education reform. *Harvard Educational Review* 47(2): 171–197.

Weick, K. E. (1985). Sources of order in underorganised systems: themes in recent organisational theory. In Y. S. Lincoln (Ed.), *Organisational theory and inquiry*. Beverley Hills: Sage.

Welsh Government. (2014). *Qualified for life: an education improvement plan for 3 to 19-years in Wales*. Cardiff: Welsh Government

Wenger, E. (1998). *Communities of Practice: Learning, meaning and identity*. Cambridge University Press.

Wespieser, K., Sumner, C., & Bernardinelli, D. (2017). *Capacity for collaboration? analysis of school-to-school support capacity in England*. Slough: NFER.

West, M., & Ainscow, M. (2010). Improving schools in Hong Kong: a description of the improvement model and some reflections on its impact on schools, teachers and school principals. In S. Huber (Ed.), *School leadership – international perspectives* (pp. 1–18). London: Springer.

West, M., Ainscow, M., & Stanford, J. (2005). Sustaining improvement in schools in challenging circumstances: a study of successful practice. *School Leadership and Management* 25(1): 77–93.

Whitty, G. (2006). Education(al) research and education policy making: Is conflict inevitable?, *British Educational Research Journal*, 32(2), 159–176.

Whitty, G. (2010). Marketization and post-marketization in education. In A. Hargreaves, A. Lieberman, M. Fullan, & D. Hopkins (Eds.), *Second international handbook of educational change* (pp. 405–413). Dordrecht: Springer.

Wilkins, A. (2016). *Modernising school governance: corporate planning and expert handling in state education*. London: Routledge.

Wohlstetter, P., Malloy, C. L., Chau, D., & Polhemus, J. L. (2003). Improving schools through networks: a new approach to urban school reform. *Educational Policy* 17(4): 399–430.

Zahra, S. A., & George, G. (2002). Absorptive capacity: a review, reconceptualization, and extension. *Academy of Management Review* 27(2): 185–203.

INDEX

Note: *Italicized* page numbers refer to figures, **bold** page numbers refer to tables.

academies: aim of 114; in England 112, 113, 116; programme 12, 114; specialist schools and 19; sponsored 35
Academies Act (2010) 115
accelerated improvement boards 47, 51–52, 53, 57, 65, 108, 133
access: to higher education 17; to high-quality educational experiences 24, 101; to information 8, 9, 74, 147
achievement: Greater Manchester Challenge 24, 101; *see also* educational achievement
Adonis, Andrew 19
agility 97
Ainscow, Mel 117, 129, 133, 166–167
alignment 97
allocation of resources 97
Andrews, Leighton 72
architecture *see* practice architecture
Armstrong, Paul 116
aspirations, Greater Manchester Challenge 24, 101
association 117
Association of Directors of Education 109
Attainment Challenge *see* Scottish Attainment Challenge
Attainment Fund 95, 100
Audit Scotland 96
Australian Research Council 156

Bales, Robert 38
barriers: collaboration as 131–133; to progress 120–121; to sharing data and intelligence 119
barriers to change 136–161; changing leadership 156–160; changing practices 149–152; changing schools 152–156; collaborative inquiry 146–148; cultural factors 141–143; decision making 143–146; making sense of 136–143; overview 136; political factors 138–141; social factors 137–138
belonging to one big school 86
Benn, M. 16
Bernardinelli, D. 124
Better Futures 33
between-school factors 156
beyond-schools factors 156
Blair, Tony 17
bonding social capital 38; *see also* social capital
Boomer, Garth 158
bricolage 71, 77
bridging social capital 38; *see also* social capital
Brighouse, Tim 18, 20–21, 30
brokered school-to-school support 77
Burgess, Simon 22–23, 35
By Schools for Schools 38, 119

Cabinet Secretary for Education and Learning 105

Campbell Collaboration 165; *see also* collaboration

Central South Wales (CSW) Challenge 70–90, 145; aim 72–73; case studies 75; collaboration and competition 80–81; collaborative activity 75, 75–78; disruptive transition 71–72; evidence 74–75; hub schools 77–78; impact 74, 79–80; overview 70–71; pathfinder path 76–77; principles 73; process 87–89; purpose 72; rationale 73–74; school improvement groups 76, 85–87; strategy group 81–85, 127; success 84; theories of change 74–75

challenges 112–135; addressing 125–133; educational reform in England 114–116; global trend 112–114; lessons learned 121–125; schools supporting schools 116–121

change: barriers to 137–138; educational 1–14; levers for 158; theories of 74–75; *see also* barriers to change

changing leadership, barriers to change 156–160

changing practices, barriers to change 149–152

changing schools, barriers to change 152–156

Chapman, C. 117–118

charter schools 112, 113

children: academic performance 16; out of school 1; poor 2, 17; primary education 1; rich 2; social skills 33

Children, Young People and Education committee 59

Children's Plan 16

City Challenge programme (England) 7, 15–40; Greater Manchester Challenge 23–39, 26; London Challenge 17–22; London effect 22–23; overview 15–17

civil servants 9, 20, 21, 24, 26, 55–56, 140, 144

clear and tangible benefits 121–122

closing the gap 17, 40

Cochrane Collaboration 165

collaboration 96, 117, 128; as barrier 131–133; competition, CSW Challenge 80–81; culture of 114; with the 'enemy' 118; within local area school 54

collaborative activity, CSW Challenge 75, 75–78

collaborative inquiry, barriers to change 146–148

collaborative leadership 84

collaborative learning 62–63

collegiality 117, 118, 160

competition and collaboration, CSW Challenge 80–81

complex and messy research 5; *see also* research-based approach

consistency 97

consortia 44, 45, 53

constructivist and sociological research 5; *see also* research-based approach

contextual analysis 128, 163

contextually astute, reticulists 7

contrived collegiality 118, 160

controlled trials, randomised 166

cooperation 117; barriers to 125; competition and 114, 118; cross-border 34; fabricated 118; between local authorities 55; between schools 12; school-to-school 116, 120, 124

coopetition 121

coordination 37, 73, 116, 118–119, 128, 144

Croft, J. 116

CSW Challenge *see* Central South Wales (CSW) Challenge

cultural diversity 24

cultural factors, barriers to change 141–143

cultural identity 43

culture of collaboration 114

Curriculum for Excellence 92–93, 106

Cyfleoedd+ 86–87

The Death and Life of Great American Cities (Jacobs) 24

decision making: barriers to change 143–146; Ontario, Canada 6; operational 74

Delivering Excellence and Equity in Scottish Education: A Delivery Plan 106

democratic and conceptual research 5

Department for Education 130

deprived students 24

Deputy First Minister 105

Directors of Education 72

disruptive transition, CSW Challenge 71–72

diversity 97; *see also* cultural diversity; social diversity

double-loop learning 155

ecology of equity 154–155

Economic and Social Research Council (ESRC) 149

edubusinesses 113

182 Index

education: fairness 2; inclusive 2, 3; minimum standard of 2; policy change in 6; primary 1, 104; quality 3; in Scotland 92–93; strategic model 150, *151,* 156–157, *157;* transformation 47
Education 2030 Framework for Action (UNESCO) 3, 168
Education Action Zones 116
educational achievement 24
educational change 1–14; fairness 2; features 9–10; generating data 7–9; inclusion 2; influencing policy-making 6–7; international change agenda 1–4; overview 1; research and policy-making 4–5
educational equity 2, 10, 42, 128
educational leadership 99, 156
educational marketplace 17, 112–135, 159; barriers to progress 120–121; benefits of 121–122; challenges 125–133; English policy context 114–116; global trend in 112–114; goals and agreements in 123–124; insiders 118; lessons from 121; promising developments 118–120; school-to-school cooperation 116–118; skilled leadership 124–125; trust between partners 122–123
educational potential 2
educational reform in England 114–116
Education Bill 110
Education Endowment Foundation (EEF) 166–167
Education Endowment Fund (EEF) 101
Education for All 3
Education for All movement 1
education policy in England 114
Education Scotland 92, 95, 97, 99
empowerment 91, 97, 108, 139
engaged researchers 5, 146, 164
England: academies in 112, 113, 116; as divided city 126–131; educational reform 114–116; Education Endowment Foundation (EEF) 166–167; education policy 114; government funding 167; Opportunity Areas 168
equity: ecology of 154–155; educational 2, 10, 42, 128
ESRC *see* Economic and Social Research Council (ESRC)
ethical leadership 156, 158, 159
Every Child Matters 16
evidence: CSW Challenge 74–75; data and 97; insiders 118

Evidence for Policy and Practice Information Coordinating Centre 165
Excellence in Cities 116
excellent networkers, reticulists 7
expectations, Schools Challenge Cymru 46

fabricated cooperation 118
failures, school improvement group (SIG) 87
fair education 2
Families of Schools 26–29, *27;* goal 29; headteachers 28; limitations 28; performance 27–28; shared leadership 29; use of web-based system 28
Finland 2; low-income student 2; national testing for education 3
Fishman, B. J. 8
flexibility 97
free schools 112
Fullan, M. 3, 164

Gallimore, R. 155–156
gap: in knowledge 116; *see also* closing the gap
GCSE 17, 51, 59, 79, 126
Global Monitoring Report 1–2
goal(s): and agreements 123–124; Families of Schools 29
go beyond talk 127
Gove, Michael 36
Governance Review: Next Steps (Scotland) 104
government funding in England 167
grammar schools 30; in Plymouth, England 126
Greater Glasgow Challenge 108
Greater Manchester Challenge 23–39, *26;* aims of 24; elements of *26;* headteachers 31, 32; impact of 25, 35–37; leadership strategy 31–32; lessons learned 37–39; move knowledge around 25–34; opportunities 24–25; participants 23; three As 24, 101; work strands 32–33
Greaves, E. 35

Hamilton 162
Hammersley, M. 165
Hargreaves, D. H. 38, 117, 141, 160
Harris, A. 6
headteachers 26; accelerated improvement boards 51–52; associate 84; CSW Challenge 72; empowerment of 91, 108, 139; Families of Schools 28; Greater Manchester Challenge 31, 32; internal competition between 86;

London Challenge 21; primary school 85; retired 110; secondary 130; strategy group 145
Hiebert, J 155–156, 160
Higher Futures for You 33
Hopkins, D. 31
House of Commons Education Committee 36
House of Commons Hansard 130
hub schools 32, *75,* 77–78
human rights 2
Humes, Walter 106, 141–142
Hutchings, M 36–37

identity *see* cultural identity
an illusion of association 117
Improving the Quality of Education for All (IQEA) 8, 93, 148
Incheon Declaration 3
inclusive education 2, 3
independence 97
independent public schools 112
Innocenti Centre 3
innovations 10, 25, 33, 37, 46, 49, 82, 144, 166
inquiry stance 159
Institute for Education 165
intensive school partnerships 53
internship 33
interruptions 149
invitation to innovate 49
IQEA *see* Improving the Quality of Education for All (IQEA)

Jacobs, Jane 24

Kemmis, S. 158
Kerr, K. 16, 166–167
Keys to Success programme 20, 29–31
Kidson, M. 19, 21
knotty implementation challenges 21; *see also* specific challenge
knowledge creation 10
Knowsley 131

labour governments 16, 149
Laws, David 7
leadership 53–54, 61–62; behaviours and practices 145; capacity 31, 84, 102, 163; changing 156–160; collaborative 84; development pro-gramme 78; educational 99, 156; ethical 156, 158, 159; local 13; man-agement quality 58; political 11, 32; professional learning and 107;

within school 61–62; shared 29, 124, 125; skilled 124–125; strategy 21, 31–32; strengthening 28, 60, 61–62; teaching and 16, 53–54
leading from the middle 164
learning: collaborative 62–63; double-loop 155; partnership 119; professional 52, 98, 107; single-loop 155; social 10; teaching and 16, 29, 79, 85
leverage 97
levers for change 158
Levin, B. 6
Lewin, Kurt 147
Lewis, Huw 46–47
Lima, J. A. 39
linking social capital 38
local area school, collaboration within 54
local authorities 33–34, 44, 45, 54–55, 73; confusions 120
London Challenge 16, 17–22
London effect 22–23
Louis, K. S. 125
Lowe, Josh 22

Macmillan, L. 35
Mansaray, A. 36–37
marketplace *see* educational marketplace
MAT *see* multi-academy trusts (MAT)
McGinn, N. F. 4
McKinsey report 34
McTaggart, R. 158
the middle tier 137
migration 2
Millar, F. 16
Minister for Education and Skills 46
Minister for School Standards 130
move knowledge around 25–34, 42; Families of Schools 26–29, *27;* Keys to Success programme 29–31; leadership strategy 31–32; local authorities 33–34; work strands 32–33
Muijs, D. 121, 122, 123
Mulford, B. 37–38
multi-academy trusts (MAT) 115, 126, 133

National Assembly of Wales 55
National College for School Leadership 21
national framework 97
National Improvement Framework 103–104
national leaders of education (NLE) 115, 124
National Model for Regional Working 72

184 Index

naughty forty 45
New York Times 131
NLE *see* national leaders of education (NLE)
No more failures: ten steps to equity in education (OECD) 2
nondeprived students 24
normative, political and interest-based research 5
Norris, E. 19, 21

OECD 2, 15–16, 43, 103, 105
Office for Standards in Education (Ofsted) 16, 22, 126
operational decision making 74
Opportunity Areas 168
optimism 119

pace 65
partnerships 29–30; grammar school 30; intensive school 53; learning 119; primary school 30, 45, 102; school-to-school 29
pathfinder partnerships 75, 76–77
Pathways to Success schools 46–47, 49–50
Patterson, S. 94–95
Payne, C. M. 137
pecking order 126
peer enquiry 75, 78
peer review 54
PISA *see* Programme for International Student Assessment (PISA)
pledges 24
Plymouth Challenge 128, 130
policy-making 6–7; *see also* research and policy-making
Policy Scotland (University of Glasgow) 107
political factors, barriers to change 138–141
political leadership 11, 32
political mandate 163
practice architecture 80
primary education 1, 104
primary schools 50, 104; partnership 30, 45, 102
problem-solvers, reticulists 7
professional boundaries 163
professional capital 6
professional development 32, 47, 48, 49, 52, 62, 115, 167
professional hour 20
professional learning 52, 98, 107
profoundly unsatisfactory 44

Programme for International Student Assessment (PISA) 92
promising developments 118–120
promotion 128
propositions 162–165
public education 113
public perceptions 5
Pupil Equity Fund 94–95, 103, 110, 145
The Pupil Offer 49
Putnam, Robert 37

quality: assurance systems 113; education 3; management 58

randomised controlled trials 166
rationale, CSW Challenge 73–74
Regional Improvement Collaboratives (RIC) 104, 105, 107
Regional Innovation Hubs 105
Reimers, F. 4
Report Card (Unicef) 3
research *see* specific research
research and policy-making 4–5; complex and messy 5; constructivist and socio-logical 5; democratic and conceptual 5; normative, political and interest-based 5; relationship between 4; technocratic and instrumental 4–5
research-based approach 162–169; overview 162; propositions 162–165; searching for solutions 167–168; what works 165–167
researchers: engaged 5, 146, 164; strategic model 146, 161
Research Scotland 96
resources, allocation of 97
reticulists 6–7
RIC *see* Regional Improvement Collaboratives (RIC)
ripple effect 46, 168
Robert Owen Centre, University of Glasgow 102–103, 107
The Room Where It Happened 162
Rumyantseva, N. 121, 122, 123

Salokangas, M 112–133
SCC *see* Schools Challenge Cymru (SCC)
Schein, E. 141
school autonomy 112
school improvement group (SIG) 75, 76, 79–80, 85–87, 122; secondary 86; success and failures 87
School Improvement Partnership Board 38

Index 185

School Improvement Partnership Programme 93, 100, 102–105
School on a Page template 47
schools: administration 113; autonomous 113; categorization 57–58; charter 112, 113; commissioner 130; external support 63–64; governance 113; image of 65–68; management 113; quality assurance systems 113; *see also* primary schools; secondary schools; teaching schools
Schools Challenge Cymru (SCC) 7, 42–69, 144; aims 45–46; barriers to progress 48–49, 66–68; complications 46; correlation to City Challenge programme 45; end of 59–60; expectations 46; impact 53–55; implementation issues 46; independent evaluation 57–59; lessons learned 61–68; national election impact 55–57; overview 42–44; Pathways to Success schools 46–47, 51; progress 48–50; school categories 57–58; second year 50–52
schools supporting schools 116–121; barriers to progress 120–121; developments 118–120; insiders 118
school-to school cooperation 124
school-to-school partnerships 29
School to School Support Fund initiative 118
Scottish Attainment Challenge 7, 91–111, 167; aims 93; allocation and spending **100**; embedding and extending 100–103; empowering 103–107; establishing of 96–100; financial support 94; future 108–110; overview 91; principles 96–97
Scottish Education Council 104, 105
Scottish Index of Multiple Deprivation 94
Scottish Parliament 92, 94, 104
Scottish Qualifications Authority 92
secondary schools 18, 30, 35, 45, 104; in Plymouth, England 126
Secretary of State for Education 114
self-improving school system 36, 38, 43–44, 70–90, 114; *see also* Central South Wales (CSW) Challenge
self-managing, reticulists 7
Senior Academic Advisor 95
shared intelligence 8
shared leadership 29, 124, 125
shared understanding 163
Sibieta, L. 35
SIG *see* school improvement group (SIG)
Simon, H. 27

single-loop learning 155
Skelcher, C. 6, 164
skilled communicators 6
skilled leadership 124–125
Smith, Katherine 4–5
social boundaries 163
social capital 6, 10, 16, 137; defined 37–38; types 38
social cohesion 2, 109, 110
social control 109
social deprivation 2, 73
social diversity 24
social factors, barriers to change 137–138
social learning 10
social skills 33
sociological and constructivist research 5
solutions, searching for 167–168
Stenhouse, Lawrence 142
Stigler, J. W. 155–156
strategic model: education 150, *151,* 156–157, *157;* practitioners and policy-makers 13, 136; researchers 146, 161
strategic orientation 7
strategic partnership board 133
Strategic School Improvement Fund 132
strategy group: CSW Challenge 81–85, 127; headteachers 145; roles 128
students *see* deprived students; nondeprived students
success: CSW Challenge 84; school improvement group (SIG) 87
Sullivan, H. 6, 164
Sumner, C. 124
support, brokered school-to-school 77
synergy 97
system leaders 31–32

teacher development 102, 142
Teacher's Toolkit 101
Teach First 22
teaching 53–54; inclusive 149; leadership and 16, 53–54; learning and 16, 29, 79, 85; schools 21
Teaching and Learning research programme 149
teaching schools 21, 32, 115, 133; confusions 120; *see also* schools
team meetings 20
technocratic and instrumental research 4–5; *see also* research-based approach
theories of change, CSW Challenge 74–75

186 Index

three As, Greater Manchester Challenge 24, 101
Tinkler, Jane 8
trusts 44; between partners 122–123
Twigg, Stephen 19, 36

Understanding and Developing Inclusive Practices in Schools 149–152
UNESCO 3, 168
United Nation's Education for All movement 1
United States, low-income student 2
University of Cambridge 148

University of Glasgow: Policy Scotland 107; Robert Owen Centre 102–103, 107

Wales 43, 47
Weick, Karl 162–163
Wespieser, K. 124
West, M. 16, 117
WEST Partnership 107, 108
what works approach 165–167
Whitty, G. 4
Wilkins, A. 115
within-school factors 156
work strands 32–33
World Forum on Education 3